NO SMALL THING

NO SMALL THING

The 1963 Mississippi Freedom Vote

WILLIAM H. LAWSON

University Press of Mississippi / Jackson

Margaret Walker Alexander Series in African American Studies

www.upress.state.ms.us

The University Press of Mississippi is a member of the Association of American University Presses.

Copyright © 2018 by University Press of Mississippi
All rights reserved

First printing 2018

∞

Library of Congress Cataloging-in-Publication Data

Names: Lawson, William H., author.
Title: No small thing : the 1963 Mississippi Freedom Vote / William H. Lawson.
Description: Jackson : University Press of Mississippi, [2018] | Series: Margaret Walker Alexander series in African American studies | Includes bibliographical references and index. |
Identifiers: LCCN 2017046044 (print) | LCCN 2017047615 (ebook) | ISBN 9781496816368 (epub single) | ISBN 9781496816375 (epub institutional) | ISBN 9781496816382 (pdf single) | ISBN 9781496816399 (pdf institutional) | ISBN 9781496816351 (hardcover : alk. paper) | ISBN 9781496818195 (paperback : alk. paper)
Subjects: LCSH: African Americans—Civil rights—Mississippi—History—20th century. | Civil rights movements—Mississippi—History—20th century. | African Americans—Suffrage—Mississippi—History—20th century. | African Americans—Mississippi—Politics and government—20th century. | Mississippi—Race relations—History—20th century.
Classification: LCC E185.93.M6 (ebook) | LCC E185.93.M6 L39 2018 (print) | DDC 323.1196/0730762—dc23
LC record available at https://lccn.loc.gov/2017046044

British Library Cataloging-in-Publication Data available

CONTENTS

ACKNOWLEDGMENTS AND DEDICATIONS
vii

Prologue **THE HARBINGER**
3

Chapter One ***INVENTIO***
13

Chapter Two **THE SUMMER BEFORE THE LONG, HOT SUMMER**
29

Chapter Three **ORGANIZING, RECRUITING, AND CANVASSING**
49

Chapter Four **THE CAMPAIGN IMAGE IMAGINED**
83

Chapter Five **FREEDOM IN FULL SWING**
97

Chapter Six **A RALLY FOR VICTORY, A REVIVAL FOR FREEDOM**
129

Chapter Seven **FROM FREEDOM DAYS TO FEDERAL LAW**
147

Epilogue **KEEPING THE FAITH**
171

NOTES
175

BIBLIOGRAPHY
187

INDEX
197

ACKNOWLEDGMENTS AND DEDICATIONS

The title of this book is not my own. In the summer of 2006 I was on the campus of the University of North Carolina, Chapel Hill, conducting research for this project. After spending a few days at the library roving through its historical archives for primary sources, I managed to make contact with a few of the volunteers who had traveled to Mississippi in the fall of 1963 and lived in the area. I was wrapping up an interview with one of those volunteers, Pete Andrews, when he suggested that I speak with a gentleman across the hall. The next thing I knew, I was having lunch with Hodding Carter III, a Mississippian who not only had been involved in state politics in the 1960s but who had also advised presidents (not to mention his father had won the Pulitzer for his editorial writing during the Emmett Till trial and postverdict). In the middle of our discussion, he stopped midsentence, looked me in the eye as if to make sure I understood with absolute clarity what he was about to say, and said, "You know, Bill, what they did was no small thing." I nearly fell out of the booth. He didn't know it then, but he had just given me the title.

What you have in your hands is the result of many years of effort. And yet I feel it's still not complete. Every time protests pop up in the news, I wonder if they have anything in common with the Freedom Vote. They almost undoubtedly do: local people organizing and speaking out for change. This trend did not start with the Freedom Vote and certainly did not end there, but it was conducted in a uniquely American manner: protest in the form of a mock election. Real participation in a fake campaign where the legality of the votes was overshadowed by the symbolic act of casting a ballot not only showed tactical innovation in protest but also empowered its participants as it educated them. During our lunch conversation that day, I was profoundly moved by how brave those involved with the Freedom Vote were, regardless of the role they played. The need for social change is not likely to ever leave us, and we would do well to remember examples like the Freedom Vote as we continue to negotiate for a better world. And so I dedicate this book in honor of all those who volunteered and participated in the Freedom Vote.

I couldn't have done this on my own. I would like to first thank my colleagues who encouraged me to pursue continuing work on the Freedom Vote. Big "thank-you's" to Davis Houck, Jennifer Proffitt, Andrew R. Opel, and Raymond Fleming. I am forever in your debt; you taught me how to find answers to questions. I must also say a grateful thanks to the editors and staff at the University Press of Mississippi. Your encouragement meant a lot to me as we worked through this process. Though I don't have enough room to list them all, I must thank each librarian, collections manager, curator, and archivist who spared their time to help me. This wouldn't have been possible without your assistance and expertise. We owe a lot to the folks who keep our libraries, archives, and collection holdings safe and accessible. Thank you. Lastly, I would like to thank my family for all their support over the years, and for actually believing me when I said I was working on a book.

NO SMALL THING

Prologue
THE HARBINGER

> Certainly this is one of the most unique voting campaigns in American history. And certainly this is the first time that people went out on the dusty roads all around some state to gather in the vote. And certainly, though we really can't realize it, history is being made right here in Jackson today, and was made all over this state this week. And certainly the real campaign that was waged in this gubernatorial election was the one that Henry and Ed King were waging and the one that was bringing for the first time to people in this state, for the first time to people all over this country maybe, an awareness of the fact that Mississippi, since Reconstruction time, has never had a free election.
> —ROBERT P. MOSES[1]

To say the 1960s was a turbulent time is an understatement. The decade witnessed drastic changes to many fundamental aspects of American culture. Initiating some of that change were social movements, each one seemingly feeding off the momentum and strategies employed by those that came before it. The decade began with the civil rights movement already well under way, generating other movements such as Black Power and the feminist movement, and the environmental movement and the antiwar movement. While each movement certainly had many differences in goals, strategies, and constitutive members, these distinct and unique movements also had something in common—protestors.

The protestor of the 1960s is not the first civil disobedient in American history. The tradition of protest is rich and extends far beyond the founding of our nation. Yet the protestor of the 1960s is markedly different than those who came before, and is still an influential model for how social movements operate today. Contemporary social movements owe much to the protestors and protests from the 1960s, specifically in the model the protestor provided: middle class, liberal, progressive, and in their twenties, with some higher education—these are the characteristics that came to mark the agents of change, not only then but today as well.

The mold for this social actor prototype can be traced back to a summer in Mississippi, simply known as Freedom Summer. Historian Bruce Watson posits that Freedom Summer kicked off and inspired what we have collectively come to think of as *the* decade of social protest. According to Watson, all we associate with the 1960s—the counterculture lifestyle, the politically charged atmosphere, the progressive and liberal changes to society—didn't actually begin until the summer of 1964.[2] This is when close to 1,000 northern college students volunteered to spend their summer in Mississippi educating local blacks about citizenship and attempting to register voters. Resistance followed, but the summer marked the end of America's naïveté and laissez-faire attitude toward civil rights.

Watson is not the only one who feels this way. Doug McAdam states, "In short, Freedom Summer served both as the organizational basis for much of the activism of the Sixties as well as an important impetus for the development of the broader counterculture that emerged during the era" (5). Tracy Sugarman, a reportorial cartoonist who spent the summer of 1964 in Mississippi, notes, "Nearly one thousand summer volunteers left Mississippi at the end of the 'long, hot summer' of 1964, and reentered the frenetic political landscape," and the lessons they learned were quickly put into practice (167). This impact did not go unnoticed. As Clayborne Carson explains, "the summer volunteers, who returned home greatly influenced by their experiences in Mississippi, would bring a measure of radicalism into the student rights and antiwar movements" (129). The protestors from Freedom Summer changed not only Mississippi, but as the quotes above bare witness, America as well.

Freedom Summer's influence on the trajectory of not only the civil rights movement but also the social movements to follow is unmistakable. The style of direct-action protest, organized and coordinated across organizations, mobilizing and unifying resources in a sustained campaign with clearly defined goals, got its start in the muggy, sweltering heat of that Mississippi summer. The "idol of the historian tribe may be called the obsession with origins," and it would appear that the beginning of what we commonly think of as the decade of protest begins with and owes its creation to Freedom Summer (Bloch 29).

This would make for a nice story, but, then again, that story would be incomplete. If the social movements of the late 1960s owe Freedom Summer a debt of gratitude, then they ought to keep paying it forward and send regards to the event that inspired "the long, hot summer," the 1963 Mississippi Freedom Vote.[3] The Mississippi Freedom Vote of 1963 was an integrated citizens' campaign to empower and promote agency for blacks within the state. With candidates Aaron Henry, a black pharmacist from Clarksdale, for governor and Reverend Edwin King, a white college chaplain from Vicksburg, for lieutenant governor, the Freedom Vote ran a platform aimed at obtaining votes, justice, jobs, and education for blacks in the Magnolia State. Though the actual campaign took place October 13 through November 4, the Freedom Vote's impact far transcends those few weeks in the fall of 1963 and extends beyond the borders of Mississippi. Campaign manager Bob Moses was right to label the Freedom Vote "one of the most unique voting campaigns in American history."[4] In terms of its overall goal, the Freedom Vote had one objective: that Mississippi blacks would vote if given the chance—and that they would also do so in large numbers. Whether major works like Taylor Branch's *Parting the Waters: America in the King Years 1954–1963* and *Pillar of Fire: America in the King Years 1963–1965*, John Dittmer's *Local People: The Struggle for Civil Rights in Mississippi*, and Charles Payne's *I've Got the Light of Freedom*, or lesser-known works like Mildred P. Walter's *Mississippi Challenge* and Frank R. Parker's *Black Votes Count: Political Empowerment in Mississippi after 1965*, the literature confirms this basic strategic end.[5]

It is here in the Freedom Vote that we find the foundation for not just Freedom Summer but all the events that followed. After 80,000 or so black Mississippians cast ballots in the mock gubernatorial election, civil rights organizations quickly realized the potential. The Mississippi Freedom Democratic Party (MFDP) was founded the following spring, and plans for Freedom Summer began. One tactic employed—the idea of utilizing northern, middle-class college students spread out at the local level across a broad region—started with the Freedom Vote, not Freedom Summer. Employing a style of protest that was instructive and educated its protestors began with the Freedom Vote, not Freedom Summer. The tactic of unifying organizations and appropriating resources and protestors to get the attention of the mass media started with the Freedom Vote, not Freedom Summer. Baldly stated, if Freedom Summer is the birth of the decade of protest and social movements, then the Freedom Vote of 1963 is the harbinger for what was yet to come.

The Mississippi Freedom Vote of 1963 is no small thing. It is a complex historical and rhetorical phenomenon worthy of in-depth analysis. While many arguments will be raised in this book throughout the analysis of the Freedom Vote, it is important to keep rhetorical agency at the forefront. The Freedom Vote of 1963 is many different things to many different people, but the promotion and execution of rhetorical agency are significant. The main assertions of this book are simple: the Freedom Vote *symbolically represents and employs* the very rhetoric it is attempting to instill in black citizens of Mississippi, an image event that actually practices what it preaches; and the tactical innovations employed by the Freedom Vote *enable* the significant historical events that follow.[6] It is precisely *how* the rhetorical forms employed by the Freedom Vote catalyze agency that is so appealing and unique. Educating people about citizenship and then providing an opportunity to practice this *phronesis* in real time created a groundswell of political activity in Mississippi. The Freedom Vote campaign employed the rhetorical tactics of image events to protest voting rights inequalities by executing a campaign that allowed participants to enact the very agency that was being criticized. The campaign turned protestors into citizens, allowing local citizens to experience empowerment, and it allowed organizers to learn valuable lessons that they would employ time and time again. Almost immediately following the Freedom Vote are a series of Freedom Days across the state and the subsequent founding of the MFDP—clear evidence that the Freedom Vote had an impact on its participants and the political landscape of the Magnolia State, and soon after on the nation as a whole.

Though overshadowed by major events in the arc of the civil rights movement, the Mississippi Freedom Vote of 1963 is an early and crucial exercise of citizenship in a lineage of racial protest during the 1960s. Because existing texts pay more attention to the March on Washington and the protests in Birmingham, or to the assassination of John F. Kennedy and the triple homicide of Andrew Goodman, James Chaney, and Mickey Schwerner during Freedom Summer, an in-depth analysis of the Freedom Vote is long overdue.

Those who participated in the event realized its significance immediately. As one of the original members of the Freedom Vote's executive committee, Dave Dennis could assess the failures and successes of the campaign from a firsthand account: "During the past three weeks, we, CORE [Congress of Racial Equality] and SNCC [Student Nonviolent Coordinating Committee] have been involved in a 'Freedom Vote Campaign.' Many people felt that this was silly and was some sort of play thing, but on the contrary, it did much more for the movement toward uniting Mississippi than anything else we have done."[7] Dennis believes the Freedom Vote accomplished its goals. "Over 82,000 Negroes voted in the Freedom Vote Campaign. Many more would have participated if it had not been for the harassment and intimidation. We had over 100 arrests, several shootings, and hundreds of threats and traffic tickets. Our campaign cost over $13,000. Three of our CORE workers were jailed. One, George Raymond, was kicked around by police. Several SNCC workers were beaten [or] shot at, and over 80 were jailed." The total sum of the votes, beatings, and money spent falls profoundly short of representing the symbolic significance of the Freedom Vote, but it does serve the purpose of quantifying some aspects of this unique moment in the civil rights movement.

Over 80,000 people cast a ballot in a mock election that proved to have very real consequences. The process of educating people and then providing a chance to exercise that knowledge empowered Mississippians in the late fall of 1963, and reminds us today how precious and powerful a thing it is to vote. The Freedom Vote worked immediately in Mississippi, but the effects rippled beyond the state in a profound way. The mock campaign proved to be a very real training ground for protest and protestors. The tactics and lessons learned in Mississippi were carried out by the participants and protestors, only to return stronger during Freedom Summer, and then the exponential explosion of protests and protestors following. Examining the legacy of the Freedom Vote involves looking at the campaign and the subsequent texts and contexts in a nuanced yet simple and straightforward manner.

To those ends, this project is a rhetorical history done in a chronological close-textual reading. Labeling the Freedom Vote as a type of image event frames the analytical perspective of the following criticism, affording the opportunity to learn more about the protest campaign and to expand upon the utility of rhetorical theory applied to social protest. Examining the Freedom Vote from an image event frame uncovers an underappreciated historical moment and allows for the further development of how the rhetorical theory of image events can continue to be applied to different forms of strategic protest that garner media attention. The participatory nature of image events is highlighted and expanded upon in the work that follows. Using the framework of image events to examine the agency employed by the Freedom Vote reveals how image events function from a practical perspective of inclusive participation at every level of the campaign. Whether it is at the level of a campaign organizer, a canvassing volunteer, those who cast ballots, the journalists who covered the event, or the range of audiences that responded to the campaign, it is obvious that the Freedom Vote got people acting, and, more important, enacting the practices of participatory citizenship.

This book analyzes a variety of texts throughout its exploration of the Freedom Vote, ranging from stump speeches to campaign posters, performances at event rallies to news reports, but the methodological approach remains constant. The most obvious of these approaches is a fusion of close-textual analysis in tandem with a perspective rooted in rhetorical history. Michel Leff recognizes the goal of close-textual analysis is to allow the critic to engage texts and examine rhetorical instances as they reveal themselves in the text. According to Leff, critics have a task at hand when analyzing rhetorical texts: "Their primary attention should remain focused on the unfolding surface" (387). Leff argues that rhetoric embedded within texts "is constrained by and refers to the order and relation of events in the world, but it also constructs a certain order and relation of elements within its own pattern of utterance" (385). This places the critic at an intersection between two notions of time. "The time in the discourse mediates our perception of time in the public world. *The central task of textual criticism is to understand how rhetorical action effects this negotiation, how the construction of a symbolic event invites a reconstruction of the events to which it refers"* (385).[8] This close-textual approach reveals the artistry behind rhetoric embedded within speeches, posters, and campaign rallies, and delineates how that rhetoric responds to both the world of the rhetors and their perceptions of changing that very world. A close-textual reading of the Freedom Vote done in a chronological manner allows for the analysis of the campaign as it happened from day to day, week to week, in the manner Leff describes as the "unfolding surface." Doing so in this manner reveals how the Freedom Vote tactically adapted to what was happening around the campaign as it was responding to the rhetorical climate around it.

David Zarefsky's article "Four Senses of Rhetorical History" defines a strong link between rhetoric and history "to open possibilities for productive inquiry" (31). He outlines four categories of study: "the history of rhetoric, the rhetoric of history, historical studies of rhetorical practice, and rhetorical studies of historical events" (26). The category that concerns his project is the rhetorical study of historical events. Zarefsky notes that the perspective of this approach markedly contrasts it from the other categories. The key difference of the rhetorical historian's perspective is that it analyzes "how messages are created and used by people to influence and relate to one another" (30). According to Zarefsky, "The focus of the study would be on how, and how well, people invented and deployed messages in response to the situation" (30.) Michel Leff's close-textual analysis, in partnership with David Zarefsky's fourth sense of rhetorical history, provides the primary lens used throughout this work to examine and understand the Freedom Vote.

Charles Stewart notes that "little progress has been made toward the goals of understanding the nature of social movement rhetoric and of constructing generalizations that apply to different movements in different periods" (152). Stewart asserts that in order to actualize historical scholar Leland Griffin's goals, researchers must first functionalize the role of rhetoric within social movements. "An approach that seems most promising for making significant strides toward Griffin's vision is one viewing rhetoric as the primary *agency* through which social movements perform necessary *functions* that enable them to come into existence, to meet opposition, and, perhaps, to succeed in bringing about (or resisting) change" (153). Rhetoric does the work of social movements; social movements need rhetoric in order to do work. The relationship is obvious, intimate, and essential. Social movements treat rhetoric as a means, as an instrumental tool. In this light, the legacy of the rhetorical tactics from the Freedom Vote extends beyond Mississippi and the civil rights movement to influence future protests of all kinds.

According to Kevin DeLuca and Jennifer Peeples, "we must consider image events, then, as visual philosophical-rhetorical fragments, mind bombs that expand the universe of thinkable thoughts. Image events are dense surfaces meant to provoke in an instant the shock of the familiar made strange" (144). The visual nature of image events not only appeals to broader audiences by doing its rhetorical work visually, but due to this visual characteristic it implants in viewers' consciousness concrete rather than abstract representations of ideographic values like justice and freedom. "Image events," according to DeLuca, "challenge a number of tenets of traditional rhetorical theory and criticism, starting with the notion that rhetoric ideally is 'reasoned discourse,' with 'reasoned' connoting 'civil' or 'rational' and 'discourse' connoting 'words'" (14). For DeLuca, image events are not "the desperate stunts of the disillusioned" (17) but rather are the way in which the business of communication is done in contemporary society:

> In today's televisual public sphere corporations and states (in the persons/bodies of politicians) stage spectacles (advertising and photo ops) certifying their status before the people/public *and* subaltern counterpublics participate through the performance of image events, employing publicity as a social medium through which to hold corporations and states accountable, help form public opinion, and constitute their own identities as subaltern counterpublics. Critique through spectacle, not critique versus spectacle. (21)

DeLuca sees social movements as activities rather than as objects. Visual ideographs can be a catalyst for exigency, efficacy, and agency. Continuing along the lines of a practical approach, John W. Delicath and Kevin DeLuca extend our understanding of how image events function, examining the rhetorical event with the understanding that "image events are best understood as a form of argumentative practice" (321). The authors highlight three specific ways in which image events work to potentially democratize argumentative processes in the contemporary public sphere. First, image events allow more individuals to participate by reaching and including subaltern counterpublics (324). This effect pairs with the Freedom Vote's strategic goal of proving that black citizens wanted to participate in politics. Second, the manner with which image events are distributed stimulates response, precisely because they are actually acts in the form of images and not words (325). This is a characteristic that other critics also find attractive. Johnson sees image events as "a type of rhetorical address that is ocular, rather than verbal," setting them apart from traditional means of protest (2). Having agency in the realm of the ocular is a key source of influence driving the rhetorical power of the Freedom Vote and what it meant to participate in it, at the level of an organizer, protestor, or voter. Finally, "image events and other critiques performed through spectacle animate the possibilities for public discourse and expand the range of relevant rhetorics in social controversies by generating new lines of argument" (Delicath and DeLuca 327). By focusing on how image events function argumentatively, Delicath and DeLuca strengthen the significance of image events as effective tools for communication. Viewing the Freedom Vote as an image event reveals insight into the real power of the rhetorical form of the campaign as a mock election. The goal of this project is to examine how that power translated to the events and decade that followed the Freedom Vote, and to make sense of how and why it is such a significant event.

CHAPTER BY CHAPTER

The narrative structure of this work focuses on the rhetoric of the Freedom Vote campaign as it unfolds chronologically. Chapter 1 begins shortly after the Civil War, during Reconstruction, when the Mississippi state legislature officially amended the state constitution to ensure that most blacks were denied their right to the franchise. Using voting as a theme, the chapter moves quickly through Mississippi's history to chapter 2: post-Reconstruction to the summer of 1963. Understanding the events that took place just prior to the Freedom Vote, both regionally and nationally, places the event in an arc of protest and counterviolence. Recognizing its place in this trajectory further solidifies the significance of the tactical evolutions of social protest occurring within the civil rights movement.

Chapter 3 explores the organizing, recruiting, and canvassing of the Freedom Vote and covers the months of August, September, and October 1963, when the campaign evolved from an idea to a tactical engagement: from the drawing board out into the field. The textual artifacts analyzed become more frequent and include news articles, internal memos, and press releases. The chapter delves into the competing representations produced by the news media and the campaign itself. Local, regional, and even a few national news sources produced and ran stories covering the campaign. These texts reveal the different perceptions of the campaign circulating in the news media, creating an interesting inside/outside thematic dichotomy.

Chapter 4 explores the visual rhetoric of the Freedom Vote. The campaign's visual artifacts afford opportunities to analyze how and why the campaign branded itself. In these texts the themes of religion, agency, and violence reveal themselves as rhetorical threads in the campaign's attack and platform planks.

The next chapter, chapter 5, finds the Freedom Vote in full swing and analyzes the final week of the campaign. Rather than analyzing isolated texts, this chapter critically examines entire rallies. Three major rallies from the last four days of the campaign resemble a series of evangelistic revivals rather than strictly political events. Chapter 6 extends this perspective by examining the final rally of the campaign. Advertised as a "Victory Rally" both by posters and the speeches given at the final event, the Freedom Vote participants are able to look back upon the campaign and on their own terms institute its significance.

Chapter 7 establishes the legacy of the Freedom Vote. The chapter posits that the campaign became a symbolic and tactical model for how civil rights organizations operated in the state and nation, ultimately influencing the passage of the Voting Rights Act of 1965. A series of Freedom Days, the formation of the MFDP, the seating challenge at the Democratic National Convention, the Freedom Vote of 1964, and the subsequent congressional seating challenges that followed in the spring of 1965 all evidence the legacy of the 1963 Freedom Vote.

The epilogue situates the Freedom Vote within the framework of contemporary politics and again demonstrates that the campaign is worthy of sustained analysis. The primary goal of the Freedom Vote, empowering citizens through the practical process of voting, is as important today as it was over fifty years ago. Voting still matters in America, and it has traction in the global political environment. The Freedom Vote, originally a mock election, is still playing a very real role in protests and politics.

As Marc Bloch reminds us, "In a word, in history, as elsewhere, the causes cannot be assumed. They are to be looked for" (197). In that spirit of curiosity and with a desire to learn, what follows is not a report on the Freedom Vote documenting every moment of the campaign, but an attempt to help make sense of it. Once we attain a better understanding of the Freedom Vote, we make better sense of how and why protest and protestors continue to be agents of change.

Chapter One
INVENTIO

The organizers of the Freedom Vote chose a political campaign as the form of protest to raise attention to the issues of inequality in Mississippi, most notably that of voting rights. The Freedom Vote's functionality as an image event draws attention to the need for change in voting rights by providing black citizens in Mississippi the very opportunity to exercise the franchise in such a manner that it would attract attention. In order to appreciate the decision of employing a campaign as an image event protesting voting rights, an examination of the contextual history of voting itself in Mississippi is required. This takes the starting point of our close-textual reading to just after the American Civil War, almost a hundred years before the Freedom Vote campaign.

At the end of the Civil War, few things were certain. What did seem definite was that the war was in fact over, the Union won, and the legal institution of slavery was dead. For a short-lived period of time, blacks participated and found success in the political process at the local, state, and national levels. Hiram Revels, Blanche Bruce, and John R. Lynch are examples of black Mississippians who quickly rose through the political structure. Revels, born free in North Carolina and educated at a seminary in Ohio, was first elected as an alderman in Natchez in 1868. After a brief stint in the Mississippi state senate, Revels became the first black senator to serve in the US Congress, fulfilling the rest of the Senate seat for the state of Mississippi previously held by Jefferson Davis (Franklin and Moss 267). In 1872 John R. Lynch served as the Speaker of the House in the Mississippi state legislature and went on to serve three terms in the US House of Representatives, representing Mississippi's Sixth District (Franklin and Moss 266). Blanche Bruce first served as a sheriff, a tax collector, and a school superintendent before being elected to the US Senate in 1874 (Franklin and Moss 267–268). Bruce was the only black to serve a full term in the Senate until Edward Brooke, a Massachusetts Republican, in 1966.[1]

Yet the promises of Reconstruction and the newly codified Thirteenth, Fourteenth, and Fifteenth Amendments to the Constitution went unfulfilled in actual practice in the South. Just twelve years after the end of the war, a "second" reconstruction began to take form. In 1877 the federal occupation of the southern states ended, and state legislatures in the South scrambled to pass Black Codes and usher in the era of Jim Crow.[2] The Black Codes, in effect, nullified the promises of citizenship and suffrage for blacks granted by the Fourteenth and Fifteenth Amendments.

LEGAL REPRESSION

Whites in Mississippi altered and ratified the Mississippi state constitution in 1890 at a state convention in Jackson. The new amendments to the state constitution included poll taxes, literacy tests, grandfather clauses, gerrymandering, and the all-white primary. Historian Neil R. McMillen notes that "Mississippi, the pioneer state in the southern disfranchisement movement, had no peer in the denial of black rights" (325). Then why did the state constitutional convention so specifically alter the Mississippi constitution around the issue of voting as a passive-aggressive act in systematic oppression?

Democratic governments are founded on the understanding that the right to rule is granted by the people. "Starting from the basic premise that our government exists by consent of the governed, the importance of preserving suffrage rights is self-evident," according to C. W. H. III, because without the guaranteed right to vote for all citizens, any democratic government's authority to rule on behalf of the governed is compromised (945). The right to vote and its relationship to the ideal of equality are foundational principles in democratic societies because an individual's vote comes to represent him or her, and that representation should be equal and afforded to all. Robert B. McKay argues, "Of all the discriminations endured by black citizens of the United States, none has more fully revealed the intent of the white majority to suppress the black minority than the pervasive and long-enduring efforts to limit access to the ballot" (103).

The amendment and ratification of the Mississippi state constitution in 1890 represent an early peak in the systemic disfranchisement of American blacks. During the 1880s, a movement initiated by conservative whites that called for the revision of the state constitution began, primarily to change the voting qualifications. Governor Robert Lowry had consistently vetoed any legislative measure calling for a state constitutional convention, but when John M. Stone was elected governor in 1889, a man known for wanting to change the constitution took office (Mabry 320). The main changes discussed during the convention concerned how to alter the voting qualifications: a switch to the Australian ballot, an educational prerequisite, an increased poll tax, gerrymandering, a property qualification, women's suffrage, lengthening residency requirements, and an examination and certification of fitness requirement (Mabry 323).

The challenge facing the Committee on Elective Franchise, Apportionment, and Elections chaired by Wiley P. Harris was circumventing the federal compact the state of Mississippi ratified in order to be readmitted into the Union. There was "a condition that the electorate of the state, as provided for in the constitution of 1868, should not be restricted" (Mabry 318). There was also the dilemma of ensuring that the proposed changes disfranchised only blacks and did not infringe upon the voting rights of the white lower classes. There was, of course, also the issue of the Fifteenth Amendment, which guaranteed suffrage for black males. Potential impacts on Mississippi's white voters split the delegates. Those delegates from "Black Belt" counties did not mind losing a few white votes so long as they could maintain power. In these Black Belt counties, the large proportion of blacks swelled the county populations, and because representation in the state legislature was based on total population, these counties had long been in control of state politics despite the fact that there were relatively few Black Belt counties. Delegates from the white counties did not want to lose any of their already meager voting totals, so any qualifications that adversely impacted the white voting class were challenged.

The Committee on Elective Franchise, Apportionment, and Elections made its report at the convention on September 2. The report proposed many voting qualifications. Under the committee's recommendations, voters would be at least twenty-one years old, sane, and a resident in the state for two years and in their election district for at least one year. A voter also would need to be registered and never convicted of any of the following crimes: bribery, burglary, theft, arson, obtaining money under false pretenses, perjury, forgery, embezzlement, murder, or bigamy (Mabry 327). In order to vote, voters would have to have paid a poll tax of $2.00 before February 1, of both the current year and previous year, proof of which must be readily available.

Section five of the committee's report includes the infamous "understanding clause." This qualification states that voters must be able "to read any section of the state constitution; or to be able to understand the same when read to him, or give a reasonable interpretation thereof" (*Journal of the Proceedings of the Constitutional Convention* 136). The "understanding clause" was a basic literacy test in which the potential voter's interpretation of a section of the state constitution was evaluated by the county registrar. Even if all the above-mentioned qualifications were met, the loophole presented in the "understanding clause" permitted even illiterate whites to pass the literacy test, but ensured that blacks would fail because the county registrar's "evaluation" had the final say, and the registrars were without fail always white.

The committee made a few other suggestions as well. For future elections, the ballots would be produced and distributed by the state, voting stalls were to be private, and voters would be permitted at least ten minutes to mark and cast their ballots (Mabry 327). Also, just as important as the literacy test in the guise of the "understanding clause" was legislative apportionment. The committee suggested increasing the number of representatives in the lower house by thirteen. In order to do so, white sections within the Black Belt counties were carved out and appointed legislative seats. The final suggestion by the committee concerned the election of the state's governor. Here the benefits of gerrymandering were carried to their limit, as the committee proposed that the governor be elected not by popular vote, but rather by an Electoral College scheme (Mabry 327). The popular vote from each county was counted, and the candidate receiving a majority got as many votes as that particular county had members in the state legislature. The office of governor was important in Mississippi for many reasons, but most important, the governor appointed the judges.

Only two amendments were made to the committee's suggestions. The first was that the "understanding clause" be put into practice in 1892 rather than the proposed year of 1896. Second, rather than a variable poll tax of $2.00 or $3.00 at the discretion of the county board of supervisors, a uniform poll tax of $2.00 was accepted. The convention accepted the suffrage and apportionment articles and ratified the completed constitution on November 1 (Mabry 331).

Mabry argues that "the convention evolved a constitution which discriminated not against the Negro but against his characteristics and his limitations" (330). Many of Mississippi's fellow southern states soon adopted similar state constitutions. The Supreme Court's decision in *Plessy v. Ferguson* in 1896 further entrenched legal segregation and disfranchisement for the next fifty years (Franklin and Moss 290). The Court's "separate but equal" ruling remained the law until *Brown v. Board of Education* in 1954.

POST-WORLD WAR BLUES

Over the next four decades, blacks in the South grew socially and culturally. Women's clubs, vocational schools and educational institutions, black fraternities, and Christian churches were outlets and sources of black culture. Institutions like Fisk in Nashville, Howard in the nation's capital, and the Tuskegee Institute in Montgomery, along with organizations like the National Association for the Advancement of Colored People (NAACP) and the Niagara Falls Conferences, provided social organization for blacks in America. Public black figures like Booker T. Washington, W. E. B. Du Bois, Marcus Garvey, Ida B. Wells, and Mary McLeod Bethune were role models for black citizenship and social involvement.[3] During World War I, through the Great Depression, and up to and including World War II, blacks in America found themselves playing a greater role in the health, maintenance, and security of the nation.[4]

Black veterans of the Second World War returned home unsatisfied with their status as citizens. Being able to die for their country but not having a say in how that country operates stirred many black veterans to action.[5] In Mississippi, this meant attempting to participate and vote in the state's traditionally all-white primary. On April 3, 1944, the Supreme Court outlawed the practice of the all-white primary in *Smith v. Allwright*. The timing of the Court's decision proved crucial in Mississippi, because 1946 was the primary in which Theodore Bilbo sought reelection for his third term as a US senator (Lewis 331). Bilbo's political career followed on the heels of James K. Vardaman, a staunch white supremacist:

> The distinctive feature of the two periods was the success of political demagoguery based on bellicose appeals to the racial prejudices of a white electorate, the great preponderance of which was educationally and economically substandard. In such a political climate, the demagogue's defense of white supremacy was a cause which relatively few "self-respecting" white Mississippians could fail to support. It was a climate in which there was little or no place for a Negro citizen's enjoyment of political privileges on the basis of equality. (Lewis 330)

Race-baiting was the norm in Mississippi politics, and with the return of World War II veterans ready and eager to participate in the Democratic Party primary (supported by the Court's decision in *Smith v. Allwright*) in the summer of 1946, Bilbo was forced to step up his efforts as well. An excerpt from one of Bilbo's speeches demonstrates his attempts at race-baiting, "I call on every red-blooded white man to use any means to keep the niggers away from the polls. If you don't understand what that means you're just plain dumb." Bilbo implies that violence and intimidation toward blacks is common sense: "I'm calling on every red-blooded American who believes in the superiority and integrity of the white race to get out and see that no nigger votes. And the best time to do it is the night before."[6] Bilbo openly called for white intimidation the night before the election. When legal means had been exhausted, supremacists turned to extralegal means, primarily violence and intimidation, to keep southern blacks from voting.

Twenty-two black Mississippi citizens filed a formal complaint with the US Senate concerning Bilbo and his campaign's approach to keeping blacks away from the polls. The Special Committee to Investigate Senatorial Expenditures convened in Jackson, Mississippi, hearing over 100 witnesses, mainly black, testify that Bilbo's speeches throughout the state contributed to the discrimination and abuses suffered during the primary. The all-white five-man panel, not shockingly, ruled that "there had been no discrimination," concluding that such discrimination as may have been practiced by the election officials "came from their deep-seated traditional conviction that the Negro has no place in the Democratic primary" (Lewis 332–333). The committee, chaired by Louisiana senator Allen Ellender, was distinctively southern and Democratic in its composition.

If the testimony of more than 100 Mississippi citizens failed to show discrimination in practice, the numbers produced by the special investigative panel's Republican minority revealed another side. The committee's investigators covered twenty-two counties, and the results showed that not only had blacks been discouraged from registering, but even those already registered failed to cast a ballot in the 1946 primary. In Leflore County, for example, there were 14,394 whites and 38,970 blacks. County records indicate that only 4,345 citizens were registered, only 26 of whom were black.[7] Of those twenty-six registered black citizens of Leflore County, not a single one cast a ballot in the primary. It is astonishing that in a county like Leflore, where the black population comprised 73 percent of the total populace, not a single member of that majority participated in the primary. In Hinds County, where the racial demographics were not as heavily lopsided, the trend persisted. In 1946 Hinds was comprised of 51,826 whites and 55,445 blacks. The county had 27,386 registered voters, of which only 414 were black. The investigative report submitted to the committee shows that only 195 blacks cast ballots in the primary, meaning that less than 1 percent of the county's black majority voted in the election. In counties like Winston County, where whites outnumbered blacks, the trend continued. Winston County had 13,638 whites and 9,062 blacks, with only 5,000 of all citizens registered. Only 25 of those 5,000 registered were black, none of whom participated in the primary.[8] The numbers clearly indicate a pattern of systematic disenfranchisement of the state's nearly half-a-million eligible adult black citizens.

Earl Lewis argues, "All reliable estimates seem to indicate that from 1947 through 1954 a steady increase in the number of Negroes who registered and voted in Mississippi elections occurred" (334). Lewis assimilates several studies conducted during this time period to make his case. He notes a study by Luther P. Jackson from the *New South* that reports that in 1947 an estimated 5,000 blacks were registered to vote in Mississippi. He compares this with a study conducted by William Buchanan in cooperation with Mississippi State College's Social Science Research Center, which reports that nearly 17,000 blacks had registered by 1952. Lewis finally references a master's thesis from the University of Mississippi by James F. Barnes, which concludes that 19,975 of the state's nearly half-a-million qualified black voters were registered in December 1954. While Lewis is able to demonstrate an increase in the registration of black Mississippians, the overall percentage of only 4 percent of the state's eligible black voters is still shockingly low. As McMillen reminds us, "Yet it is well to remember that voter registration is not voter participation" (372). This statement is more than a cliché; as reflected in the numbers above, it was the political reality.

In 1954 the Supreme Court's landmark ruling in *Brown v. Board of Education* catalyzed both sides of the segregation issue into action. The Court's opinion states:

> What ever may have been the extent of psychological knowledge at the time of *Plessy v. Ferguson*, this finding is amply supported by modern authority. Any language in *Plessy v. Ferguson* contrary to this finding is rejected. We conclude that in the field of public education the doctrine of "separate but equal" has no place. Separate educational facilities are inherently unequal. Therefore, we hold that the plaintiffs and others similarly situated for whom the actions have been brought are, by reason of the segregation complained of, deprived of the equal protection of the laws guaranteed by the Fourteenth Amendment.[9]

This passage from the Court's ruling states in straightforward language that inequality was clearly unconstitutional, and therefore illegal. The Court is linking its decision to the equality clause of the Fourteenth Amendment, which guarantees citizens equality in matters of law and rights. Though the *Brown* decision deals with education, other institutional practices and policies were to follow. Violent white reactions followed the ruling, and the urgency with which the ruling was carried out came under scrutiny.[10] The Court essentially gave resisting school districts a loophole by never giving a specific time period by which districts had to adhere to the ruling. Lewis argues that after the increase of black voter registration up to 1954, a downward trend began shortly thereafter. He notes that the two major factors in that decline were "those forces which have been set in operation under color of law" and "a wide range of extralegal and illegal factors" (336).

What made whites in Mississippi feel justified in these actions of intimidation, violence, and outright murder? Lewis notes, "The most fundamental factor in the entire scheme of racial relations in Mississippi, as elsewhere in the South, is the widespread assumption by white Southerners of the inherent inferiority of Negroes to whites. It is against this background of pervasive belief in white supremacy that extralegal and illegal conditions, institutions, and practices which prevent or delimit Negro political participation have developed" (343). The attitude toward black citizens was a broadly applied and generalized stereotype not of indifference, but of racial superiority. This attitude penetrates not only political behavior but also the realm of people's quality of life from day to day.

Contributing to the maintenance of racial segregation and disfranchisement was the creation of the Association of White Citizens' Councils, an organization of "white males dedicated to the preservation of segregation" (Lewis 343). After its creation on July 11, 1954, in Sunflower County—the same county where Senator James O. Eastland maintained his plantation home—the Association of White Citizens' Councils established chapters in all of Mississippi's eighty-two counties. A letter from the White Citizens' Councils to potential members outlined the functions of the organization's various operating committees. The statement of the Political and Elections Committee reads: "It will screen all candidates in local and state elections against those who might be seeking the Negro vote. If necessary, organize a white private election within the group to combat the Negro bloc vote. Discourage Negro registration by every legal means."[11] While Dittmer claims that the individuals who joined the White Citizens' Councils "were not interested in starting a Klan Klavern," the upper-middle-class attorneys, business owners, and local officials who joined were interested in maintaining the racial status quo of segregation (45).

Thomas P. Brady and Robert B. Patterson played major roles in the establishment and creation of the White Citizens' Councils. Both men were Mississippians who lived in the Delta. Patterson was a former football star at Mississippi State and a paratrooper in World War II, and Brady was a Yale-educated Mississippi circuit judge. After the *Brown* decision, both were outraged and "convinced that national salvation required nothing less than total white solidarity" (McMillen 17). Brady delivered an address known as the "Black Monday" speech, which functioned as an attack on the Supreme Court's "disdain" for legal precedent. The speech quickly became popular enough in segregationist circles that it was published as a booklet and served as the primary text of the White Citizens' Councils. McMillen writes, "Typically, an organizer such as Patterson or Brady would be invited by a sympathetic member to address a Rotary, Kiwanis, Civitan, or Exchange Club luncheon in an unorganized locality. After explaining the Council's nature and purpose, he met with interested individuals to arrange a second and larger meeting" (20). It was at these second meetings where a local chairman and steering committee were nominated and approved, establishing the basic foundation of a local chapter of the Citizens' Council.

Due to their positions within their local communities, White Citizens' Council members could both punish blacks and protect whites without fear of legal consequences. As leaders and business owners, the White Citizens' Council members controlled institutions and local economic, legal, and political practices. Avoiding the use of hooded violence, these "respectable" members preferred subtler and more sophisticated forms of resistance, including propaganda, economic reprisals, and other forms of interfering with civil rights organizations. Whites could violently or economically react to any blacks thought to be involved with the movement without suffering any consequence. When assessing the control and influence of private organizations formed to counter *Brown*, McMillen writes, "None was more powerful than the Citizens' Council, which in the course of a few short years would claim among its members governors, congressmen, judges, physicians, lawyers, industrialists, and bankers, as well as an assortment of lesser men who crowded membership rosters packed with municipal auditoriums to dedicate themselves to the preservation of 'states' rights and racial integrity'" (11). The influence of the Citizens' Council had integrated itself into every facet of political and social life in Mississippi. This created a climate of fear and intimidation in which black citizens could never be sure from what quarter of society or from what direction retribution and intimidation would come.

What further empowered the White Citizens' Councils was their relationship to the state legislative entity known as the State Sovereignty Commission. The commission was formed shortly after the Dixiecrats walked out of the 1948 Democratic National Convention to help ensure that states' rights were preserved in Mississippi. The Mississippi State Sovereignty Commission acted as a treasury for the White Citizens' Councils across the state (Katagiri 30–33). This created an atmosphere of impunity for racist whites and their behavior. The Sovereignty Commission also symbolically represents the marriage of legal and extralegal institutions and practices, a symbolically powerful linkage.[12] There seemed little recourse or room for response for citizens in Mississippi.

THE NORMALCY OF KILLING AND VIOLENCE

Reverend George W. Lee was vice president of the Regional Council of Negro Leadership (RCNL) and was known for his activism with the NAACP. The RCNL was organized by T. R. M. Howard, a successful doctor in the all-black Delta community of Mound Bayou. The RCNL held a mass meeting in the spring of 1955; around 10,000 blacks came to hear several speakers, including Congressmen Charles Diggs from Detroit and Reverend Lee (Dittmer 55). Two weeks after Reverend Lee spoke at the rally encouraging blacks to register to vote, near midnight he was murdered on the streets of the south Delta town of Belzoni. He was driving his car when a convertible pulled up from behind and fired into Lee's car, causing him to crash. He died on the way to the hospital from gun blasts that had torn off the lower side of his face.

On Saturday morning, August 13, 1955, sixty-three-year-old farmer Lamar Smith was shot on the courthouse lawn in Brookhaven, Mississippi (Dittmer 54). The World War I veteran had been encouraging blacks to get involved with the upcoming Democratic primary. Smith had ingeniously devised a way for registered blacks to participate via absentee ballots, which permitted registered blacks to vote without experiencing the violence or intimidation they faced at the polls. Even though the sheriff admitted to seeing a white man leave the scene with blood on him, three suspects were never indicted by a grand jury. Despite the crowd that was on the courthouse lawn that day, a witness willing to testify about the shooting could never be found.

Later that summer a story spread across the national news wire that shocked the world. The abduction and killing of fourteen-year-old Emmett Louis "Bobo" Till cast a spotlight on Mississippi.[13] On a Wednesday evening late in August, a group of kids sat outside Bryant's Grocery and Meat Market in the tiny Delta town of Money, Mississippi. As usual, the boys played checkers and talked about girls. Till, who was visiting from Chicago for a few weeks, boasted about a girlfriend back in Chicago who was white (Dittmer 55). Upon a challenge from one of the other boys, Emmett went into the store and allegedly made "ugly remarks" to and wolf-whistled at the white female clerk tending the counter. Whether it was a whistle or a simple "bye, baby," Till unwittingly broke the most sacrosanct rule below the Mason-Dixon Line. When the white woman, Carolyn Bryant, ran out to get a pistol, the group of boys grabbed Till quickly, speeding out onto a county road to escape.

Days passed and no backlash came from the incident at the Bryant Store until early Sunday, August 28. Carolyn's husband, Roy Bryant, and his half-brother, J. W. "Big" Milam, entered the home of Moses "Preacher" Wright, Till's great-uncle, and took Till from his bed. What exactly happened after the kidnapping party left Wright's home is still under debate, but the result of whatever occurred that early morning is not up for deliberation. Till's bloated and disfigured body was found three days later in the Tallahatchie River, weighed down by a seventy-five-pound cotton gin fan tied to his neck with barbed wire. Less than a month later, an all-white jury found the two defendants not guilty.[14]

In November 1955 another shooting took place in Belzoni. Gus Courts, a sixty-five-year-old grocery store owner who had testified to the Special Senate Committee in Jackson the previous year, was shot in his grocery store (Dittmer 45). Courts had already given into pressure from the Belzoni chapter of the Citizens' Councils by resigning his presidency of the local NAACP chapter, but he still used his grocery store as a place where blacks could pay poll taxes and discuss political issues. Courts was forced to move to Chicago shortly after recovering from his wounds. Courts testified later in 1957 before a subcommittee of the Senate that the morning following the murder of Reverend Lee, a representative from the local White Citizens' Council came to his store warning him, "If you don't go down and get your name off the register, you are going to be next" (Lewis 344). Courts went on in his testimony to counter the statements of then Mississippi governor Coleman's testimony before the subcommittee:

I understand that Governor Coleman, of Mississippi, when testifying before the House Judiciary subcommittee last week, said that he assumed that failure to pay poll taxes was one of the reasons why the Negro vote had been reduced. The governor knows that this is not so. I now tell this committee that the Negro vote in Mississippi has been reduced because of intimidation, violence, and fraud on the part of those who operate the election machinery and their associates. (Lewis 345)

Courts clearly blamed white supremacists' institutional and structural control of the political process for blocking and inhibiting black involvement. Singling out Governor Coleman by name directly links supremacists' behavior with the political institution of the state, showing the cooperation occurring between the two. It was not necessarily the individual acts of violence and intimidation that blacks were forced to suffer, but rather the systemic and institutional policies that provided support for and encouraged these moments of violence that made matters worse.

Amid the hostility and violence, there was some action on the part of the federal government, albeit very little and very ineffective. An eighty-two-year absence of federal legislation relating to civil rights ended with the passage of the Civil Rights Act of 1957. The act consists of four main parts: the creation of a Civil Rights Commission, the addition of an assistant attorney general, the further protection of voting rights, and the elimination of the requirement that federal jurors be competent as such under state law (Winquist 625). One of the major problems facing the enforcement of the act is found in the basic premise of the Tenth Amendment, which states that "those powers not delegated to the United States by the Constitution nor prohibited by it to the States" are given to the state and its people (C. W. H. 950) It is here in this phrasing of the Tenth Amendment where the constitutional legitimacy of "states' rights" is found, deferring to each state the right to enact and enforce laws as it sees fit so long as that legislation does not violate federal law. Another problem stems from the prevailing interpretation of the Fifteenth Amendment that action is appropriate on the part of the federal government only to prevent discriminatory state action and not individual acting against individual (C. W. H. 951). The legislation protects citizens from the state, but not from other citizens.

Two developments in the Civil Rights Act of 1957 are worth mentioning: the establishment of the Civil Rights Commission and the (re)enforcement of already existing voting rights protections. The commission's duty was to investigate written and sworn complaints that "United States citizens were being denied rights of suffrage by reason of their color, race, religion, or natural origin" (C. W. H. 957). The major protection added by the Voting Rights Act "was the power given the Attorney General to seek preventative relief in the form of an injunction on behalf of persons denied the right to vote because of race, color or previous condition." The creation of the commission, in light of this newly appointed power of injunction, theoretically allowed the attorney general to enforce already established and codified voting rights protections.

Yet the resulting number of federal investigations was nowhere near staggering. In his first report to the president, Assistant Attorney General William Wilson White appeared to prefer "conciliation to litigation." McMillen notes that "although the United States Commission on Civil Rights found overwhelming evidence of a region-wide pattern of suffrage denial, the Civil Rights Division during White's tenure filed only three voter-discrimination suits, none of them in Mississippi" (McMillen 355), evidence that the Magnolia State wasn't even on the radar of the federal government. Harold Tyler Jr., White's successor under Eisenhower, failed to file a single case to enforce federal voting statutes in Mississippi, further turning a blind eye to the violence and intimidation in Mississippi.

The 1950s ended with the NAACP forced underground, little to no activity on the part of the newly created Civil Rights Commission, and Mississippi blacks weary of the white backlash and resistance to change. If change was going to come to Mississippi, it would not arrive in the form of civil rights icons like Martin Luther King Jr. and his Southern Christian Leadership Conference (SCLC), which had generated success in Montgomery, Alabama, and elsewhere, or from the involvement of the federal government. Yet despite this, change was needed, but what wasn't clear was from where it would come.

MOSES AND THE LOCAL PEOPLE

Robert Parris Moses arrived in the north Delta town of Clarksdale, Mississippi, in the summer of 1960.[15] Ella Baker, working out of the SCLC office in Atlanta, sent the introspective Harvard graduate student on an exploratory mission to assess potential black leaders for an upcoming conference to be held in the fall (Dittmer 102). Moses got off the Greyhound bus in Clarksdale and was greeted by Aaron "Doc" Henry, a successful pharmacist in the community. Moses then ventured south to the town of Cleveland, where he began his friendship with the man who served as his liaison to Delta blacks, Amzie Moore (Branch 330). They talked about how to bring about meaningful change to Mississippi. Moore convinced Moses that political power—the vote—was more important and tenable than direct-action desegregation campaigns.

Dittmer claims that "Robert Parris Moses' journey from the streets of Harlem to the dirt roads of southwest Mississippi is part of the folklore of the black freedom struggle" (102). Born and raised in Harlem, Moses attended Hamilton College before getting a master's degree at Harvard in 1957 (Burner

16). In the summer of 1960, while visiting an uncle who taught at the Hampton Institute, Moses participated in a demonstration in Newport News, where he heard Wyatt Walker give a speech about an upcoming SCLC rally in New York City (Burner 18). Moses returned briefly to New York to work with Bayard Rustin, who realized Moses's leadership potential and sent him south to Ella Baker and the Atlanta SCLC offices. The student sit-ins from that spring had a deep impact on Moses. "As yet they were only spontaneous acts of rebellion, lacking the theoretical and conceptual power that Moses, the disciple of Camus's morality of voluntary autonomous political action, would give them," the sit-ins shaped the young civil rights worker's perception of leadership (Burner 18). At the sit-ins, Moses saw local people organizing and acting on their own, without any help from the mainstream or iconic individual leaders like Martin Luther King Jr.

The summer Moses arrived in the Mississippi Delta, Congress passed the Civil Rights Act of 1960. The main focus of the act came in the provisions of the Federal Enrollment Officer Bill (C. W. H. 968). This bill combined the initiatives of appointing federal registrars and referees to oversee voting procedures and policies. What hurt the overall effectiveness of the act, though, was that registrars and referees could be appointed only after a federal court "found a pattern or practice of racial discrimination" (C. W. H. 968). This left the enforcement up to the discretion of federal judges, including William Harold Cox of Mississippi's Southern District. Cox was a former college roommate and friend of Senator James O. Eastland, chairman of the powerful Judiciary Committee (McMillen 357). So while the act may have had potential, ambiguous wording and reliance on the personal discretion of southern judges like Cox stripped the legislation of any real impact.

While direct-action efforts like the Freedom Rides of 1961 highlighted the violent white reaction to civil rights activity common in the South, they did little to ensure the long-term success of meaningful change represented by the ballot. In return for a bargained "cooling off" period, the Kennedy administration helped set up foundations that would channel money into voter registration drives (McMillen 359). Coordinating this effort, the Voter Education Project (VEP), organized by the Southern Regional Council, directed funds from the Taconic and Field Foundations and the Edgar Stern Family Fund (McMillen 359–360). In exchange for these funds, SNCC and CORE promised to shift their efforts from direct-action campaigns to voting rights and registration drives.

The VEP issued a news release on March 31, 1963, in an attempt to make some of the national Sunday papers.[16] The news release documents sixty-four acts of violence and intimidation against Mississippi blacks who had attempted to register to vote from January 1961 to March 1963. While the list may not be comprehensive, it is a solid reflection of the environment leading up to and contemporary with the Freedom Vote. Wiley Branton, director of the project, states in the report that while the list does not include the riot at Ole Miss, or the subsequent harassment of James Meredith,[17] "it does demonstrate conclusively, however, the pattern of discrimination and violence which exists in Mississippi, and makes Constitutional rights virtually inoperative in that state."[18] The last entry details the arrests of James Forman and Bob Moses in Greenwood on March 27, 1963, along with ten other registration workers. The recent surge in voter registration activity in Greenwood stemmed from increased and localized efforts from SNCC, CORE, the SCLC, and the NAACP that had started on the first of March, with the announced goal "to get every qualified Negro in LeFlore [sic] County registered to vote, if he or she has any desire to do so."[19] COFO's efforts were having an impact, but was it enough? Keeping the different organizations focused on voting needed measurable results.

Despite the optimism of workers and organizations, the number of registered voters barely changed. McMillen notes that in the summer of 1962 in Leflore, 268 of the county's 13,567 black adults were registered; in January 1964 that number increased by only 13, or "no appreciable increment" (McMillen 362). Other counties faced equally bleak numbers. Efforts in Amite, Pike, and Walthall Counties had almost no effect on registration totals. The percentage of eligible blacks registered in those counties increased by a mere 0.03, 2.2, and 0.1, respectively (McMillen 360).

Soon after the report was issued, the VEP pulled its financial support from efforts in Mississippi. The voter registration drives had registered less than 4,000 new black voters in almost two years of work, and at the expense of over $50,000 (McMillen 362). Despite the collapse of the Delta campaign sponsored by the VEP, McMillen contends "that the idealistic crusaders for black suffrage emerged from two years of utter defeat with a healthy sense of realism" (364). McMillen posits that this newfound sense of realism forced leaders to understand that significant and meaningful change would only come from federal intervention, and that intervention was likely to occur only with sweeping public support. Voting efforts temporarily stalled, but the movement did not stop moving.

Through the examination of the historical arc in this chapter, what is clear is an established legacy of suppressing the black vote in Mississippi. As illustrated throughout this chapter, protests and the subsequent legal and extralegal responses to said protests created an environment that severed black citizens from the protections of the Constitution. More specifically, Mississippi blacks in the 1960s had been so thoroughly conditioned not to exercise the franchise that they had become disconnected from their own hard-fought attainment of the ballot. After being guaranteed access to the ballot with the ratification of the Fourteenth Amendment in the 1860s, blacks still struggled to exercise that right for the next hundred years.

This chapter has explored the historical disenfranchisement and climate of fear that Mississippi blacks faced for a hundred years after the Civil War.[20] Changes to the state constitution, murders of black citizens brave enough to challenge the status quo, and failed attempts to bring black voters back to the polls represent a stagnant atmosphere marked by violence and fear. This historical background is important—without it as a reference point, the rhetorical tactics employed by the Freedom Vote are hollow and isolated—and strengthens the relevance of its successes. After exhausting what appeared to be every available means to them, the stage was set for activists and protestors to change tactics in order to achieve the strategic goal of the franchise. That shifting of tactics would not happen overnight, but it would keep voting as the primary theme and telos.

Chapter Two
THE SUMMER BEFORE THE LONG, HOT SUMMER

The Freedom Vote emerged from a flurry of national and regional activity. Examining the months leading up to the campaign introduces some of the people and organizations directly involved with the event. This chapter examines artifacts ranging from photographs to newspaper stories, and the initial speech text of the Freedom Vote. Readers will engage the rhetorical happenings in the summer before the campaign as they chronologically unfold, starting first with the Jackson sit-in and the photograph that captured that protest, moving next to the death of Medgar Evers, then the discourse that went in to the planning of the Freedom Vote, and finally a recruitment speech Allard Lowenstein delivered in the early fall on the campus of Stanford University. This close-textual reading of these texts and moments provides the foundational understanding of how and why the tactical use of a traditional political campaign as a form of protest utilized image event concepts. This chapter begins to trace the legacy of the Freedom Vote and its tactical innovations back to the wellspring.

• • •

Getting your name, let alone your picture, on the front page of the *New York Times* is a hard thing to do. Most of us will never experience the fame or infamy of being disseminated via one of the historically most-trusted sources of news information not only in America, but arguably the world. For some, getting their picture on the front page of the *Times* is just a matter of being at the right place at the right time, but for others it's the result of careful strategic planning and timely tactical execution. For Memphis Norman, it proved to be a bit of both.

On May 29, 1963, Norman found himself on the front page of the *New York Times* not once, but twice, and in very different poses.[1] Under the headline "Negro Is Beaten and Kicked at Lunch Counter in Mississippi's Capital," Norman appears in two drastically different photos; in the first photo, Norman is seen sitting at the Woolworth's downtown lunch counter in Jackson.

Norman is sitting with another black student from Tougaloo College with a sign advertising $0.70 roasted turkey dinners and Coca-Cola hanging behind them. The accompanying image is not so Rockwellian; Norman is seen lying on the ground as former police officer Benny Oliver kicks him, surrounded by a group of onlooking white men. The crowd appears unimpressed and unmoved—one man smokes a cigarette while watching. The photos take on the quality of montage at this point, aided by the simple captions; we know, or at least think we know, that Norman was removed from his stool and then beaten and kicked by Oliver. Our minds do the sequencing for us. Here we see on the front page of the *New York Times* evidence of racial violence and hatred in the American South.

This was not the only photograph taken of the previous day's sit-in. Fred Blackwell, shooting for the *Jackson Daily News*, took what would be one of the more iconic photos of not just the student sit-ins that swept across the country but of the civil rights movement itself. Blackwell's photo, which ran in *Newsweek* the following week, remains in the visual consciousness of our civil rights memories. Pictures of dogs and hoses unleashed on young Birmingham protestors mix with images of Martin Luther King Jr. marching arm-in-arm in Selma to create an almost photo-album-like history of the civil rights movement. This moment from the Jackson sit-in forever captured by Blackwell shares one key thing with other iconic civil rights photos: it wanted to be taken; it was designed to be taken. This image from the Jackson sit-in is the result of a careful, well-executed plan designed to draw attention. What the photograph captures and communicates is of great importance: contained within the photo is a moment that transformed a boycott into a direct-action campaign, which would continue on into the summer in Jackson. Like many of the images from the civil rights movement, this photograph of the protest captures an image event with rhetorical consequences. Specifically, the photograph functions as a source of evidence to refute the myth that violence and intimidation were not everyday experiences in the South; the photograph has a constitutive function by depicting both black and white agents in social movement activity; and the photo also works as a flashpoint for the tactical developments the Freedom Vote campaign utilized in a more sustained manner. That pictures and photos are powerful influencers on our beliefs and attitudes is of little doubt, but what is ultimately more significant is how the meaning and symbolism of what we see turn into cognitive activity and potential behavior—in short, how and why we translate the pictures we see into the pictures in our heads. Before examining Blackwell's photograph, first we must define and discuss the meaning behind labeling the event an image event.

THE SHOCK OF THE FAMILIAR MADE STRANGE

According to rhetorical critics Kevin DeLuca and Jennifer Peeples, "We must consider image events, then, as visual philosophical-rhetorical fragments, mind bombs that expand the universe of thinkable thoughts. Image events are dense surfaces meant to provoke in an instant the shock of the familiar made strange" (144). For the Jackson sit-in and its iconic photo, the familiar is the lunch counter, an all-American experience immortalized by Norman Rockwell's paintings, which cast the lunch counter as an idealistic and patriotic experience, an almost sacred place. This is our image event's familiar. The shock comes from what is happening in this familiar space; intruders are trespassing. An image event is a visual contradiction that triggers cognitive dissonance; here the scene is familiar, but the action and activity are strange.

Examine Fred Blackwell's photograph as an image event with rhetorical consequences. "Image events," according to DeLuca, "challenge a number of tenets of traditional rhetorical theory and criticism, starting with the notion that rhetoric ideally is 'reasoned discourse,' with 'reasoned' connoting 'civil' or 'rational' and 'discourse' connoting 'words'" (14). For DeLuca, image events are not "the desperate stunts of the disillusioned but rather the way in which contemporary society communicates" (17). Image events exercise their agency by "employing publicity as a social medium through which to hold corporations and states accountable, help form public opinion, and constitute their own identities as subaltern counterpublics. Critique through spectacle, not critique versus spectacle" (21). Image events do not confront ideology outside of popular mainstream media; instead, they use the very same means of distribution to spread their own counter ideological messages. The use of the American lunch counter as a vehicle or delivery method for rhetoric is not to be missed. The sit-in organizers knew the American lunch counter would make a powerful delivery method for their protest rhetoric.

While the Jackson sit-in did not receive as much attention as other iconic civil rights image events, such as Martin Luther King Jr.'s Birmingham campaign or the March on Washington, it does provide a model of protest and resistance built from the ground up at the local level without the aid of iconic leaders or national organizations. Scholar Davi Johnson explains, "Image events are often orchestrated by social movements, and they are defined as deliberately staged spectacles designed to attract the attention of mass media and disseminate persuasive images to a wide audience" (2). This function of image events was of great import to activists and organizations working in Mississippi, where they sorely needed media attention.

Johnson explains how images from social movements work, noting, "Photographs can be epiphanic, forcing a psychic transformation of the citizenry by rupturing imagined conceptions of identity" (8). This transformation, this rhetorical psychology of images and image events, creates within us our own unique experience and understanding, which then influences the ways we think and act. "Images, then, are important not because they represent reality but create it," especially for viewers who were not there to experience the image event firsthand (DeLuca and Peeples 133).

It is important to remember that the organizers design image events to appear on the "public screen," an extension and evolution of the public sphere. "The public screen is a constant current of images and words, ceaseless circulation abetted by the technologies of television, film, photography, and the Internet," according to DeLuca and Peeples (135). It is access to the public screen, much like similar critiques of the public sphere, that generates problems of control and cultural hegemony. DeLuca and Peeples point out three rhetorical constraints facing citizens who want to participate in the discourse of the public screen: "1) private ownership/monopoly of the public screen, 2) Infotainment conventions that filter what counts as news, and 3) the need to communicate in the discourse of images" (136). As we analyze the Jackson sit-in and Blackwell's photo, we see how these same constraints faced activists and organizations. This is further evidenced by Davi Johnson's work on the Birmingham campaign of 1963 and Christine Harold and Kevin DeLuca's work on the image of Emmett Till's corpse. The next section shows how a trend in literature focusing on images and image events from the civil rights movement is already well under way.

"READING" THE IMAGES FROM THE JACKSON SIT-IN

Think of the images in this book as a visual rhetorical history. The rhetorical historian's perspective analyzes "how messages are created and used by people to influence and relate to one another" (Zarefsky 30). According to Zarefsky, rhetorical historians focus on "how, and how well, people invented and deployed messages in response to the situation" (30). This study utilizes this perspective but applies it to visual artifacts. Christine Harold and Kevin DeLuca, in "Behold the Corpse: Violent Images and the Case of Emmett Till," examine how the symbolism contained in images of Emmett Till's corpse impacted the black community (Harold and DeLuca 263–286). They explore the motivating power and influence that images of Till's corpse had on the contemporary civil rights movement.

Shaping the visual rhetorical history of the work that follows are two articles by Gallagher and Zagacki, in which they analyze how visual rhetoric influenced (and continues to influence) viewers' perceptions of the civil rights movement.[2] They argue that visual rhetoric "evoked common humanity by visually disregarding established caricatures," "evoked common humanity by creating recognition of others through particularity," and "reminded viewers that abstract political concepts were always relative to the individuals or groups whose lives were most directly influenced by their presence or absence" ("Visibility and Rhetoric" 180). Gallagher and Zagacki analyze how individual visual artifacts provide rhetorical sources and resources for viewers to actually engage with the experience of others. A rhetorical perspective focuses on "how images interrogate viewers so as to invoke self-awareness about the conscious lived experience of the other" ("Visibility and Rhetoric" 182). Looking at photographs, images, and art from a rhetorical perspective opens up these artifacts to examine the rhetorical functioning embedded therein. This allows for a different interpretation of historical events and shapes public knowledge of the past by "reading" visual artifacts. The state of Mississippi has few historical markers concerning the civil rights movement, but one of them is in downtown Jackson and indicates where the Woolworth's used to be—the Blackwell photo is on the back of the marker. The Blackwell photo becomes the authoritative and preferred representation of the sit-in protest by physically occupying the very space captured in the photograph. This photo then also becomes part of our collective memory of the event, further solidified when the protest is reified by the marker's presence.

A STATE IN TACTICAL EVOLUTION

By the time of the Jackson sit-in in May 1963, workers and organizers in Mississippi had tried just about everything. Violent oppression in the 1950s, including the murders of Reverend George Lee, Emmett Till, and Mack Parker, had driven the National Association for the Advancement of Colored People (NAACP) underground and left the civil rights movement in Mississippi in a state of disarray and inactivity.[3] Bob Moses and the Student Nonviolent Committee (SNCC) began voter registration drives in the early 1960s that for all the time, money, and effort spent registered far too few black voters. When the Freedom Rides rolled into Jackson, the riders quickly found themselves in the state's infamous Parchmen Penitentiary, known locally as the Parchmen Farm. James Meredith integrated Ole Miss only with the force and coercion of the recently mobilized National Guard. Activists in Mississippi had tried almost every tactic available at the time: voter registration, testing the Interstate Commerce Commission (ICC) ruling, and even school desegregation.

It was a natural progression for the movement in Mississippi to incorporate a previously used tactic, the sit-in. The first sit-in was in Greensboro, North Carolina, in February 1960, and it too has a photograph to accompany the event, though the image is not as shocking as the one from the Jackson sit-in. The Mississippi organizers deployed the tactic at the perfect time. The movement in Mississippi had stalled, and local leaders were unsure in which direction to go. There was no single iconic leader to look to or major organization that made the decisions. Mississippians had never attempted a direct-action campaign of this size and scale. The birthplace for mass demonstrations and direct-action campaigns in Mississippi was the lunch-counter stools of the downtown Jackson Woolworth's.[4]

PHOTO ANALYSIS

On May 28, 1963, students and professors from historically black Tougaloo College sat at the Woolworth's lunch counter for nearly three hours as a white mob of almost 200 harassed them. To look at the photo, you would think that John Salter, Joan Trumpauer, and Anne Moody just showed up and sat down for lunch when a white mob developed and harassed them as they calmly sat and Fred Blackwell clicked away with his camera. But that's not how it happened.

Planning for the demonstration had been going on for weeks before the actual sit-in. When the actual day of the demonstration arrived, every protestor involved knew exactly what to do. At 11:00 a.m. Anne Moody, Pearlena Lewis, and Memphis Norman walked into Woolworth's through the rear entrance and separated, spreading out through the store (Moody 286). At 11:15 a.m. the three black students from Tougaloo met and sat as planned at the lunch counter. Within a few minutes, whites sitting at the counter got up and left, waitresses abandoned their customers, and the clientele were replaced by newsmen and onlookers. Protestors held, in a clever means of divergence, a faux demonstration at 10:45 a.m. in front of the J. C. Penney store. Organizers had previously informed reporters about a planned demonstration early in the day but withheld the location so that local authorities could not prevent the demonstration. This planning demonstrates the strategic design of the sit-in, one of the primary features of any staged image event.

Anne Moody recounts that not much happened, and newsmen almost left after forty-five minutes, but then a local high school let out for lunch at noon. The high school students arrived at Woolworth's and instantly began taunting

Figure 2.1. Photograph of the Jackson sit-in at the downtown Woolworth's counter. AP photograph taken by Fred Blackwell, 1963

the three demonstrators, chanting derogatory slogans and even making a hangman's noose out of rope meant to cordon off the area. At this point Memphis Norman suggested to Moody and Lewis that the three of them pray together. Moody remembers, "We bowed our heads, and all hell broke loose" (Moody 287).

Benny Oliver, a former police officer in Jackson, pulled Memphis Norman from his stool to the ground and began kicking him savagely in the head. After a few kicks, a plains-clothed policeman identified himself and arrested both Norman and Oliver. Moody and Lewis had also been pulled down from their stools but were not beaten, and they returned to their seats after the arrest of their colleague. Joan Trumpauer, a white student from Tougaloo, joined the two black women at the counter. As the harassment continued, the first of two Tougaloo professors joined the demonstrations. Lois Chaffee sat down, bringing the total number of protestors at the counter to four, all of them women. This is when the mob began peppering the protestors, literally. Ketchup, mustard, salt, pepper, and even sugar containers were emptied on the protestors. John Salter, a white professor from Tougaloo, sat down at this point, and a member of the mob instantly greeted him with a pair of brass knuckles, adding his blood to the mixture. Walter Williams, a CORE worker from Jackson State College, sat down while the mob emptied ashtrays on the demonstrators. The blood on Salter is hard to miss. So, too, are the looks on the faces of the onlookers: old and young alike are watching closely—some in anger, some in concern. Note the face of a young white woman in the top-middle of the frame; gender is here, both in the crowd and at the counter. The presence of different genders strengthens and increases the potential appeal (and disgust) of not only the photograph but the protest event itself. Several different age groups are represented in the mob—older gentlemen with ties and hats mix with high school students; a true social gathering is unfolding.

It was some time shortly after this that Fred Blackwell took the photograph that has been in major works on the civil rights movement and reprinted in collections of the most important photographs of the twentieth century.[5] From an aesthetic perspective, the photo has it all: it is well-framed and well-lit, it focuses on the dramatic action, and it engages the viewer in a very active nature because action is being captured. The photo has depth and action; it's an easy picture to look at and engage not only for its aesthetic qualities but also the depiction of dramatic action. The photo has the character of direct cinema, where the camera acts like a fly on the wall, strictly in an observational role. Because of documentary-like characteristics such as this, there is fairness and balance in what the image captures. The appearance of accuracy and objectivity is important for the photographs that capture moments from the movement. What the image captures actually seems rather unfair, but it is a fair documentation of the event as it happened.

The easy engagement comes from not only the aesthetics of the photo but also the locale of the context of the photo. Here is an all-American scene, the lunch counter, but what's happening here seems very un-American. The photo asks the viewer several intimate questions: "Does this happen to you during your lunch?" "Is this common at your local lunch counter?" The viewer is confronted with an everyday context, lunchtime at a lunch counter, where extraordinary action is taking place. Protest is a very democratic and patriotic thing, but the reaction of the mob, as evidenced by blood and condiments, is quite the contrary. These patriots are being punished, and we are seeing it. Image events must use the discourse of images that create cognitive dissonance, and this photo does so with chilling effect.

This is more than just a great picture at work—this is a moment of change being played out. Contained within the photo is a moment that transformed a boycott into a direct-action campaign, which would continue on into the summer in Jackson.[6] This photo captures and suspends a link in the legacy of protest in Mississippi. The photo portrays what Sean Patrick O'Rourke calls "instances of rhetorical somatics" in that the very bodies of the protestors, rather than their words, are acting rhetorically (688).

As previously stated, the photograph of the protest functions as an image event with rhetorical consequences; specifically, the photograph functions as a source of evidence to refute the myth that violence and intimidation were not everyday experiences in the South. Understanding these functions of the photo provides insight as to how and why visual rhetorics of display have such influence, and why social movements consistently employ and include image events as tactical options.

The photo is myth busting in that it shows a common everyday experience, getting lunch at a lunch counter. The photo is evidence, visual proof, that violence and intimidation were normal aspects of daily life for blacks in Mississippi. In the top-right corner of the photo are a few American flags, not the Confederate Stars and Bars, but the flag of the unified nation. The picture transmits a disconnect as very antidemocratic behavior on the part of the mob contrasts with the protestors exercising a sacred American right that dates back to the Boston Tea Party.

The photo disproves the notion that everything was fine in 1960s America, that blacks faced no violence and intimidation in their daily lives across the South. The photo is a direct contradiction to that myth, and like other mediated image events, this photo helps us *to see* it in a shocking and jarring manner. The photo serves as a synecdoche for what daily life was like for blacks and protestors in Mississippi by portraying just one part of their day. Showing a normal day's activity, like eating lunch, allows viewers to connect a *pars por toto* that blacks face this kind of violence and intimidation all the time, every day, and not just during lunch.

The myth that violence doesn't happen is further shattered because of the fact that we are witnessing an act of violence—we are actually seeing intimidation in action. The outstretched arm of the white youth grasping the empty shaker speaks without saying a word; so too does the grin in his eyes as he surveys his work. There are a lot of smiles and grins in the photo, signaling approval on the part of the mob. It is strange to see other people taking joy watching something you yourself despise yet are powerless to stop. Or is that the point of the photo as an image event? Wayne Santoro notes, "When the audience is willing to look the other way or holds little sympathy for the recipients of violence, violence used by the stronger of the combatants usually works" (1395). He found three key aspects that the audience witnessing violence, or images portraying such, must have in order for the audience to want the termination of violent actions: attention, sympathy, and involvement (Santoro 1395). When audiences contain high levels of these three aspects toward the victims, they are far more likely to express their distaste and actually seek means to end such discrimination. But when the audience's attention, sympathy, and involvement are low, violence by the superior group is often a successful response to protests.

A second rhetorical function of Blackwell's photo is the unifying nature of the image. It would be inaccurate to read it as an "us-versus-them" dialectic, a simple black-and-white rendering. To look at the image and say "these people hate those people" misses the chance to identify not only with the protestors but also with the mob, and possibly with other people around the country viewing the same image. Breaking down the protestors to one black female student, one white female student, and a white male college professor is a start, but even those classifications neglect the nuances and individual makeup of each protestor. Extending the image's first function as myth-busting, one common misbelief was that all protestors were from out of the state, or commonly referred to as "outside agitators." In actuality, the protestors are all from Tougaloo, the nearby historically black college, and therefore have an investment in the community. Technically speaking, two of the protestors are "southerners"; Moody is from Mississippi, and Trumpauer is from Virginia. Salter, raised in Arizona, is too far of a stretch to be considered a "southerner," but another interesting layer of his identity is that one of his parents was Scottish and the other a Native American. Gender and age help here too, as Trumpauer's bun of hair occupies the focal middle point of the picture.

The constitutive function here is not one that parcels off particular groups from a larger population or community, but rather is one of unity through plurality. A black Mississippian, a white southerner, and a Scotch–Native American are together for a common cause despite differences in gender, age, race, and ethnic backgrounds. It is not their actions in the photo but the behavior of the onlooking mob, our fellow compatriots, that is repulsive. In the 1960s viewers may not have immediately marched down and fought to desegregate their own lunch counters (though some may have), but would they want to be counted among the mob? Shame and guilt, sadness or disgust, arise from comparing the onlookers' grins with Anne Moody's facial expression. She looks disappointed, let down, not by her own actions but by those of her fellow Mississippians. "Before the sit-in," Moody recalled, "I had always hated the whites in Mississippi. Now I knew it was impossible for me to hate sickness. The whites had a disease, an incurable disease in its final stage" (290). The fact that we can't see the protestors' eyes is another interesting feature of the photo. This ambiguity allows the viewers to imagine themselves or people they know in the scene.

A third rhetorical function of the image is as the pedagogical flashpoint for Freedom Vote tactics. This relates to the first function of myth-busting for viewers back in the 1960s but also teaches contemporary viewers about historical acts of democratic protest. The photo preserves the context of civil rights in Mississippi by depicting a historical protest. It also instructs us about the people and individuals who did the protesting and those who resisted the protestors. But we also learn more than just dates, places, and names. We learn about where our country has been and how far it has come since then. We learn essentially about ourselves, about what we are capable of, both good and bad.

It is hard to merely look at civil rights photography, especially when it's in black and white—somehow the lack of color adds another layer of credibility to the photo's depiction of reality. You don't glance at these photos; they sink in. The viewer contemplates them; even if viewers don't know all the details of specific names and dates, they drink in every visual detail and cue, and, if no caption is provided, they enthymematically fill in details for themselves.

The two gentlemen at the far end of the counter played significant roles that often are overlooked. The gentleman sitting at the counter is Tougaloo president Daniel Beittel. For the last hour of the sit-in, Beittel ran in and out of Woolworth's trying to get the ninety or so police officers outside to break up the riot going on in the store.[7] The chief of police consistently told Beittel that he would not enter Woolworth's unless the manager of the facility requested it. The frustrated sixty-three-year-old then joined his students and faculty member at the lunch counter. It was only after the mob began smashing and breaking anything they could get hold of that the manager turned off the lights and shut down the store (Dittmer 162). The man speaking with President Beittel is Ken Toler, a reporter for the *Memphis Commercial Appeal*. Toler covered the mass meetings that followed during the next few evenings, and he approached Salter and complimented him and his fellow protestors for their tenacity and courage. "Significantly," Salter recounts, "he did this in full view of Mississippi lawmen and Mississippi newsmen."[8]

The protestors were escorted out of Woolworth's, protected by police officers, who created a barrier between the protestors and the crowd that had gathered. As mentioned earlier, many historians view the sit-in as a catalyst for the mass demonstrations that followed and spread into the summer. The sit-in was as a successful image event. Communicating via the discourse of Blackwell's images, the event gained access to the public screen through "the shock of the familiar made strange." The image creates a state of cognitive dissonance in the minds of Americans and challenges viewers now, much as it did then.

KEEPING THE MOVEMENT MOVING

The sit-in sparked a demonstration by high school students from the four all-black Jackson high schools a few days later.[9] As the students marched, carrying American flags toward the capitol itself, they were met by eighty-seven police officers. Many were beaten, most were arrested, but the movement was moving in Jackson, at least for a while.

Being familiar with the environment and state of affairs in Mississippi before, during, and after the Freedom Vote is crucial to understanding how important the campaign was to the advancement of civil rights in Mississippi. A comprehensive history of violence in the state against blacks or civil rights workers is not necessary, though, because that history never really stopped in Mississippi until later. Workers and volunteers were reminded of this a little more than a month after the Woolworth's demonstration.

Early on the morning of June 12, 1963, the movement in Mississippi lost one of its greatest proponents. Medgar Evers, as he returned home late from a long day of meetings and planning sessions, was shot in the back by Byron De La Beckwith. Evers was the NAACP Mississippi field secretary, a veteran, and a longtime crusader for justice on behalf of Mississippi's black citizens. Evers's wife and three children watched as he died in the carport. Coincidentally, President Kennedy just a few hours earlier had addressed the nation in a televised speech asserting that Americans faced "a moral dilemma." Kennedy's address specifically cited the recent forced integration at the University of Alabama but also touched on national and worldwide trends of democratic freedom. The president posed some difficult questions to the nation: "The heart of the question is whether all Americans are to be afforded equal rights and equal opportunities, whether we are to treat our fellow Americans as we want to be treated. If an American, because his skin is dark, cannot eat lunch in a restaurant open to the public, if he cannot vote for the public officials who will represent him, if, in short, he cannot enjoy the full and free life which all of us want, then who among us would be content to have the color of his skin change and stand in his place? Who among us would then be content with the counsels of patience and delay?"[10] The murder of Medgar Evers further highlighted the urgency and necessity behind the president's soul-searching questions.

The assassination of Evers temporarily stalled efforts in Mississippi. The voter registration projects in the Delta, along with the demonstrations in Jackson, had gained some national attention, albeit often due to violent white reactions. The assassination of Evers created extreme tension in the capital city. Evers's death signaled the end of direct-action campaigns in Jackson for a time. Dittmer notes that more conservative members joined the steering committees of civil rights organizations operating in Jackson (168). Despite Evers's death and organizational leadership issues, the movement in Mississippi needed to keep moving.

INSPIRATION IN MOURNING

A "voting day" project sprang up in conversations between Allard Lowenstein and Bob Moses. Lowenstein arrived in Mississippi in July 1963, coming from his teaching position at North Carolina State, and for a few weeks observed the climate in Mississippi.[11] Lowenstein saw the potential for a unique opportunity in Mississippi: "I remember that I had been in South Africa on Election Day. The African National Congress had called a day of mourning so that blacks would demonstrate their discontent. So I thought, in South Africa, where blacks can't vote, they have a day of mourning, but in Mississippi they are supposed to be able to vote. So why not have a day of voting" (Viorst 390–391). Lowenstein and Moses formed plans to test the idea in the upcoming August primaries. Law students volunteering for movement organizations in Jackson had found a loophole in the Mississippi Constitution that allowed the casting of protest ballots during any primary (Burner 112). Nearly 1,000 blacks, mostly in and around Greenwood, cast "freedom ballots." During the Democratic primary runoff election a few weeks later, organizers quickly created opportunities for blacks to vote in their churches, businesses, and other community gatherings to let blacks feel as if they too were participating in the runoff. More than 27,000 local blacks cast ballots. Moses deemed the vote a success, and organizers started planning for a statewide "freedom vote."

In August, during the all-white primaries in Mississippi, the March on Washington stole the nation's attention. The history texts and news concerning the event tend to focus on Martin Luther King Jr.'s famous "I Have a Dream" speech, but also of note is a shorter and more controversial speech that the new chairman of SNCC, John Lewis, made. This particular speech was altered, arguably censored by event planners, at the last minute. The censored speech contains toned-down statements in three sections where Lewis originally had included more passionate, provocative, and explicit language.[12] There is, however, a brief passage in the middle of Lewis's speech that pertains to the Freedom Vote:

> My friends, let us not forget that we are involved in a serious social revolution. By and large American politics is dominated by politicians who field their career on immoral compromises and alliances to the open forum of political, economic, and social exploitation. There are exceptions of course. We salute those. But what political leader can stand up and say, "My party is the party of principles"? For the party of Kennedy is also the party of Eastland. The party of Javitz is also the party of Goldwater. Where is our party? Where is a political party that will make it unnecessary to march on Washington? Where is the political party that will make it

unnecessary to march in the streets of Birmingham? Where is a political party that will protect the citizens of Albany, Georgia?[13]

Lewis's questions function as public demands for a political party that represents and serves the interest of black Americans. The phrase, "Where is *our* party?" became a powerful public call and declaration. It was a decree for an opportunity to afford blacks a means of participation in the political process through the formation of a political party. Lewis insinuates that neither the Republican Party nor the Democratic Party seemed willing to shoulder the causes of black America, and by asking "Where is our party?" he is asking for blacks to organize themselves into their own political party. With the planning for, and the eventual execution of, the Mississippi Freedom Vote of 1963, Lewis's questions had an initial answer.

LOWENSTEIN REACHES OUT

Allard Lowenstein's speech at Stanford University on October 2, 1963, along with correspondence, meeting notes, and reports from organizations operating within Mississippi, clearly illustrated the planning that went into the Freedom Vote as a strategic image event. Both Lowenstein's address and the archived sources paint a picture of a well-organized and motivated effort, which had been discussed tentatively since the end of August.

Lowenstein, designated the chairman of the campaign's advisory board, utilized his connections around the country to round up support and resources for the Freedom Vote. Lowenstein was able to convince northern white college students from both Yale and Stanford to give more than their money to the effort. Through speeches and meetings on campus, much like the one on October 2, Lowenstein painted a picture of violence and intimidation as the norm in the Magnolia State. He motivated the students and challenged them to become participatory citizens.

Lowenstein begins his speech with a series of jokes, addressing rumors concerning his status as a Communist. Before really getting into the topic of his speech, he shares with the crowd, "I think my favorite rumor of the day, which I'm told is the imaginative contribution of one of my greatest admirers in the political science department, is that my present ambition is to become the first Jewish President of the United States of America." The crowd responded with laughter, and Lowenstein continued to make light of the rumor. "I want to deny the charge simply because what Harry Golden said in connection with the present campaign, which I agree with, and that is that I've always known that the first Jewish President of the United States would be an Episcopalian." Lowenstein often used humor to start his speeches, which displaces some of the tension inherent in such a moment and allows him to connect with an audience through self-disclosure and sharing a laugh.

Lowenstein then puts the joking aside as he immediately turns to his topic and takes his identification to the intimate and personal level. "I don't think that Mississippi is a foreign country in our midst—and I think one reason it's important to talk about Mississippi is it is very much *ourselves* in our midst."[14] This is a theme that runs throughout the speech, one with which Lowenstein constantly reminds his audience that the problems and issues in Mississippi are their problems and issues as well. Lowenstein connects to the students in his audience as he poses questions of personal morality: "How many of us haven't in our own hearts accepted the implications of the fact that because Mississippi is 42 percent Negro—and parts of it 70 percent Negro—that therefore Mississippi does have special problems which excuse the white behavior, not because we like brutality or because we agree with white supremacy, but because, after all, we have to expect that the white race is always really going to rule things? I think most of us are guilty of this kind of thinking." Lowenstein accuses his audience of stereotypical thinking and complacency with the status quo. He uses statistical information, in a section on racial demographics, throughout his address to supplement the credibility he already possesses from his experiences in Mississippi.

He again turns toward his theme of inclusion and identification when he refers to Mississippi as a "sick place": "It's so sick that to go to Mississippi is to leave America in the way that we think of America and to see America in a grotesque mirror in which all our warts are magnified. But they are our warts. It is us. It is our racial sickness, not some foreign breed, although you do feel occasionally surprised when you go into a store and discover that you don't have to change currency to buy something." The constant reminder that the problems faced in Mississippi concern all Americans makes the audience take ownership and responsibility for those issues. In doing this, Lowenstein empowers his audience and pushes the crowd to action.

Lowenstein shares with the crowd what he felt was the most useful thing he could do in preparing for a half-hour talk about Mississippi: "What I did was to jot down little episodes." These "little episodes" operate less as stories and more as a powerful and compelling narrative that instills a sense of exigency in the audience, planting mind bombs in their consciousness. These verbal narrative mind bombs can be just as powerful as their visual counterparts due to the similar enthymatic nature of their interpretation. Within another rhetorical framework, these episodes operate much like a religious witnessing or a testimony. In a long statement, Lowenstein explains to the audience his decision to tell them little episodes: "I felt that the most useful contribution a person can make who has been in Mississippi to people who have not been in Mississippi, perhaps, is to go into the specifics of what is now going on and hope that out of this will come more than a statistic, will come in your hearts a feeling that you are involved in Mississippi, not only for the residual reasons of world prestige and not only because your conscience bothers you to know that there's injustice." Lowenstein clearly tells the audience his intentions: to get them "involved in any way." He does so through verbal illustration, mind bombs in the form of stories. He is motivating the audience to action, instilling in them a cause; through his little episodes, Lowenstein attempts to communicate to the Stanford students a moral obligation to participate and enact agency, shocking the students into action.

The bulk of the rest of Lowenstein's address is the actual telling of these little episodes. The twelve stories he shares are from experiences all over the state, but stories from the Delta and Jackson comprise the majority. He tells of how the Episcopal bishop of Mississippi was beaten in his home in Jackson. He tells of how just four weeks after the assassination of Evers the citizens of Leflore County raised $1,500 to help fund the defense for Byron De La Beckwith, his killer. Lowenstein shares that during the three weeks he was in Mississippi that summer, four blacks had been killed, three by police officers. He tells of how in Tchula, Hartman Turnbow was arrested for firebombing his own house. Lowenstein depicts an environment in which death, violence, and intimidation are the norm; he shares with the audience the gruesome ramifications for those who attempt to participate in the most basic of democratic practices.

He also touches on the failures of the judicial system and the political corruption within Mississippi. He highlights the relationship between Judge William Harold Cox and Senator James O. Eastland—Cox is the federal judge in Mississippi and a former law partner of Senator Eastland, who heads the Judiciary Committee. Lowenstein recalls witnessing Judge Cox in action during a trial earlier that summer. During the trial, witness after witness testified to seeing a deputy sheriff of Rankin County beat blacks attempting to register at the courthouse. Lowenstein describes the judge's reaction: "And Judge Cox, having heard all the evidence—a federal district court judge—not only dismissed the suit against the sheriff and the deputy sheriff on the grounds that there was no proof that the beatings were connected with their effort to register—although nobody ever adduced any evidence that they were connected to anything else—but he also dismissed the perjury of the deputy sheriff on the grounds that, after all, the evidence had been improperly received in the courtroom and therefore it was improper to consider whether perjury had been committed in improperly produced evidence." Lowenstein asserts through this particular episode that the problems in Mississippi are social and systemic, not isolated to mere incidents of localized white violence or intimidation. The political system and other social institutions are not neutral in Mississippi, if they are anywhere, but rather they are controlled, influenced, and clearly interconnected by a network underwritten by white supremacy. Again, Lowenstein's speech is functionally similar to the tactics of image event generating mind bombs.

One of Lowenstein's more personal episodes tells of when he was in Clarksdale wearing a black suit and holding a briefcase on the steps of a church. He remembers, "I went up to the church steps and there I was, standing there in this attire in the hot sun, with the police driving around in their helmets and Confederate flags and whatnot. And I was really astonished to discover that as the day wore on and the heat got worse, they got more and more polite. And this whole thing mystified me until finally a photographer came over to me and said, 'Is it true that you're in the FBI [Federal Bureau of Investigation]?'" The audience erupted with laughter at this image. "The local gendarmes had told him this. They had said, 'Those god-damn feds've even got an FBI agent standing up there with all them niggers.'" While this episode further strengthens Lowenstein's credibility by physically placing him in Mississippi, and therefore potentially in harm's way, it also relates the mentality and outlook that motivated local white authorities.

Lowenstein saves his most powerful episodic mind bomb and testimony for last. He tells of standing at the same church the very next day and overhearing an eighty-four-year-old black woman ask, "What did we did, what did we did that made 'em hate us so?" as she watched protestors being hauled away in paddy wagons. Lowenstein recounts:

> Then she said, "I gave them my two boys; one of them they took off into a war and killed, and now I can't even go on the streets of my own city." And I reached over and just took her hand and she, I think for the first time, saw there was a white person present. And she broke up, and I did. And we went in and sat down in the church. And then she told—one wishes one could have the gift of poetry that comes naturally to some people—the story of her life in Clarksdale. And I suppose if there's anything that's permanently with me from Mississippi it was this woman, who had been cleaning white people's houses through the rear doors for all these years, whose children, one of them now dead, had been good enough for her country to take, but who was unable to walk in the streets of her town, saying, "What did we did that made 'em hate us so?"

This episode crystallizes the issues Lowenstein has been speaking of throughout his address into a compelling and emotionally moving story for his audience to relate to. That simple phrase uttered by the elderly woman is a powerful one; it is the same introspective and rhetorically reflective question any oppressed individual would ask. Her question is not literal; it is symbolic in that it represents a plea for reason, for understanding and justification. "What did we did that made 'em hate us so?" then becomes not a question, but a demand to know.

Lowenstein includes this story perhaps to force the students to ask themselves what they are willing to do to change her perspective and counter her demand. He moves from this last episode into his closing remarks. This final section of his speech is a clear call-to-action for his audience: "When you list all the possible ways of trying to break through this nightmare in Mississippi, when you consider the fact that you cannot picket, that even boycotts produce tremendous retribution and are conducted with tremendous difficulty, that you can't vote, that you can't mass-demonstrate, that there isn't any way you have of expressing protest, it leads to the necessity of figuring out something else that can be done." This is where Lowenstein shares with the Stanford students two options that organizations in Mississippi were considering. "One is this mock vote." Without going into much detail, Lowenstein argues that the campaign is an opportunity for blacks in Mississippi to demonstrate how badly they want the rights that all Americans are supposed to have. He is unmasking the sustained image event campaign, another anchor in the arc of the Freedom Vote's legacy. The other option he makes available to the students is on a grander scale; Lowenstein calls this option "a mass assistance campaign from outside Mississippi" planned for the next summer—what would later be known as Freedom Summer.

Lowenstein's final remarks remind his audience why he is speaking to them and encourages their participation. He concludes:

> So this is what our hopes are in Mississippi. It's not an optimistic forecast of the situation. I couldn't honestly be optimistic now about Mississippi except that I think you know, and I know, that we are going to win in Mississippi, that the feeling that somehow there is no progress is wrong. And that from the perspective of the United States and of the world, this little island of embittered people, shooting and beating and turning to brute force to terrify, are in the backwater of civilization and are going to be lost. Mississippi is not a foreign country in our midst—it's the foreign part of all of us in our midst. And we help ourselves, I think, as we help Mississippi. Thank you very much.

Lowenstein effectively ends his speech as he began it: reminding the audience that the problems in Mississippi are not outside their own lives and experiences as American citizens. The issues facing Mississippi concern and belong to all Americans. The speech is a personal plea for help and assistance. Lowenstein, speaking on behalf of organizers and participants of the Freedom Vote, appeals to the students on a level of moral obligation and duty. This speech is the first to touch upon the themes found throughout the rhetorical artifacts of the Freedom Vote.

The Freedom Vote did not randomly appear; rather, as this chapter demonstrates, it was an organized response to an environment of injustice. Examining the events immediately leading up to the Freedom Vote contextualizes the texts produced by protestors and participants, shedding light on why they responded with a mock election. Chapter 3 establishes how this response was put into action. It also details the recruiting and canvassing of the campaign, along with the media's initial response, or rather, lack thereof.

Chapter Three
ORGANIZING, RECRUITING, AND CANVASSING

Change came in many forms during the Freedom Vote, often in subtle ways. Yale Divinity student Jim Vaughn challenged the code of segregation unknowingly while working for the Freedom Vote in Greenwood, Mississippi. He and two Student Nonviolent Coordinating Committee (SNCC) staffers stopped at a burger stand for lunch. Vaughn went up to the counter, ordered, and brought the food back to the car to find wide eyes and dropped jaws. One SNCC staffer, Nate, told Vaughn that it was the first time that blacks had ever been able to eat from that restaurant.[1] Moments like this connect to the overall goal of the Freedom Vote in not-so-obvious but important ways, still contributing to the change needed in Mississippi.

This chapter moves through the first three-and-a-half weeks of October 1963, when the rhetoric of the Freedom Vote was mobilized and put into action by organizers. During this time, the Council of Federated Organizations (COFO) officially sponsored the Freedom Vote, which required intense organizational planning along with recruitment and initial canvassing. By synthesizing speech texts with visual counterparts, critiquing the media coverage, and exploring oral histories and archived documents, this chapter analyzes the initial rhetorical and tactical execution of the Freedom Vote. It is important to remember that the Freedom Vote symbolically represents and employs the very rhetoric it is attempting to instill in its audience, specifically regarding the agency of the vote via the implementation of the image event criteria that creates a "critique through spectacle, not critique versus spectacle."

The organizers' actions in this time period also reveal precisely *how* they attempted to achieve their ultimate goal for the Freedom Vote. Remember that the organizers of the Freedom Vote claimed as their goal that if given the chance, blacks would vote, and do so in large numbers. The Freedom Vote cited specifically for its goal a total of 200,000 votes, or roughly half the state of Mississippi's black population. The tactical decisions employed throughout the Freedom Vote in pursuit of its strategic goal are a significant part of the overall rhetoric. Think of the social actors of the Freedom Vote as characters in pursuit of a goal; the focus of analysis is on exactly *how* these characters pursue success. Ultimately, as will be discussed later, the tactical decisions that the Freedom Vote organizers employed are still prevalent in social activism today, particularly the function of image events to capture media attention via visual rhetorical mind bombs.

The organization, recruitment, and initial canvassing of the campaign involved many texts. This chapter begins by exploring internal reports and memos from the campaign and then analyzes the initial patterns of media coverage. Close-textual analysis reveals internal textual details in relation to their context. What links all these various forms of rhetoric and their subsequent analyses is their shared pursuit of a goal. The pattern and presence of the media coverage generated evidence the success of one of the campaign's main goals, notably to bring attention to the fact that blacks would vote if given the opportunity but also the success of the tactical image event designed to garner media attention.

ORGANIZING INTERNALLY

With the official state gubernatorial election a few weeks away, plans for the Freedom Vote came into sharp focus in early October 1963, as evidenced by the level of detail in organizational reports, meeting minutes, and correspondence.

The "talk" of the Freedom Vote became action when COFO approved plans to hold a mock election during the regular state gubernatorial election. This unified the civil rights organizations operating under COFO and allowed for the appropriation of staff, funds, and resources needed to run the Freedom Vote; as such, the Freedom Vote moved from the ideational to a real and potentially powerful political demonstration.

The archived sources utilized in this chapter are detailed, outlining and defining the policies and procedures that would carry the Freedom Vote to fruition. Details include, but are not limited to, an outlined budget for the campaign, mission statements and goals, conduct and procedures for workers at polling places, brief biographies of the candidates, current voter registration numbers by district, and even a handwritten itinerary for candidate Aaron Henry during the two-week campaign.

A news release issued by COFO on October 7 announced the organization's intent to run a "Freedom Vote." The headline of the release reads: "COFO MAPS VOTE FIGHT: HENRY RUNS FOR GOVERNOR IN FREEDOM BALLOT CAMPAIGN." The release starts:

JACKSON, MISS., Oct. 7—A state-wide meeting here of the Council of Federated Organizations (COFO) mapped plans yesterday to run a Negro gubernatorial candidate in a Freedom Vote prior to the Nov. election.

Dr. Aaron Henry, 42-year-old President of COFO, agreed to campaign throughout the state in the next three weeks in an effort to bring out a record Negro vote for his candidacy in the unofficial balloting.

COFO's Freedom Vote campaign is directed at potential Negro voters, regardless of whether they are registered. The plan is to place ballot boxes in churches in nearly 20 cities during the week prior to Nov. 4, to give Negroes an opportunity to cast ballots in support of COFO's program.[2]

The release goes on to say that COFO's goals for the Freedom Vote were to challenge the literacy tests required for citizens to register to vote and to help future attempts and elections for all national and state offices. The release announces the Freedom Vote's candidate and labels the campaign the "Freedom Vote."

Civil rights organizations regularly issued releases to media services; it was the legitimate and preferred means of disseminating information via news outlets and therefore lent credibility to the organizations and their activities. Media attention is also a means for generating broader public support. It joins the goal of the Freedom Vote to evidence black citizens wanted to vote with the image event characteristic of capturing attention. They both do so in a performative and mediated manner.

An eight-page COFO internal memo simply titled "The Freedom Ballot" further details the campaign. The memo is from the Committee to Elect Aaron Henry Governor of Mississippi and is organized into three sections with various subsections. The first section defines the Freedom Vote and its goals. Under the heading "Why Are We Holding a Freedom Vote?" the memo states, "The Freedom Vote, in which all citizens may cast ballots, will show the world that there are thousands of Mississippians who are dissatisfied with their government, but who are powerless to do anything about it."[3] The statement asserts that the state and local governments of Mississippi do not represent everyone and their interests. The memo highlights five specific problems that needed to be addressed in Mississippi: "Only 6% of Mississippi's qualified voters participate in general elections," "the illiteracy and poverty of Mississippi people, black and white," "our educational standards are deplorably low," "our economic problems are overwhelming," and "there is no equality before the law, or civil liberties in Mississippi."[4] After citing these problems, the memo then clearly outlines the Freedom Vote candidates' platform:

1. That universal suffrage be established immediately.
2. That all schools be desegregated by 1965.

3. That a crash program be begun to improve all phases of our education.
4. That a State Fairness Commission be established to insure non-discrimination in jobs, public places, and public accommodations and to work for equal justice before the law.
5. That the following steps be taken to insure full and fair employment in Mississippi:
    a) An extensive public works program,
    b) A job retraining program,
    c) A just minimum wage, and
    d) The repeal of anti-labor laws, particularly the right to organize unions.

These outlined goals became the Freedom Vote's platform as well as the main rhetorical themes in campaign materials ranging from posters to the candidates' speeches. The themes center on jobs, education, justice, and suffrage. At the very bottom of the page, after the list, is the phrase "ONE MAN—ONE VOTE," centered and in all-capital letters. The memo has literal content that is to be taken at face value, but its presence is also symbolic in that it represents structure, legitimacy, and prudence on the part of the campaign and its organizers.

The next section of the memo is a detailed budget for the campaign, broken down into the five basic categories of office, promotion, transportation, workers, and reserve fund. The overall estimated cost and total budget for the Freedom Vote comes to $20,795.36. The single most expensive item listed in the budget is for funding fifty workers in the state's five congressional districts at an estimated $6,000. Within each section of the budget is an itemized account for costs, with a subtotal. For instance, under the "office" section are listed six items ranging from rent to telephone costs, with postage being the most expensive item at an estimated $600. This planning and level of detail depict a serious campaign, organized by participants who had a plan and were well organized. The cumulative effect of these memos and documents speaks directly to the ethos of the campaign, making it look like any other campaign in America.

Two other items from the budget section highlight significant funding needs for the campaign. The first is within the "promotion" subsection of the budget. Here an estimated $3,990 is allocated for radio and television time. The campaign organizers planned on airing a thirty-minute program on two separate television stations: WLBT in Jackson, and WDIA in Memphis. The memo even reports that a time slot is available at WLBT on Monday, November 4, from 9:00 to 9:30 p.m. Campaign organizers, however, never actually aired the program because neither of the local television stations would sell them the air time. This later contributed to the *Office of Communications for the United Church of Christ v. Federal Communications Commission* case in 1966, which eventually opened up the licensing renewal process and catalyzed the consumer advocacy movement.[5]

A handwritten observation on the memo brings immediate attention to the desperate financial challenge facing the campaign and its organizers. Near the bottom of the first page in the budget section is written, "Will not be able to raise amount needed. Only $2,000.00 has been raised thus far." The organizers and planners of the Freedom Vote realized the challenge they faced in obtaining the fiscal resources to execute the campaign.

The final section of the memo contains a one-page biography for each of the two freedom candidates. Each bio includes basic information like date and location of birth, educational background, profession, military service (Henry was stationed in Hawaii from 1943 to 1946), and family. Aaron Henry was born in Clarksdale, Mississippi, on July 2, 1922. He received a bachelor's degree in pharmacy from Xavier University in 1950 and was active there in student politics and pharmaceutical associations. Henry was married to Noelle Michael, and had a daughter named Rebecca. Ed King was born in Vicksburg, Mississippi, in 1936. He had an associate's degree from Millsaps College in sociology in 1958, a bachelor's degree in theology from Boston University, and a master's in theology in 1963, also from Boston University. King married Jeannette in 1960, shortly before being ordained as a minister in the Methodist Church.

A subsection entitled "civil rights record" stands out among the others; this section details the activities of each candidate two to three years previous to the campaign. Each candidate's "civil rights record[]" is essentially an arrest record, providing dates, locations, and reasons for arrests. The records speak to each candidate's willingness to sacrifice and suffer for the issues they stand for; they delineate their careers in protest and resistance, an interesting and necessary addendum to any freedom fighter's résumé.

Note how the Freedom Vote is performing in the image and practices of a traditional political campaign. It gains recognition and credibility by acting like any other real campaign; this means issuing memos, staging press conferences, and producing campaign materials and all the other trappings expected of a political campaign in America. This component of the Freedom Vote works nicely with the visual nature of image events to rhetorically achieve its goal.

A handwritten, two-page itinerary for Aaron Henry lays out the campaign trail for the gubernatorial candidate.[6] Listed first is a political rally in Jackson on October 13, followed by a swing through the Gulf Coast starting on the fourteenth. Next is Vicksburg on the eighteenth, followed by a busy day on the twentieth, when Henry is to stop at Batesville during the day and then Holly Springs in the evening. Then, for the next twelve days in a row, Henry is to make campaign stops in cities throughout the state, starting on the twenty-first in Columbus; then Greenwood, Clarksdale, Greenville, and Yazoo City on the twenty-fifth; Noxubee, Meridian, Laurel, Hattiesburg, and Clarksdale again on the thirtieth; followed by Biloxi; and finally concluding the stretch in Jackson on the first of November. Note that Henry's itinerary avoids the southwest corner of the state, where the deaths of Lamar Smith, Mack Parker, Herbert Lee, and Roman Duckworth took place. That portion of the state had a reputation for being particularly violent and unchanging on segregation and is where Moses and SNCC had labored so hard with little progress. In that corner of Mississippi, the ratio of blacks to whites in each county was not nearly as high as those found in the Delta region, where Henry ultimately spent most of his time during the campaign. Considering the limited time to organize and execute the campaign, it was crucial that efforts and resources be utilized in the most efficient manner for the highest yield of vote totals.

Correspondence from the subject file of the Freedom Vote at the Mississippi Department of Archives and History shows that local leaders were contacted by organizers prior to the execution of the campaign. A cover letter in an information packet concerning the Freedom Vote reads: "Because of your standing in the community and the respect which people of the area have for you, we are sending you a statement of our belief and purpose here in the hope that you will be able to help improve the relations between people of all colors who live here."[7] This statement attempts to motivate the recipient by invoking a sense of obligation and duty. It asks the recipient to get involved and to make a difference in the local community. The belief statement is a two-page letter detailing the goals of the campaign. The letter is signed by Annell Ponder of the Southern Christian Leadership Conference (SCLC), Samuel Block of the Student Nonviolent Coordinating Committee (SNCC), Andrew L. Jordan of the National Association for the Advancement of Colored People (NAACP), and David J. Dennis from the Congress of Racial Equality (CORE). The final statement on the letter is the phrase "We'll Never Turn Back." By signing their names and indicating the organizations that they represent, the signers of the letter demonstrate cross-organizational support for the Freedom Vote. Recipients of the letter then see a careful plan being put together by a cooperative of civil rights groups rather than just a single leader or organization.

What may appear as mere paperwork to some is in fact an important characteristic of the Freedom Vote and other image events. Image events are strategic in that they are planned; there is a design in mind, meaning that there is also a desired end state or goal behind the whole enterprise. Like all image events, the Freedom Vote was carefully planned and coordinated. The previous memos and reports released by the campaign prove this fact and link it as a form of protest to other image events.

Correspondence, memos, and reports issued and circulated by the Freedom Vote varied in form and content, but their purpose was unified in attempting to make the campaign a success. Some of these documents, such as the cover letter and mission statement, were passionate and personal; others were the dry and impersonal documents necessary for the day-to-day operations of the campaign. A report titled "Planning Details for Freedom Vote of Governor," dated October 10, 1963, outlines how the Freedom Vote was to be carried out.[8] There are six sections to the planning details report: ballot, polling places, polling procedure, personnel at the polling places, appearance of the polling places, and publicity for the Freedom Vote. Reports and memos illustrate how well organized the Freedom Vote was before it was put into action, down to the details of the ballot's appearance. This contributed to the Freedom Vote's credibility, both externally to the voters, participants, and any government authorities observing the campaign and also internally to the organizers and planners by formalizing and regulating conduct.

Note the "realism" of the campaign thus far, its appearance and operation like a real campaign. Herein lies the genius of using the form of a traditional political campaign (with all the trappings of planning committees, candidates, posters, stump speeches, and so forth) as the vehicle of protest to bring attention to voting rights issues. It utilizes one of the powerful rhetorical effects of image events described by DeLuca and Peeples when they argue, "Image events are dense surfaces meant to provoke in an instant the shock of the familiar made strange" (144). The familiar is the traditional campaign form, the strange aspects are who is running the campaign and who is participating in the campaign. This use of "the shock of the familiar made strange" became more and more obvious as the campaign progressed and carried out its performance. It was important that the campaign prove itself (and, more important, appear) as a legitimate demonstration: the efforts and results of the Freedom Vote were to be taken seriously. What had yet to be seen was how the press would treat the Freedom Vote.

"READING" THE PRESS'S FREEDOM VOTE

The media representation of the Freedom Vote played an important role in shaping the character, success, and impact of the campaign. Of rhetorical significance is *how* the news media's framing of the Freedom Vote potentially impacted the audience's impression of it. Despite the often negative nature of the news coverage of the Freedom Vote, audiences receiving *any* coverage of the Freedom Vote played a significant strategic role in attempting to establish and influence broader public support for the movement in Mississippi. Was the news coverage concerning the Freedom Vote biased? Undoubtedly, but what is important is that the media acknowledged the Freedom Vote at all. Of course, the positive and negative connotations communicated to their varying audiences potentially affected the symbolic meaning of the Freedom Vote, but "good news" or "bad news," considering the contextual environment the Freedom Vote operated in, was still publicity.

This section analyzes periodicals ranging from local to national, from both traditionally conservative and progressively liberal media outlets. Nine Mississippi daily newspapers are analyzed from October 7 to November 12, 1963: the *Meridian Star*, the *Delta-Democrat Times*, the *Clarksdale Press Register*, the *Clarion-Ledger*, the *Jackson Daily News*, the *Jackson Advocate*, the *Greenwood Commonwealth*, the *Enterprise Journal*, and the *Hattiesburg American*. Articles from the *Nation* and the *New South* are compared along with the scant coverage provided by the *New York Times*, the *Commercial Appeal* in Memphis, and the *Washington Post*. The *Yale Daily News* is also utilized to provide yet another perspective and layer to the media coverage of the Freedom Vote. Alternative perspectives represented by the black-owned and -operated weekly *Mississippi Free Press*, SNCC's monthly paper the *Student Voice*, the *Chicago Defender*, and the *Southern Patriot* are also analyzed.

Of particular interest in the analysis of the media coverage is how the rhetorical lenses of framing, labeling, and naming impact the representation of the Freedom Vote. Cultural scholar Stuart Hall argues, "Representation through language is therefore central to the process by which meaning is produced" (1). How does language do this work? According to Hall, "language is able to do this because it operates as a *representational system*" (1). The language employed to report on the Freedom Vote therefore has a rhetorical influence on the meaning audiences attach to the event, its activities, and the agents conducting and participating in these activities. Language, in this sense, is a "signifying practice," having consequences on the representation of what is being signified; in the case of the Mississippi Freedom Vote of 1963, "representation, here, is closely tied up with both identity and knowledge" (Hall 5).

In her book *Making News: A Study in the Construction of Reality*, Gaye Tuchman states that "news is a window to the world," and "the news aims to tell us what we want to know, need to know, and should know. But, like any frame that delineates a world, the news frame may be considered problematic" (1). The framing of events offered by the news is problematic, according to Tuchman, because by attempting to disseminate information that people "want to know, need to know, and should know," that framing "imparts to occurrences their *public character* as it transforms mere happenings into publicly discussable events" (3). The language that the media use to frame stories actually labels and defines for its consumers the very nature of an event's "public character," which also impacts the publicly perceived value of covered (and also *non*covered) events.

Tuchman reminds us that because "news imparts a public character to occurrences," news is "first and foremost a social institution" (4). Tuchman supports this assertion with three observations: "news is an institutional method of making information available to consumers," "news is an ally of legitimated institutions," and "news is located, gathered, and disseminated by professionals working in organizations" (4). These characteristics reinforce Tuchman's notion that "the act of making news is the act of constructing itself rather than a picture of reality" (12). The labels, definitions, and very presence or coverage of these social constructions in/by the news are symbolic.

As Charles Kauffman points out, "names are strategic in the sense that they attempt to remedy perceived problems in a situation; they provide an 'orientation' or a way of coping with a difficult and complex problem" (273). Kauffman also reminds critics that "names are stylized because, as tropes, their structuring of situations favors certain symbolic orientations over others" (273). In terms of the Freedom Vote, the consequences of how the various news outlets "named," or "labeled," the campaign are significant. Most sources tended to use the phrase "mock election," and the cost of such a designation must be explored. Edward Schiappa's *Defining Reality: Definitions and the Politics of Meaning* also adds depth to understanding the rhetorical significance of labels. Schiappa suggests that two sorts of questions be asked of labels and the meanings that they imply: questions of purpose and interest, and questions of power (177–178). The media's varying portrayals undoubtedly impacted the public's perception of the Freedom Vote, as they still do to this day.

News critic Todd Gitlin speaks more of how the role of the media shifted during the 1960s. He argues, "By the sixties, American society was dominated by a *consolidated* corporate economy, no longer by a *nascent* one" (2). The growing free press with many available sources for information then became a sort of information monopoly. With this tighter rein of control, the media's influence also shifted and changed:

> They name the world's parts, they certify reality *as* reality—and when their certifications are doubted and opposed, as they surely are, it is those same certifications that limit the terms of effective opposition. To put it simply: the mass media have become core systems for the distribution of ideology. That is to say, every day, directly or indirectly, by statement and omission, in pictures and words, in entertainment and news and advertisement, symbol and rhetoric, through which ideology becomes manifest and concrete. (Gitlin 2)

This ideology is evidenced by the very language that the media use to cover news, in the discourse that forms around and creates the media's coverage. Hall defines discourses as "ways of referring to or constructing knowledge about a particular topic or practice" and, more important, how: "These *discursive formations*, as they are known, define what is and is not appropriate in our formulation of, and our practices in relation to, a particular subject or site of social activity; what knowledge is considered useful, relevant and 'true' in that context; and what sorts of persons or 'subjects' embody its characteristics" (6). Remembering Tuchman, what makes the mediated discursive formations surrounding the Freedom Vote important is that they come to represent the "public character" of the event and the participants. What is crucial to recognize is not only *how* the media talked about the Freedom Vote but also the fact that the media actually said anything on the subject at all.

Gitlin is able to bridge Hall and Tuchman. The notions of "discursive formations" and the "public character" of social movements as portrayed by the mass media have important consequences. Gitlin claims, "In such quiet fashion, not deliberately, and without calling attention to this spotlighting process, the media divide movements into legitimate main acts and illegitimate sideshows, so that these distinctions appear 'natural,' matters of 'common sense.' What makes the world beyond experience look natural is a media *frame*" (6). Gitlin brings the importance of media frames right back to Tuchman's doorstep. He defines media frames as "*persistent patterns of cognition, interpretation, and presentation, of selection, emphasis, and exclusion, by which symbol-handlers routinely organize discourse, whether verbal or visual*" (7). According to Gitlin, the "symbol handlers" are able to impress upon the public through the media their preferred ideological notions and ideals. Citing Antonio Gramsci, Gitlin notes the hegemonic consequences of mediated discourse, most notably control. Tuchman also notes this control and influence: "I propose a theoretical formulation of news as a social construction and social resource. That formulation, I suggest, may also apply to other forms of organizationally and professionally produced knowledge. And I conclude that through its routine practices and the claims of news professionals to arbitrate knowledge and to present factual accounts, news legitimates the status quo" (14). This notion of maintaining the status quo on the part of a privileged and segregated society within Mississippi further underlines how and why local news outlets covered the Freedom Vote in the manner that they did.

There are a few important things to note before undertaking an analysis of the media's portrayal of the Freedom Vote. A change in the medium of analysis does not necessarily change the rhetorical method of analysis. If a rhetorical theme used in a speech also appears in songs and campaign posters, that theme is relevant to rhetorical analysis of all three. Violence is still present in the media's discourse today; so too is the idea of agency and citizenship, albeit now the sources of these rhetorical themes have different designs than did the social actors carrying out the Freedom Vote. That is why it is important to bring Kaufman and Schiappa, along with Tuchman, Hall, and Gitlin, into the analysis. The rhetorical naming, labeling, defining, and framing of the Freedom Vote have important consequences; even the mere presence of the Freedom Vote in the media's discourse is significant, representing the partial achievement of the Freedom Vote as it functions like an image event.

The Freedom Vote certainly represented a struggle between the forces of change and those that supported Jim Crow on the physical streets and public spaces in Mississippi, and yet the same battle raged in the mediated reality of the news. While this analysis examines the rhetorical themes of violence, citizenship, and agency, also prevalent is the theme of knowledge and its use or dissemination to instill a state of exigency and efficacy in various audiences throughout the nation.

There is a complex matrix working on the "knowledge" of the Freedom Vote. Each level of production, reproduction, and circulation of this information has its own agents and audience. The "facts" about the violence during the Freedom Vote vary between what source was reporting them and which audience was receiving the information. The social activists and agents within the Freedom Vote wanted to capture the attention and impact the behavior of qualified black Mississippians, but they also wanted to convey the state of affairs in Mississippi to a broader national audience. Complacent white and black audiences received representations of the Freedom Vote through various news outlets. This is not a study of reception of the rhetoric employed by or about the Mississippi Freedom Vote of 1963; it is a study of the symbolic meaning of the Freedom Vote through the analysis of rhetorical artifacts and how the Freedom Vote enabled other significant historical events that followed. This chapter specifically seeks to unpack the symbolism of the mediated representation of the Freedom Vote and acknowledges the rhetorical significance of the mere presence of the Freedom Vote in the "discursive formations" of the news media.

In examining the historical relationship between the press and the civil rights movement in Mississippi, two sources are crucial: Gene Roberts and Hank Klibanoff's *The Race Beat: The Press, the Civil Rights Struggle, and the Awakening of a Nation* and Julius E. Thompson's *The Black Press in Mississippi, 1865–1985*. Thompson's work is an excellent source for tracing the foundation, growth, and progress of black-owned and -operated periodicals in the Magnolia State. Thompson traces the first successful black newspaper to Vicksburg in 1867, when Henry Mason established the *Colored Citizen* (2). Soon after, in

November of the following year, James D. Lynch founded the *Colored Citizen's Monthly* in Jackson (Thompson 3). By the end of Reconstruction, however, only two black papers were in circulation in Mississippi: the *People's Advisor* in Jackson and the *Mississippi Republican* in Vicksburg (Thompson 7). This is a pattern in Mississippi's history of the black press—papers often were established to live short public lives. For instance, the *Free State* was a four-page weekly in Brandon published from only 1898 to 1905, and the *Golden Rule* from Vicksburg circulated from 1898 to 1907 (Thompson 21). Religious papers often sprang up, and by the end of World War II blacks were working at twelve different commercial papers throughout the state, with the McComb *Mississippi Enterprise*, the Greenville *Delta Leader*, and Percy Greene's *Jackson Advocate* obtaining the highest circulation rates (Thompson 25).

The post–World War II relationship between the press and the civil rights movement is the focus of Roberts and Klibanoff's *Race Beat*. The authors begin their study by summarizing the findings of Gunnar Myrdal's *An American Dilemma* before covering the major civil rights–related media events, from *Brown v. Board of Education* to Selma. Roberts and Klibanoff point out:

> At no other time in U.S. history were the news media more influential than they were in the 1950s and 1960s, sometimes for better, sometimes for worse. From the news coverage came significant and enduring changes not only in the civil rights movement but also in the way the print and television media did their jobs. There is little in American society that was not altered by the civil rights movement. There is little in the civil rights movement that was not changed by the news coverage of it. And there is little in the way the news media operate that was not influenced by their coverage of the movement. (Roberts and Klibanoff 7)

Roberts and Klibanoff begin their exploration of the news coverage surrounding the Mississippi civil rights movement with the coverage of Gus Courts and Reverend George W. Lee, following with a chapter devoted to the Emmett Till trial (77–108). The book does not discuss Mississippi again until later chapters covering Meredith at Ole Miss, the murder of Medgar Evers, and Freedom Summer.[9] Interestingly enough, neither Thompson's *The Black Press in Mississippi, 1865–1985* nor Roberts and Klibanoff's *Race Beat* mentions the Freedom Vote.

In "The Contemporary Study of Public Address: Renewal, Recovery, and Reconfiguration," Medhurst argues that contemporary rhetoricians "have recovered the truth that rhetoric's primary domain is in the public sphere generally, and the world of public affairs in particular" (498). This supports the notion that rhetoricians are public affairs scholars who use specific lenses to examine topics and events and "that the study of rhetoric is inherently interdisciplinary" (Medhurst 499). As this book examines different texts, keep in mind Medhurst's notion of reconfiguring rhetorical archaeology, that is, "digging up from the residues of the past rhetorical artifacts that have been lost, misplaced, unrecognized, or never catalogued—ought to be a first-order priority for scholars of rhetoric and public affairs" (504).

GOING PUBLIC

On October 13, 1963, two Mississippi papers broke the story of the Freedom Vote: the *Delta Democrat-Times* in Greenville and the *Clarion-Ledger* in Jackson. The *Delta Democrat-Times* (*DDT*) is unique among the commercial newspapers of Mississippi. Though the paper generally was not considered radically liberal, its editor, Hodding Carter Jr., had won the Pulitzer Prize in 1946 for his editorial writing attacking bigotry across racial, economic, and religious boundaries (Thompson 39). The *DDT* ran an article on its second page with the headline "Aaron Henry May Run for Governor."[10] The article is attributed to the Universal Press International (UPI) news wire service. It quotes Henry as saying, "I think I will be a write-in candidate," and labels him a "Negro civil rights strategist." It also quotes John O'Neil as stating that Henry is an NAACP-sponsored candidate to "spearhead a 'freedom balloting' designed to show unregistered Negroes' 'desire' to vote." The article goes on to state that "Henry did not reveal whether he would, if a candidate, conduct a serious campaign" and mentions a planned rally in Jackson on the eve of the regular election. The article functions rhetorically by providing the information that forms a reader's initial conception of the Freedom Vote. The language and information contained in the article, like in other news articles to follow, are important because they influence the perspective with which readers evaluate the campaign.

The coverage in the *Clarion-Ledger* is exactly the same except for two details: the headline and the article's position in the paper's layout. The *Clarion-Ledger* ran the story with the headline "Aaron Henry Being Run for Governor by NAACP" and buried the article on page fifteen of the issue.[11] While the *Clarion-Ledger* did not alter the UPI article in terms of its factual information, the placement of the article suggests that it was not as newsworthy of an event to its readers as the *DDT*'s placement implies. In comparing the two headlines, note how the *Clarion-Ledger* links Henry with a specific civil rights organization, the NAACP. White and black readers in Mississippi were familiar with the organization and its reputation. The NAACP had long been the only civil rights organization able to maintain a presence in Mississippi and therefore had acquired the label of a meddling, even Communist, organization by

Mississippi whites; by associating Henry with the NAACP, the article links him to that reputation as well. Reporting that the NAACP was the organization responsible for running the campaign is wholly inaccurate; as previously established, COFO was the primary organization in charge of the Freedom Vote.

Rhetorical patterns are already at work here in the coverage. The newspapers ran articles that labeled the social actors and linked them to specific organizations. Throughout the coverage of the events surrounding the Freedom Vote, note who in the article is allowed to speak, what organizations they are associated with, how they are labeled (both the individual and his or her organization), and how they are quoted. In the UPI article, only Henry and O'Neil give quotes, and both are linked to the NAACP. The Freedom Vote was a collaborative effort between four major civil rights organizations and was not the sole work of the NAACP.

Now with some media coverage, and with the official support of COFO and the organizations that it unified, the Freedom Vote was able to further organize. A formal press conference was held by Freedom Vote organizers on October 14 to publicly announce the campaign and its candidates. The day before, Reverend Edwin King had accepted the invitation to run as the lieutenant governor, despite many misgivings. In his memoir, King remembers his reaction to Bob Moses asking him to join the Freedom Vote: "I was surprised—and frightened." He feared for his own safety as well as that of his immediate family and his wife's family. He was still in bandages and weak from a car "accident" that summer, and he was unsure of whether a religious figure like himself belonged so directly involved with politics, but he still accepted the nomination. "I knew immediately that I could not refuse him," King said of Moses, "that I so valued his thinking that on almost any plan I would be his disciple. I had known of the idea of a mock election from the start and he knew that I thought the plan was excellent."[12]

The following day, on the fourteenth, the *DDT* ran a story entitled "Henry to Speak Here."[13] The story is not credited to a wire service and is placed on page eight of the issue. The four-paragraph article informs the reader that Henry will be speaking in Greenville on the twenty-fourth. This time, however, Henry is associated with the "Mississippi Council of Federated Organizations" instead of the NAACP. In fact, the article never even mentions the NAACP. This could be due to the public news conference the day before in which Henry and COFO officially announced their plans for the campaign. The story labels the campaign as both "unofficial balloting" and a "mock election," minimizing the potential impact of the Freedom Vote through this framing. The story also mentions Bob Moses, who reportedly states, but is not quoted, that the aim of the campaign is to highlight that Mississippi "Negroes" want to vote and would do so if given the opportunity. The article ends with the specific time and place that Henry would be speaking. The triggering of the campaign's mind bombs are being mediated: campaign as familiar, candidates and voters as strange.

On October 15 more Mississippi newspapers announced the Freedom Vote. Again, the *DDT* ran a UPI story at the top of page two, this time entitled "Henry Announces for Governor."[14] The story is only four paragraphs long and labels Henry a "Negro integration leader." The article is also careful to point out that Henry's running mate, Reverend Ed King, is "a white Methodist minister." From a rhetorical perspective, these labels frame the candidates as challengers to the status quo. Labeling Henry an "integration leader" casts him as a challenger to the traditional practice of segregation. The article casts King in an agitator role by specifically reporting on the color of his skin; his presence in the campaign as a white southerner challenges the status quo of segregation.

The most interesting part of the story is a statement that highlights the illegitimacy of the campaign for those considering voting for the Freedom Vote ticket during the official election: "The secretary of state's office said, however, that write-in votes will be voided unless all the official candidates die before the election"—grim accounting already for the Freedom Vote and its participants based upon this UPI story. The article dismisses the legitimacy, and therefore the value of the Freedom Vote, and labels it a pointless endeavor. Either the press did not comprehend the symbolic significance of the Freedom Vote or they were hoping to completely void it. Such editorializing impacted the potential results of the Freedom Vote. The goal of the campaign was to obtain 200,000 votes. With time and resources in short supply, negative media coverage could have kept blacks from participating, adding fuel to the segregationists' fire. The Freedom Vote organizers were trying to reach as many potential voters as possible, and the news media played an important role in that process, albeit not always a positive one.

Three other papers ran the same UPI story but, again, with different headlines and in different positions. The *Meridian Star* ran the article with the headline "Negro Is Candidate But Doesn't Expect to Get Many Votes" and put the story at the bottom of page three.[15] The only change to the article between the *DDT* and the *Meridian Star* was the *Star*'s inclusion of a final statement at the end of the article that read, "Henry indicated he does not expect to receive too many votes on a write-in basis in the general election on Nov. 5." This statement minimizes the potential impact of the Freedom Vote, and raises the question if the newspaper story isn't putting words in Henry's mouth. Notice that this negativity was attributed not to an editor but rather to one of the candidates in the Freedom Vote—Henry, arguably the most important participant in the Freedom Vote.[16]

A few patterns emerge from the coverage on October 15. Most Mississippi papers did not run long, in-depth articles covering the Freedom Vote, a trend that extended to the national papers as well. Few stories printed about the Freedom Vote can be labeled in-depth analysis or commentary. Few Freedom Vote articles ever occupied the front page of any Mississippi commercial paper. Another interesting trend emerges among the four papers in the source of their stories. Most of the articles credit either the UPI or the Associated Press (AP) newswire services. These articles are picked up, edited for length and content, and then given a headline. A pattern of recycling the same stories developed throughout the coverage of the Freedom Vote. The papers end up reporting essentially the same narrowly pessimistic story, creating an "echo chamber" effect.

For example, on October 17 both the McComb *Enterprise-Journal* and the *Greenwood Commonwealth* ran the same AP story. The story announces the involvement of Yale students in the "Negro candidate for governor mock election." The story features quotes from Al Lowenstein and Tim Jenkins, a black law student from Yale who had worked in Jackson the previous summer, who reiterates the goals of the campaign. Jenkins is quoted as saying, "No change can come within Mississippi from its own accord." Here, the theme of a walled city begins in the Mississippi papers' coverage; the paper promotes an "us against them" mentality as it casts the northern activists as outsiders. Both Lowenstein and Jenkins are linked to Yale University, a northern liberal school, and Jenkins's quote would not have sounded friendly to the average Mississippi reader. Though the headlines are different—"Yale Students to Help State Negro 'Candidate'" and "Yale Students to 'Campaign' for Henry"—they both attack the perceived legitimacy of the campaign through the use of scare quotes around the words "candidate" and "campaign."

The next day the *Meridian Star* and the *Jackson Daily News* ran the same AP story, also with varying headlines—"Yale Students Coming Down to 'Aid' Aaron Henry" and "Yale Students to Campaign for Henry," respectively—and much like the headlines from the previous day, these do rhetorical work. The headlines all announce the impending arrival of outsiders and link these outsiders to the activities associated with the "mock election." What is interesting across the four articles is that the news of outsiders got front-page coverage. Freedom Vote coverage rarely won front-page status, but the papers deemed the activities of "outsiders" worthy of the spotlight.

The black-owned and -operated *Jackson Advocate* barely covered the Freedom Vote at all. Not only is the coverage sparse, with the paper running only two articles ever on the Freedom Vote, but the paper was late in delivering the news as well. The *Advocate*'s founder, Percy Greene, was a dominant figure in the Mississippi black press. He established the *Jackson Advocate* in 1938 and served as publisher until 1977. Thompson labels Greene "the most controversial black journalist in twentieth-century Mississippi" (29). Greene earned this distinction for his conservative views during the 1950s and 1960s and also for accepting direct payments from the State Sovereignty Commission, whose aid helped the *Advocate* stay alive while many other black-operated newspapers failed (63). The *Advocate*, a weekly, did not run a story announcing the Freedom Vote until October 19. A story on page eight, only four paragraphs long, labels Henry a "local Negro druggist" running as "a write-in candidate." The story in the *Advocate* even misnames Henry's running mate as "Rev. Samuel D. King." The final passage of the article echoes the pessimism and illegitimacy of other papers: "The main purpose of their running, according to Henry, is to deny the Negro vote to both the Democrat and the Republican candidate."[17] This final statement frames the activity of the campaign in an even darker light; it claims blacks were actively denying something that they were already systematically denied in order to harm the mainstream candidates. The wording here frames the Freedom Vote efforts in opposition to the democratic process instead of in accordance with democratic practices and behaviors. Rather than focus on the fundamental issue of blacks being denied the right to vote, the article draws attention to whom blacks are *not* voting for, thus casting blacks as a threat to the mainstream democratic process.

But the initial coverage of the Freedom Vote did not get much better treatment in regional or national papers, either. The October 15 issue of the *New York Times* reports under the headline "Write-In Drive Started":

> JACKSON, MISS., Oct. 14—A Negro civil rights leader, Aaron Henry, began his campaign today as a write-in candidate for Governor in the Nov. 5 general election although Mississippi does not count write-in votes.
>
> He said that the Rev. Edwin King Jr., a white Methodist minister at Tougaloo Southern Christian College, would be a write-in candidate for Lieutenant Governor.
>
> Mr. Henry is the state president of the National Association for the Advancement of Colored People.[18]

The coverage is sparse, to say the least, and is buried on the thirty-second page of the issue. What is missing from the *Times* article that is present in the Mississippi papers is why Henry is starting this "write-in drive." The Freedom Vote is not a "write-in drive" since the candidates are technically not legal candidates in the eyes of the state; labels matter. The article does not even clearly establish the fact that Henry is running *with* Reverend King; that is left to the reader. The legitimacy of the Freedom Vote is already cast into doubt and futility. While it is easy to criticize the scant coverage here, at least the *Times* recognizes the effort. This is a significant success for the Freedom Vote because the *Times* is the nation's newspaper of record; readers consider it as a news source that is credible and is able to reach a large national audience. The Freedom Vote, though depicted in a not-so-flattering manner, reached beyond the borders of the Magnolia State in the black-and-white print of the *Times* and functioned like an image event.

The Memphis *Commercial Appeal* affords the Freedom Vote a little more column space in announcing the start of the campaign on the same day as the *Times*. In a UPI-sourced article entitled "Negro Starts Drive for Write-In Votes," the *Commercial Appeal* provides the goals of what it labels a "serious campaign." This article also quotes Henry as stating, "We're going to pitch on four issues—justice of courts, education, economics, and voting rights." Few newspapers gave the social agents participating in the Freedom Vote print space for quotes, let alone a quote like Henry's that outlines the campaign's platform. The article does issue a statement paraphrasing the fact that the state will void all write-in votes unless the official candidate dies. While the article does not appear on the first page of the *Commercial Appeal*, it is even-handed and balanced in its coverage, which was crucial considering that Memphis is regionally located near the Mississippi Delta.

Then there is the coverage by the *Mississippi Free Press*, a vital alternative source of information for Mississippi residents while it was active from 1961 to 1973. The *Free Press* was a weekly periodical usually four to eight pages long, with a circulation ranging from 2,000 to 3,000 (Thompson 74). Thompson notes "the *Free Press* offered Mississippi readers a more progressive voice than the *Jackson Advocate*, the *Mississippi Enterprise*, or the *Clarion-Ledger*" (74). The *Free Press* had a tradition of not only covering civil rights activities and organizations in Mississippi but also doing so in a favorable light, often with extensive and exclusive coverage. The August 10, 1963, headline across the top of the front page reads "733 Vote for Freedom" and is accompanied by an article detailing the event. As previously mentioned, during the Democratic primaries, some blacks were able to vote by affidavit after law students working for SNCC found a loophole in the state's 1890 constitution. According to the article, "Under the little-known law, a citizen may swear out an affidavit claiming that he has been illegally denied the right to register; then he must present it at the polls and mark his ballot."[19] The article then details how many individuals in certain communities participated and in what communities people were barred from the polls. The article extends from page one to page four of the issue. The coverage in the *Free Press* is by far the most complete and thorough of all outlets reporting on the campaign.

The August 24 issue also covers the voting activity during the Democratic primary. Just beneath the top headline of "Ole Miss Graduates Meredith" is a story entitled "Negroes to File Freedom Votes." The article begins by informing readers that Mississippi blacks would "take part in a state-wide vote for Freedom election Sunday, August 25. Citizens will mark their choice for governor on unofficial ballots and put them in ballot boxes located in churches and other community centers."[20] The article labels the event and activity a "vote for Freedom" and goes on to explain why the event is important to readers: "Since this election is not official and will not be counted by state employees, there is no risk of arrest for those who choose to vote. Campaign leaders hope to make the U.S. Congress and state politicians aware of the rising bloc of politically interested Negroes in Mississippi." The story takes note of "the rising bloc" of potential black voters, unifying black voters and indicating their potential for political influence. Statements like these never appeared in the mainstream and commercial newspapers.

The August 31 issue includes a picture on the front page of an elderly black woman actually casting her "vote for freedom ballot" at a church in Jackson. The headline across the top of page one reads "Negroes Mount Massive Protest," and the subtitle reads "27,689 Cast Ballots Miss. Didn't Want."[21] Like the other articles covering voting activity in previous issues, this story goes into the details of particular communities across the state by reporting specific numbers from those polling places. The wording is again very positive: "More than 27,000 Negro citizens of Mississippi stood up last weekend and said they were not satisfied with second-class citizenship, expressing themselves through the Vote for Freedom ballot." This type of wording frames the event positively; there is clearly articulated support in the coverage's labeling. Here we have "citizens" who "stood up" by participating in "the Vote for Freedom ballot."

The *Mississippi Free Press* broke the story concerning the Freedom Vote almost an entire month before any other news source. The headline across the top of page one in the September 21 issue reads "200,000 Negroes to Vote," and is accompanied by a lengthy two-page article reporting on the upcoming campaign in November. Halfway through, the article states: "Between 3 and 4 times as many Negroes are expected to demonstrate to the people of the state and the nation what the Negro's voting strength ought to be. The powerful demonstration will show the desire of Negroes to wield that strength. The November election will follow the pattern set by the August Vote for Freedom where over 27,000 unregistered Negroes of voting age cast special protest ballots. However, the coming campaign, with an early start on state-wide organization, should produce far greater results."[22] The optimism is apparent in word choices like "voting strength" and "powerful demonstration." The future tense of the article also speaks to a more editorialized function rather than a mere report of hard news.

Starting with the October 5 issue, a pattern emerges with the *Mississippi Free Press*'s coverage of the Freedom Vote. For six issues in a row, the Freedom Vote is the main front-page story, and a photo—sometimes more than one—complements each story. In the October 5 issue, the headline reads "Negroes Pick Candidate," with the subtitle "Convention to Set Off Mighty Freedom Vote." The article reports that the convention and campaign are COFO's work and includes a lengthy quote from Bob Moses. Of particular interest is the following passage: "Since only unregistered Negroes of voting age and people who have not paid their poll tax will be allowed to vote, the Freedom ballots will not be counted in the official returns. Yet it is the very fact that so many Negroes are not registered which gives the Freedom vote its power."[23] This is a drastically different perspective on the legitimacy and significance of the Freedom Vote when compared to the coverage in the mainstream commercial presses. Other newspapers report the fact that the votes do not count, but their commentary stops there. In the *Mississippi Free Press* that futility is turned into a powerful demonstration on the part of black citizens. The picture with the article is of COFO leaders Aaron Henry, Charles Evers, Reverend R. L. T. Smith, Matt Suarez, and Bob Moses.

The October 12 issue signals the kickoff of the Freedom Vote. Alongside a rather large picture of Henry sitting behind a desk in a suit, the headline across the top reads "We Shall VOTE FOR FREEDOM." The article presents the goals of the campaign, and the bulk of the article contains quotes from Henry, such as: "We are staging this campaign to show everyone that Negroes do not have any real choice of candidates in the regular November election."[24] The coverage is obviously supportive and in favor of the campaign. The Freedom Vote is working like an image event through the visual nature of its performance; it is very visible, it is very real.

At the top of the October 19 issue is a montage of three photos of blacks completing the voter registration process. The montage makes a powerful visual argument as it communicates how black citizens completed the registration process. The headline to the article is a quote from Reverend Ed King: "We Will Be Free." The article reports on COFO's recent nomination of King for lieutenant governor. The article, similar to the one on Henry in the previous issue, features quotes from Reverend King. Due in part to the large photo montage across the top, the pictures, headline, and article are all that occupy the front page.

The coverage by the *Mississippi Free Press* functioned rhetorically like its commercial counterparts to frame and label the Freedom Vote, but it did so from a more sympathetic and supportive point of view. The coverage by the *Free Press* was so positive that the Freedom Vote campaign volunteers actually distributed the paper much like any other campaign pamphlet or materials. The *Free Press* was active from 1961 to 1973, financed primarily by donations from northern middle-class whites and edited by progressive white Mississippians like Charles

Butt and Lucy Komisar (Thompson 74). As the campaign progressed, northern whites would take on an even more significant role in the Freedom Vote.

LETTERS OF INTENT

The first car of Yale volunteers left New Haven on October 18 and arrived in Jackson on the twentieth. Many volunteers who came down ascribe to several motivating factors. The inspirational meeting on October 16 at Yale led by Lowenstein and Chaplain William Sloane Coffin, and the subsequent report the next day in the *Yale Daily News*, provided the spark. The *Yale Daily News* confronted readers with in-depth, front-page reporting on the Freedom Vote, often complemented by photographs.[25] Richard Van Wagenen recalled, "I found out about the Mississippi campaign through an article in the *Yale Daily News* and decided to go down for a week."[26] The October 17 issue of the *Yale Daily News* has the headline "Thirty Yale Students to Go to Mississippi in Protest Campaign," and the report notes that in a speech at a meeting the previous evening, Al Lowenstein talked of a letter from the campaign manager, Bob Moses, asking for help. This letter is an important rhetorical resource for the Freedom Vote. Bruce Payne recalls that it was this very letter that motivated him to leave Yale and go to Mississippi.[27]

In Moses's first letter addressed to Lowenstein, dated October 17, the heading in the top-left corner reads "FREEDOM BALLOT FOR GOVERNOR" and lists the headquarters' address on Lynch Street in Jackson.[28] Immediately following is Lowenstein's title as chairman of the Advisory Committee to Elect Aaron Henry Governor and Lowenstein's New York City address. The letter begins "Dear Al" and then informs the reader that on the fourteenth, Henry formally launched his campaign for governor. The letter includes some brief biographical information about Henry and King and then states the goal of the campaign: "to obtain more than 200,000 signatures of unregistered Negroes in a Freedom Ballot." Moses states, "The Freedom Ballot will show that if Negroes had the right to vote without fear of physical violence or economic reprisal, they would do so." The crux of the letter comes at the end in the form of Moses's plea for assistance: "We need your help—desperately. The operating budget for this campaign, for campaign literature, materials, TV and radio time and newspaper space, office supplies and equipment, and the cost of feeding and housing workers throughout the 20 cities of the state in which we are organizing for this campaign, runs just over 20,000 dollars. There are only two weeks left in the campaign. We will not be able to utilize the basic information media–posters, leaflets, and the news outlets unless we can pay for them. We need your help."

The letter closes "Yours sincerely" and is signed "Bob Moses." The letter is a plea for financial assistance, and this particular supplication comes from Moses, who holds a powerful reputation for credibility and legitimacy in the eyes of other civil rights volunteers for the time and work he had already put into the Magnolia State. By writing this letter requesting assistance, Moses has given Lowenstein a sort of rhetorical capital to spend—the character of Moses's name and reputation. This is not just anybody asking for help; it is Bob Moses. Lowenstein can show potential financial donors this letter with Moses's signature on it and use it as a persuasive tool. It ceases to be just a personal letter from Moses to Lowenstein and becomes a rhetorical device, a recruitment tool in the form of a personal appeal.

Another letter from Moses to Lowenstein echoes and generalizes the plea, this time on formal "AARON HENRY for Governor" letterhead dated October 18, 1963.[29] The letter begins the same way, with information about the candidates and the goals of the campaign. The letter also discusses the need for funding to provide campaign materials and support workers and has almost the same ending as the previous letter. There is but a slight difference: "We believe that if we obtain this amount of money quickly, the impact of this campaign can be maximized and its value to the effort to obtain equal rights for all Americans in Mississippi and throughout the Nation, can be unique and substantial." This ending generalizes and extends the goals of the Freedom Vote; it stretches the influence of the Freedom Vote beyond the borders of Mississippi. Help was needed not just in the form of volunteers, but also in financial terms.

A flyer from the Yale campus evidences the Freedom Vote's support network outside the Magnolia State, as it provides specific budgetary and financial information pertaining to the Freedom Vote.[30] Across the top in bold black lettering reads "How Much Does the Right to Vote Cost?" The flyer lists: "An SNCC worker is paid $9.64 a week, a fish fry in Holmes County costs $200, the phone bill for Henry-for-Governor is $500, a 30-second radio announcement costs $50; altogether it will cost $20,000." The bottom of the flyer reads "HOW MUCH WILL YOU GIVE," and says that donations will be collected Wednesday through Friday. The poster provides specific and detailed information about how and where the donations would be used. The flyer addresses the reader directly and personally by asking exactly how much "you" are willing to give, operating reflectivity by asking readers a question. An accompanying fact sheet provides the essential information about the campaign and its goals. There is an interesting note at the bottom of the fact sheet: "You will be asked why northerners are meddling in southern matters. It must be remembered that what is going on in Mississippi is a national problem, a national disgrace, and that the southern whites are almost without exception unwilling or unable to work for the Negroes' equality. Whites who have tried have been intimidated and run out of the state." This passage again categorizes the problems in Mississippi as issues that concern every American, a major theme that Lowenstein used during his speech at Stanford, which he delivered again on the Yale campus. This refutative design contains an obligatory component that compels persuasion. The statement also notes the presence of violence to stop the efforts of those fighting for equality, showing that the students' help is necessary.

The Freedom Vote organizers also used letters from the chairman of the campaign's policy committee, Dave Dennis, to help mobilize networks within Mississippi. Two letters calling for general assistance from local ministers and businessmen further mobilize the Freedom Vote's network of aid. The first letter to ministers provides direction by outlining two specific ways that the ministers could help with the Freedom Vote. The letter reads: "You can help by doing the following: 1) You can announce to your congregation the fact that the Freedom Ballot is going to be held, explaining to them exactly what it is, and why they should participate. 2) You can permit your church to be used as a polling place so that your members may more conveniently participate. (A card also accompanies this letter so that you can indicate that your church can be used on the above-mentioned days in this struggle for freedom. Also feel free to write or call us any time for more literature.)"[31] The letter concludes, "In the name of FREEDOM," and is signed by Dennis. This letter does two things for the Freedom Vote: first, it helps inform people about the Freedom Vote, and second, by asking the ministers to lend their churches to the cause, it establishes the physical locations for Freedom Vote polling places. Dennis is relying on the ministers' credibility and influence, understanding that congregants may be more likely to work with their pastors than a with an unfamiliar campaign worker. Some ministers refused to support or encourage participation in the Freedom Vote, as demonstrated by the canceled campaign rally in Yazoo City covered in the following chapters. Not every black community in Mississippi welcomed the Freedom Vote; even though it was billed as a mock election, participation in the Freedom Vote could still bring serious consequences.

Dennis's second letter targets local business owners. Like its counterpart for ministers, the letter opens with a brief statement about the Freedom Vote and its goals. Keep in mind that the ever-present surveillance conducted by the White Citizens' Councils and the State Sovereignty Commission put pressure on black business owners to maintain the segregated status quo. Publicly supporting or encouraging the Freedom Vote could bring economic consequences and even violent reactions for the business owners. The letter's requests for local businesses echo the sentiments addressed to the ministers, but with slight variations: "You can participate in the effort by doing the following: 1) You can announce to your patrons and friends that the Freedom Ballot is being held, explaining to them exactly what it is and why they should participate. 2) You can display posters publicizing the election and our candidates (Henry and King) in your place of business. 3) You can permit your place of business to be used as a polling place so that your customers may more conveniently participate. (A card accompanies this letter so that you can indicate that your place of business can be used on the balloting days in this struggle for freedom. Also feel free to write or call us (948–0690) any time for additional literature.)" The campaign organizers here again are relying on word of mouth, like business owners telling customers, and local community networks to help disseminate information about the Freedom Vote. Having businesses hang Freedom Vote posters also helped spread interest in the Freedom Vote. Both letters also ask the recipients to lend their physical spaces to the cause as polling places. It is one thing to ask ministers and business owners to talk about the Freedom Vote; it is another to ask them to hang Freedom Vote posters or literature; and it is yet another to request their physical space as a Freedom Vote polling place. The campaign was asking local people to commit at various levels, but each level could come at a price for those who volunteered their voices or their places.

As the northern volunteers began to arrive, the campaign shifted into higher gear. Yale volunteers dispersed to various communities, mainly in the Delta region, where they performed the day-to-day tasks of running the Freedom Vote campaign along with the SNCC and CORE staff. The Delta communities of Greenville, Clarksdale, and Greenwood, as well as the southeastern town of Hattiesburg, served as bases from which workers could spread out into smaller communities such as Indianola and Cleveland. The state capital of Jackson needed a significant number of workers to staff the campaign's headquarters. All these communities were in parts of the state where blacks comprised a large percentage of the population; volunteers targeted these areas because they could potentially yield high voter turnout.

Spreading the Yale volunteers throughout the state maximized their impact, generating media coverage through their presence and providing sheer manpower. "A quick way to tell that one is in a colored neighborhood is to look at the public properties such as sidewalks, if any exist."[32] Jim Vaughn remembers helping to organize rallies, contacting store owners and churches to serve as polling places, and campaigning door-to-door over the course of the weekend to "help get out the vote." While in jail for distributing leaflets, Yale junior Frank Basler was more afraid of what would happen to him in jail than out of it. He was worried that once his fellow inmates found out why he was in jail, he would face physical consequences.[33] To his surprise, his inmates were polite and intelligent, sharing cigarettes and talking. Vigo Nielson recalls his interactions with the Sunflower County registrar, Martha Lamb, on the twenty-third and twenty-fourth, as he escorted elderly women to attempt to register. Nielson kept a detailed diary of his stay in Mississippi from the twenty-second to the twenty-sixth. While back at the Freedom House in Greenwood after a rally on the evening of October 23, Nielson recalled he had "listened to a conversation at the office in which Willie Peacock, the number-two man under Sam Block, was telling Will Rogers about the importance of high school education. It was no different than in my home."

At this point in the campaign, all the parts were in motion. Careful planning and organization began to pay off as the volunteers and candidates started electioneering at full pace. The campaign was already generating publicity, both friendly and hostile, proving that designing the campaign in line with image event tactics was proving successful. At this point in our chronological unfolding, the theme of inside/outside continues to dominate the mediate news narratives, and continues to be one of the rhetorical frames used to influence audience perceptions of the campaign.

A WAR OF WORDS

From October 23 to the end of the campaign in the first week of November, campaign coverage in Mississippi commercial papers focused on the Yale student volunteers and their activities. The *Enterprise Journal* from Natchez ran an AP story titled "Police Hold 14 Negro Leaflet Distributors" on October 23. The brief article mentions that those arrested "included two Yale University students who were among 15 who came to the state to campaign for Henry."[34] It is interesting that the article includes a hard count of just how many Yale students are in the state campaigning, as if readers are to be informed that the northern college students are being kept track of. The article, keeping with language patterns that the mass media commonly employed to depict the Freedom Vote as illegitimate, also mentions that state law did "not provide for write-ins." The *Greenwood Commonwealth* ran the same AP story with the headline "14 Are Jailed." Both papers ran the story on the bottom half of their front pages, further establishing that if Mississippi newspapers were to grant the Freedom Vote front-page status, it would be only when those involved, particularly the outsider Yale students, were arrested or otherwise linked to illegal activities.

Media reporting concerning the Yale students follows a predictable pattern. In the October 24 edition of the *DDT*, the headline on a page-fourteen story reads "Yale Students Jailed in Two State Towns." The students are specifically named with their hometown, a pattern repeated almost every time a student's arrest is reported. Naming arrested individuals and reporting where they are from is a powerful rhetorical move; it frames those individuals as outsiders and therefore as illegitimate political or social agents in Mississippi. Highlighting the fact that these individuals arrested for illegal activities are "not from around here" creates an association between outsiders and trouble.

Unable to rely on the media to portray the Freedom Vote accurately, campaign organizers developed new strategies. Internal memos and reports provide behind-the-scenes access to organizational activity. Joan Bowman, field secretary for SNCC in Mississippi, issued a five-page report to the national office in Atlanta on October 23 summarizing the activities of the Freedom Vote up to that point. She notes that the campaign was "beginning to look and act more and more like a genuine political campaign, run by an organization which expect[ed] to be a permanent fixture in Mississippi politics."[35] She mentions the dissatisfying results of a recent press conference held to announce the Freedom Vote: "At the press conference the world was to learn of the first integrated political ticket in Mississippi, as far as anyone knows, since Reconstruction days. The press conference was a disappointment, however, because only Mississippi Free Press and local press attended. (The story was buried, however, and the press has in effect boycotted us.)" Here, the campaign organizers are well aware of their struggle against the media to establish the campaign's legitimacy. She mentions that funds were needed and that northern college students were beginning to trickle in by groups of three or four, noting that it was "strange to see TR's and MG's and VW's running errands in Negro neighborhoods."

Then, Bowman's report takes a turn toward tragedy, detailing one of the first "accidents" to happen to Freedom Vote volunteers during the campaign.

> Over the weekend a major tragedy occurred which was to affect us personally, as well as inhibit the progress of our work. Mike Miller, former SNCC field worker in Greenwood, and Lee Hill, who had arrived from California at the invitation of Moses to work on the campaign, and Gene de Alissy, an engineer for Station KSFO in San Francisco, currently donating his vacation time to the Movement, were involved in an automobile accident early Sunday morning the 20th as they were returning from Clarksdale. Miller and de Alissy were critically hurt; Lee suffered from shock and cuts.

Bowman states that as the car was driving through a deserted stretch of road near Tchula, an oncoming car crossed the center lane, striking the volunteers' vehicle and forcing it off the road. Miller would have a ruptured spleen removed, and his arm was broken in two separate places. Bowman notes that Holmes County police confiscated all the campaign materials in the car, and the Freedom Vote organizers had little hope of getting them back without a court order. The materials were invaluable to the campaign already stretched thin when it came to resources: a tape recorder, tapes, speech manuscripts, and documents of campaign plans.

Bowman is encouraged, though, as she mentions that the campaign has finally picked up pace, with Henry making regular speaking engagements. She reports a few trends on the part of local police to impede the campaign's efforts, notably the jailing of workers for "distributing leaflets without a permit" and "violating curfews." She concludes her report to the SNCC headquarters with some challenges and goals the campaign would like to achieve: "It is not clear yet what our impact has been on the other candidates, or on the state at large. Because the Jackson press is boycotting us, and the Mississippi press in general, we have no way of measuring this impact." Bowman understood the importance of press coverage to the campaign. "The general response by the press to our activities has been disappointing as well. It is hoped that in the short 10 days remaining to the campaign that we can improve on all these areas and get the nation alerted to what we are doing in Mississippi. If we are to build a continuing organization on the campaign, this must be done."

Other internal memos and press releases reveal further acts of violence and intimidation. Yale junior Nelson A. Soltman detailed his own experience in a statement he issued on October 24:

> Two "Freedom Vote" campaign workers and I entered the city limits of Yazoo City, Mississippi, at 4 p.m. on October 23. We called on two Negro ministers in the city. All five went to the downtown section of the city to speak with a Negro community leader.
>
> At about 4:30 p.m. the Yazoo City police telephoned the office where the five were speaking to the Negro. The officers told the man that they were aware that he had five people in his office, and that they were certain that at least one of the individuals worked for CORE. They further noted that they were waiting outside of the office for the group to appear.[36]

Soltman goes on to state that the "Negro" leader "did not feel it would be advisable to attempt to carry the 'Henry for Governor' campaign into Yazoo City because of the possible repercussions, for both the Negro and the white citizens of the city." Soltman closes his report by saying that the leader advised the three "non-residents" to let the police escort them to the city limits, or otherwise "there was no guarantee of what might happen to them, including physical violence."

Statements like Soltman's helped garner attention for the campaign and the goals organizers hoped to achieve. The campaign workers used these reports and statements in press releases and also in correspondence with federal authorities. The northern college students brought attention to efforts in

Mississippi simply with their presence. This rhetorical presence captured and maintained the attention of friends and family members back home or at their respective schools. Though the potential for violence and bodily harm that volunteers faced was deplorable, the campaign was able to break some of the public silence by turning a bad situation into good press, which in turn helped generate much-needed broader public support, but it still came with the costs, or potential for physical suffering.

Campaign rhetors mentioned, or witnessed, these episodes of physical harm to meet rhetorical goals specific to each situation. Accounts of violence provided evidence for an argument being made, established a rhetor's credibility with an audience, or helped audience members find grounds for identification. From the perspective of the agent, these episodes could also stimulate audience members to act by encouraging them to think, "If the speaker is willing to sacrifice and endure this pain, shouldn't I also be willing to act?" It is impossible to account for each audience member's interpretation of news similar to episodes like Soltman's, but that does not stop rhetors from employing this tactic of witnessing, nor does it inhibit audience members from interpreting these stories of violence. Violence became a major rhetorical theme in Freedom Vote materials, from press releases to campaign speeches.

REPORTS FROM THE FRONT LINES

As the final days of the campaign, when voters would actually cast Freedom Ballots, drew near, campaign workers continued to report their activities. In the final weekend of October there was little over a week left in the campaign, but there was plenty of action. An October 26 report from campaign worker Donald White in Columbus shows how some community leaders refused to accommodate the Freedom Vote campaign. White's report states, "Campaign literature to promote the candidacy of gubernatorial candidate Aaron Henry may not be distributed in this city, the Mayor ruled today."[37] The report specifically cites the mayor's and police chief's refusal to issue the permits necessary to distribute leaflets and campaign materials or grant White permission to use a sound truck. White quotes the mayor as having told him, "Aaron Henry can't prove a goddamn thing."

A press release from campaign headquarters, also from October 26, reports that Lieutenant Governor Paul B. Johnson had recently given a speech in which he declared, "We can and will organize and unite the liberty-loving citizenship of conservative America into a strong and forceful unit dedicated to preserving the integrity of the white race."[38] This is nothing more than southern segregationist reasoning further supporting the status quo of inequality. The release states that Henry "lashed out at his opponent" by asking, "How can a gubernatorial candidate from a state with a population which is so heavily Negro win on a platform such as this?"

The next day, a press release issued by Freedom Vote headquarters detailed Henry's reaction to the recent arrests of two Chicago ministers who had conducted a "pray-in" at the Capitol Street Methodist Church in Jackson. The report quotes Henry saying, "No day goes by when somewhere in this state the police act in a manner more befitting a totalitarian state than the United States of America. Who can decide what man is more equal before God? For these hypocrites to deny the house of God to their fellow men because of the color of their skin is not only a crime against humanity but a sin before God."[39] This labels the actions of the local police as violating basic Christian fundamentals and of having eternal consequences. It is a very serious charge that Henry is making, and he again highlights the hypocritical nature and reasoning of segregated policies.

A statement that Al Lowenstein issued to federal authorities in the Department of Justice further illustrates the environment in which the campaign was operating. The Department of Justice was an important audience for the Freedom Vote; as the ultimate source of political authority, the federal government could enforce change. Lowenstein states:

> Campaign workers for these candidates have discovered that it is impossible to function in Mississippi with the minimum safeguards that are assumed in any free society. People are arrested for distributing leaflets, for violating curfews while trying to enter hotels, for committing the most imaginative variety of non-existent traffic violations. Ministers who offer the use of church facilities for meetings are threatened. Negroes known to have talked with campaign workers are told—sometimes by private citizens, but more frequently by officials of the community—"not to let it happen again." In short, the atmosphere of this campaign is more nearly reminiscent of a campaign under communist tyranny than of an election in the United States of America. In such a situation the courage of the people who are continuing their efforts in the campaign cannot fail to impress and move those of us who have come from other parts of the United States.[40]

Lowenstein's statement both informs the federal authorities about the conditions in Mississippi and reaffirms the commitment of the campaign to continue on in spite of the tyrannical atmosphere. He specifically notes police tactics of arresting campaign workers, labeling one of the tactics as "the most imaginative variety of non-existent traffic violations."

The final paragraph of Lowenstein's statement is also rhetorically powerful. He states: "We shall tell what we have found in Mississippi wherever we go when we leave, and we shall not leave until we have seen through the rest of this dismal experience. We shall submit evidence of what we have found to the Civil Rights Commission and the Members of the Congress of the United States in the faith that the American people, once they know the facts, will not long be willing to allow tyranny to wrap itself in the American flag in an American State." Lowenstein utters a promise to tell the rest of America, especially authority figures such as "the Civil Rights Commission" and "the Members of the Congress." This is important because it shows a relationship between the conditions in Mississippi and a general lack of awareness on the part of the rest of America. Knowledge of "the facts" is a liberating and powerful force. He's also letting those in the federal government know that the campaign won't let them just sit back and ignore this problem.

The accumulative power of all the reports, statements, and letters from and by the campaign prove that it was generating attention. It is also doing this at many levels of communication and through many means. The letters and statements are written by individuals, addressing issues and concerns at a personal level. News stories and reports work at a public level, between institutions and individuals. This is a rhetorical function of image events that can work beyond the televisual sphere once individuals consume, interpret, and then discuss the issues that concern them.

Campaign workers drafted personal letters as a means to influence press coverage, such as a letter dated October 27 from Yale University student Jonathan Middlebrook, an exchange student from Cambridge, to the editor of the *Berksire Eagle* in Pittsfield, Massachusetts. Middlebrook openly appeals to the editor "to demand from your wire services that they give you news of the mock election being held in this state."[41] Middlebrook's letter is typed on "Aaron Henry for Governor" letterhead and is a little over two pages long. Middlebrook anticipates the response of readers in Massachusetts: "Perhaps the first reaction of people living in Pittsfield, Stockbridge or Lanesboro, when they read of a mock election, an election which can elect no candidates to office, is a rather rueful smile at wasted effort: long hours, arrests, trials—all as a gesture without practical effect. The bitter irony we live with as long as we are here is that this gesture, which is likely to provoke a smile from a Northerner, is in fact a dangerous, authentic expression of courage from an oppressed citizenry." Middlebrook's framing of the Freedom Vote as "a dangerous, authentic expression of courage" is an attempt to convince the editor that the campaign was serious and newsworthy. In the final paragraph of his letter, Middlebrook makes one last appeal to the editor:

This is a letter written in anger and shock at what I could not have believed could happen in a country I have traveled for years and admired from the perspective point of Europe. By being silent, the rest of this country pretends that it is not responsible for what happens in Greenwood, Meridian, or Yazoo City. This is not so; we are a nation proven so by a war that at one time the North considered it had won. The battle, I now know, is still being fought, and the country needs to know about it.

By breaking the silence, Middlebrook argues that knowledge and awareness of what is going on in Mississippi means accountability and action on the part of the rest of America. A lack of knowledge can no longer excuse complacent Americans. This echoes some of the rhetoric Lowenstein employed in his recruitment speeches to instill moral obligation and civic duty.

A letter from another Yale volunteer employs the same rhetorical appeals to the audience's sense of duty, further emphasizing and promoting the agency of citizenship. Yale student Kenneth Klotz wrote to his state senator on October 28. In the letter, Klotz informs Senator Birch Bayh of Indiana of Klotz's experience in Mississippi thus far with the Freedom Vote campaign. He writes, "My experiences here in two days of field work have bordered on the unbelievable. In Hattiesburg, police followed our car into the Negro neighborhood at one o'clock in the morning, then barged in on us at 8:00 a.m. and took us down to the police station. We were under arrest, although our only conceivable crime was sleeping overnight in a Negro neighborhood."[42] Klotz describes how a friend of his, a Yale divinity student, was arrested after being in Hattiesburg for less than an hour. The divinity student was accused of stealing his own car and resisting arrest. Klotz makes a final appeal in his closing statements:

> I have been told that I am an outside agitator, meddling in the affairs of others because I am from Indiana and not from Mississippi. Senator Bayh, as a human being and as a citizen of the United States of America, this *is* my business. Something must be done to change the despicable condition of justice under which the Negroes and their white supporters labor in the South.
>
> Washington is far away, I know. Perhaps the abstract phrase "police intimidation" dulls the urgency of what really is going on. But after seeing it face to face for the first time in my life, I am shocked and disappointed to say that this occurs in the United States of America. I beg you to work with all your fervor and influence to alleviate this shameful perversion of law and order.

Klotz takes responsibility as an American citizen and provides testimony of the racial problems in Mississippi. He requests that his senator also answer his duty as an American citizen, let alone as a leader. Again, by providing knowledge and awareness of what is happening in Mississippi, campaign workers hoped to stimulate a reaction from the rest of America.

There were plenty of accounts and stories to share with the nation to help generate that action. A report titled "Summary of Events, October 22 through October 28," issued from campaign headquarters in Jackson and distributed to the national offices of the cooperating organizations operating underneath COFO, details some of the intimidation and violence encountered in the previous week of the campaign.[43] The report outlines thirteen separate instances across communities statewide. The first instance reported notes that in Indianola, between October 22 and 25, twenty-two campaign workers were arrested. The next occurrence mentioned is from Clarksdale on the twenty-fourth, when Lowenstein and two Yale students were arrested for violating curfew. The third and fourth instances were Nelson Soltman's experience in Yazoo City and Donald White's clash with local authorities in Columbus that were detailed earlier in this chapter. The fifth occurrence was the arrest of the two Chicago ministers in Jackson. The sixth involved the Freedom candidate for lieutenant governor himself: in a single afternoon in Jackson, Ed King "was fined for four separate traffic 'violations.'"

Next, the report summarizes the consistent harassment of campaign workers as they traveled to and from campaign headquarters on Lynch Street in Jackson. The eighth point was Ken Klotz's experience with Hattiesburg police, and the ninth was a quick note that in Greenwood "a white lady who [had] been working on the campaign was arrested on a number of traffic violations" and was "in jail on $1,000 bond." The tenth point listed churches and other facilities that had rescinded their permission for the campaign to hold events at their locations. The remaining points concluded with evidence of phone tapping, threats, and escalating violence from "non-official persons."

Amid all these reports and press releases from the campaign headquarters, a prominent national newspaper ran a significant editorial on the Freedom Vote, an important piece of media attention given how little time was left in the campaign and how much work still was needed to achieve the Freedom Vote's goals. The *Washington Post* ran the longest story published by a commercial newspaper on the Freedom Vote on October 27. Staff writer Robert E. Baker's editorial included a picture of Aaron Henry and was titled "Miss. Negroes Plan 'Private' Election." Baker begins by noting how the governor's race in Mississippi was unique that year because, for the first time, a Republican candidate was challenging the traditional one-party system, but "the Johnson-Phillips donnybrook is not the full story of this election. There is another ticket running—the unofficial 'Freedom Ballot.'"[44] Baker is one of the only reporters to ever grant the Freedom Vote the label used by the participants and organizers of the campaign itself. Baker explains, "The idea of the Freedom Ballot is to bring out a record number of Negro votes in an unofficial balloting to show they would vote in official elections in Mississippi if they were allowed to." Baker even includes details of Mississippi's state constitutional convention in 1890, highlighting the tactical changes aimed at disenfranchising the state's black citizens. Baker notes at the end of his article that if the "Freedom Ballot" were able to reach its goal of 150,000 black votes, it would surpass the total number of voters in the state's last gubernatorial election of only 58,000. Does Baker editorialize about the Freedom Vote? Absolutely, and what is significant is the manner and tone of his editorializing. Baker's writing is far more optimistic and encouraging than the majority of the press's coverage. Also significant is that Baker's words come from a widely read national news source, the *Washington Post*. This is the kind of coverage the Freedom Vote needed and intended to get by design—image event tactic achieving strategic success.

Attempting to gather further support through correspondence with federal authorities, Henry's campaign board crafted a message for the highest office in the land. A telegram from the Henry/King ticket sent to President Kennedy and the attorney general of the United States requested federal marshals to protect the campaign workers and citizens attempting to participate in the campaign. The telegram reads:

DEMAND IMMEDIATE DISPATCH OF FEDERAL MARSHALS TO PROTECT CAMPAIGN WORKERS FROM GROWING HARASSMENT THROUGHOUT MISSISSIPPI STOP OVER 200 INCIDENTS INVOLVING POLICE VIOLATION OF CONSTITUTIONAL RIGHTS HAVE OCCURRED IN LAST TEN DAYS STOP BETWEEN MIDNIGHT AND THREE A.M. IN JACKSON TODAY ONE WORKER WAS STRUCK BY A POLICEMAN AND HELD AT GUNPOINT FOR "INTERROGATION" FOR 20 MINUTES STOP FIVE OTHERS HAVE BEEN STOPPED AND THREATENED HERE IN LAST FEW HOURS STOP CAMPAIGN RALLIES HAVE BEEN DISRUPTED BY POLICE OR WHILE POLICE STOOD BY IN BILOXI, HATTIESBURG AND YAZOO CITY STOP FOUR YALE STUDENTS HAVE BEEN ASSAULTED BY POLICE OR WITH APPARENT POLICE CONNIVANCE IN VARIOUS PARTS OF THE STATE STOP TWO WORKERS HAVE BEEN DRIVEN FROM NATCHEZ BY ARMED MEN WHO FIRED SHOTS THAT LEFT THREE BULLET HOLES IN THEIR CAR STOP POSSIBILITY OF FURTHER SHOOTINGS LEADING TO DEATH AS WELL AS WHOLESALE INFRINGEMENTS OF BASIC RIGHTS MAKE IMMEDIATE ACTION ON YOUR PART IMPERATIVE [45]

The telegram is signed with seven names: the two candidates, Henry and King; campaign manager Robert Moses; chairman of the Policy Committee David Dennis; Speakers' Bureau chairman Charles Evers; the Reverend R. L. T. Smith acting as the finance chairman; and Advisory Committee chairman Allard

Lowenstein. In keeping with the campaign's strategy of spreading information, the telegram provides evidence of the violence blacks faced in Mississippi.

With only a week left, the Freedom Vote was beginning to look and operate like a real political campaign. The organizing and recruiting were beginning to pay off as Henry spoke at rallies throughout the state and as campaign workers and volunteers continued to recruit as many potential voters as possible. What also unifies the texts from this chapter with those in the next chapter is their shared telos, or end goal—that of empowering black Mississippians through a symbolic enactment of citizenship. The Freedom Vote was far from forecasting an assured victory though; the most intense and trying days still lay ahead.

Chapter Four
THE CAMPAIGN IMAGE IMAGINED

One of the main tasks facing the Freedom Vote and its campaign workers was simply getting the word out. Volunteers distributed leaflets, flyers, and other campaign materials such as posters and pamphlets as one means of achieving that mission. This chapter looks exclusively at texts of a visual nature, specifically the posters and flyers produced as campaign materials for the Freedom Vote.

So far the Freedom Vote has been seen performing in many different ways; it has been in the public sphere through news reports, it has been functioning like a campaign through meetings and other organizational events, and it has been performing as a form of direct action protest. "The significance of direct actions is in their function as image events in the larger arena of public discourse" (DeLuca 6). Part of the campaign's rhetorical performance as a direct action protest is found in the pamphlets and posters distributed throughout the state.

Though the pamphlets, flyers, posters, and photos that follow are far from the status of iconic granted by Hariman and Lucaites, a similar approach to analyzing these visual artifacts provides a guide. "We define photojournalistic icons as those *photographic images appearing in print, electronic, or digital media that are widely recognized and remembered, are understood to be representations of historically significant events, activate strong emotional identification or response, and are reproduced across a range of media, genres, or topics.*"[1] Again, the following images and visual artifacts are far from the iconic status, but they do share some features of the definition beyond being visual. While the artifacts were certainly not widely recognized and remembered, or yet to be reproduced across a range of media, genres, or topics, the other characteristics still apply. The remainder of this chapter borrows from the approach utilized by Hariman and Lucaites to analyze the artifacts that follow: "First, a close reading of the patterns of visual display and audience identification in the image itself" (9). Be they flyers, pamphlets, or posters, this general approach to campaign materials provides a basis for critique.

One of these campaign materials is a general informative flyer. At first glance, it looks like a standard political campaign poster, but the flyer is a unique and significant source of rhetoric. If rhetorical modes of analysis can be extended to critique the visual, "reading" the flyer in a close-textual manner reveals its function as a persuasive tool. J. Anthony Blair supports the analysis of visual images as sources of rhetoric: "It turns out that, in spite of their historical association with language, arguments *in the traditional sense* can be visual as well as verbal. It is much more interesting if it can be shown that visual communications can be legitimate tools of rational persuasion" (45–46). Submitting the flyer to a close-textual reading not only brings out visual rhetorical details but also orients the reader to internal and external contextual matters. In other words, the issues and ideas addressed in the flyer were a response to the societal conditions of Mississippi.

The campaign poster provides basic information on the Freedom Vote's platform and goals, which are clearly articulated in the text of the poster, but an alternative reading of the poster's visual cues provides insight into how the Freedom Vote was a source of social protest and civil disobedience. The poster does not hint at the biracial platform with words but rather visually pairs a black candidate with a white candidate by including their pictures, side-by-side. The poster becomes a public, visual display of protest by challenging the segregated traditions of politics in Mississippi. It also shows a native black Mississippian *in* political action. Henry literally has put his face out there. This demonstrates one of the characteristics that the artifacts from the Freedom Vote have in common with iconic photographs in that they are "understood to be representations of historically significant events" (Hariman and Lucaites 27). This poster labels and defines the Freedom Vote; more than a mere representation, it is the rhetoric of campaign itself in action.

Structurally and organizationally, the flyer follows a top-down, left-to-right reading. Starting at the top of the poster, then, the reader is immediately confronted with one of McGee's traditional ideographs: freedom. In America, freedom is a god-term, and in this instance, it is made even weightier by the poster's context. Since the time of Reconstruction in Mississippi, blacks had been systematically denied their legally granted and protected role in the democratic process. Since the American Revolution, the concept of freedom had been intrinsically linked with that of the vote, self-autonomy, and democracy. The term "freedom" appears twelve times on the flyer, often linked with other less-abstract ideographs, and more commonly associated with other aspects of the democratic process, like voting. This gives the poster and the Freedom Vote a distinct patriotic flavor by association.

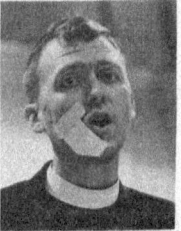

Figure 4.1. Freedom Vote poster, COFO, 1963. This was also used as a mailer.

The flyer's headline complements the immediately preceding text and images, offering further insight by connecting the issues brought forth in the text with an image of the candidates who stand for and support those ideas. Neither appears more important than the other; no one section of text is any bigger than the images. Granted, the pictures take on a certain importance due to their location on the flyer. They rest on the upper third of the flyer, and almost every aspect of the flyer adheres to the general "rule of thirds" commonly found in visual media. This is when the visual composition follows a format similar to a tic-tac-toe board. There are middle and lower horizontal thirds that complement the upper third, and even within the lower third, the "rule of thirds" is apparent in the three organized columns.

The details of the photos of the "freedom candidates" are worthy of closer analysis. Complementing the individual photo of each candidate is his name and the position he is running for. The photos are intimate in that they are close-ups and confront readers directly, face to face. Again, the rule of thirds is in action here: each candidate's eyes rest closely on a line near the upper third of the frame, with each head firmly anchored within the middle column. What would shock most Mississippians in 1963 is that the faces on the flyer are "integrated" ones. Pharmacist Aaron Henry from Clarksdale had long been involved with civil rights in Mississippi, and he would continue to be. What is intriguing about Henry's portrait (and the same can be said for Ed King's next to him) is that since the photo is a close-up of the candidate's face, it asserts a bold "publicness"—it demands intimate and immediate recognition. Not only could potential Freedom Vote participants recognize Henry on the street, but so too could oppositional forces involved with Mississippi politics. Despite this danger, the photos show the candidates' willingness to appear in direct relationship with the Freedom Vote. Another way to "read" the photos is as a matter of accountability; the candidates are acknowledging responsibility for their political actions.

What did it mean for Henry, a black Mississippian running for governor, to have a white running mate? This is a precedent-breaking moment. This is symbolic in many ways. It shows the integrated nature of the campaign's fundamental ideals for all citizens in the state of Mississippi to have better lives. It is also interesting to note that Ed King, as the lieutenant governor candidate, is subordinate to Henry. This hierarchical inversion represents the symbolic power that image events have when "the shock of the familiar made strange" is highlighted. The Freedom Vote is disseminating a message with the juxtaposition of the two portraits with the deliberate use of visuals that counter the racial status quo, signaling that this campaign, though familiar in form, is different due to the constitutive nature of its candidates, and arguably by extension all others connected with the protest. Johnson's notion that the "reflexivity of the image event, or the knowledge that many others are able to view the event," is a key source of any image event's rhetorical capacity (7). Given the context in which the Freedom Vote, as an image event, was staged, this reflexivity runs through the campaign and extends through the participants and out to a broader audience through the media and artifacts like the flyer. Johnson notes, "Photographs can be epiphanic, forcing a psychic transformation of the citizenry by rupturing imagined conceptions of identity" (8). Viewers of the flyer are confronted with a "mind bomb" that explodes what could be possible in American race relations and the roles that black citizens can play in those political and cultural relationships.

Ed King's photo next to Henry's also does more rhetorical work visually. Religious themes dominate many of the rhetorical artifacts examined throughout this book, be it in songs, speeches. or posters. The presence of Reverend King at any Freedom Vote event directly involved the presence of the Judeo-Christian tradition; he is a direct link to that rich and compelling discourse. His body and service therefore become powerful rhetorical warrants.

Note that King wears a clerical collar, a powerful source of religious credibility that was particularly influential in the black community. The presence of Judeo-Christian discourse is unmistakable here; it was literally and visually inserted on purpose. King's service and clergy is not to be taken lightly, given the nature of the audience the Freedom Vote attempted to reach.

The photo of King's face is careful to show the bandage that covers his right cheek and extends down his jaw to his chin. The bandage is unmistakable, and adds yet another level of rhetorical action. Civil rights veteran John Salter recounts how King was wounded:

> At 11:30 a.m. on Tuesday, June 18, 1963, on Hanging Moss Road on the north end of Jackson, Mississippi, the Reverend Ed King and I were heading back to Tougaloo College following a meeting with one of our lawyers, Jack Young.... I was driving my blue '61 Rambler and we were passing through the white area in fairly steady bothways traffic. Police had been following us as we headed north, but now, suddenly and inexplicably, they disappeared. Suddenly, from a side street on my left came a car driven by a young white. He drove right through the stop sign and forced a large, heavy oncoming third car directly into our path. We hit head on. When I regained consciousness, my car was destroyed. The windshield was smashed and part of Ed King's face clung to it. We were both blood-drenched, and Ed was still unconscious. Standing all around us was a growing crowd of grinning and laughing whites. The police were standing with them.[2]

Later it would be learned that the driver who ran the stop sign was the son of a prominent member of the White Citizens' Council. The visual presence of the bandage reminds readers of sacrifice—not just the sacrifice King made in terms of bodily harm, but a broader sense of sacrifice that motivated, and still motivates, social movement participants. The bandage also inspires at a level of obligation. The bandage signaled that King likely endured a wound for standing up for what he believes in; it communicates that he is willing to suffer for the cause and asks viewers what they would be willing to suffer and sacrifice. It obliges the viewer to act because King has already acted. Another side of this may be that the bandage angers viewers, because it reminds them of the injustice, which would also drive them to act. The bandage is a symbol for the wrongs they've all endured.

Campaign workers had many options for distributing the flyer as a matter of utility. Campaign workers folded them into thirds, addressed them, and then mailed them to potential Freedom Vote participants. They were also distributed as a sort of handbill or leaflet on city sidewalks and during door-to-door canvassing. The flyer was also used as an informative poster hung in both public and private venues.

The issues addressed in this flyer parallel those mentioned in Franklin Delano Roosevelt's well-known 1941 State of the Union address, popularly known as the "Four Freedoms" speech. The concepts of votes, justice, jobs, and education illuminated by the Freedom Vote flyer dovetail with FDR's four freedoms outlined in his famous address:

> In the future days, which we seek to make secure, we look forward to a world founded upon four essential human freedoms. The first is freedom of speech and expression—everywhere in the world. The second is freedom of every person to worship God in his own way—everywhere in the world. The third is freedom from want, which, translated into world terms, means economic understanding which will secure to every nation a healthy peacetime life for its inhabitants—everywhere in the world. The fourth is freedom from fear, which, translated into world terms, means a world-wide reduction of armaments to such a point and in such a thorough fashion that no nation will be in a position to commit an act of physical aggression against any neighbor—anywhere in the world.[3]

The overall themes are remarkably similar: freedom from fear harmonizes with justice; freedom from want entails jobs and education for citizens; like the vote, freedom of religion and freedom of speech relate to freedom of expression. Throughout the Freedom Vote campaign, these four freedoms were at the forefront of the campaign's rhetoric.

POSTERS AND PLATFORM PLANKS

Cara A. Finnegan argues that there are three things critics must account for when analyzing the visual: production, reproduction, and circulation (199). Images like photography and political campaign posters are not natural in that they are manufactured and distributed, and Finnegan's basic typology reminds the critic to view images as "both practical and representational" (201). In the case of the Freedom Vote, the posters are practical in that they inform viewers how they can *participate* in the actual Freedom Vote, and they are representational because they frame how viewers define, understand, and formulate an opinion *about* the Freedom Vote.

One of the posters is actually a composite of four other posters used in the campaign; it is a sort of meta-sign in that it is a poster of other posters. The four included posters are laid out with minimal text across the upper third, which reads "Mississippi Freedom Ballot." The date along the left edge of the poster is "Nov. 2–4, 1963." The real analytical work needs to be done at a more micro level of each poster. At the top is a picture of a white authority figure; it is not clear whether he is a state trooper or a different representative of authority, but he clearly holds a position of power.[4] He is the literal and symbolic focal point; he is sharply in focus in the foreground with arms crossed and a watchful gaze. The viewer does not need to know his intentions or assume that this man is even threatening, but the helmet is a marker of power that connects him to an institution of control and authority. The accompanying text asks the question, "IS HE PROTECTING YOU?" The issue is whether the viewer feels safe, asking viewers to examine how they feel about the issue. Again, though not iconic, this visual artifact does "activate strong emotional identification or response." Yes, the image of the guard or officer does seem intimidating, but the photo and question linked together address equality and safety rather than violence on the part of authority figures in general. It does so in a manner that could not be more personal, one's own sense of safety. Though the authority figure is just standing in the foreground, there is action going on around him; he is in a social setting where people are in action. His role in that action seems to be one of surveillance, or "keeping the peace." The image forces viewers to reflect on their own experiences with, and perceptions of, public safety.

A black slate at the bottom of each poster provides basic information about the Freedom Vote. Fine print at the very bottom of the box reads "Committee to Elect Aaron Henry / 1072 Lynch St., Jackson, Miss." This last line is significant because it affirms who is responsible for the poster, or, in Finnegan's terms, its production, reproduction, and circulation. It is important as a point of authorship, and it provides the physical address of those responsible for the poster

Figure 4.2. Freedom Vote compilation poster, COFO, 1963. This meta-poster combines four posters used during the campaign.

and its message—a clear indication of accountability on the part of the campaign and its organizers.

While we learn about the Freedom Vote through its artifacts, we also learn about the context it was responding to. Gallagher and Zagacki argue that photographs function at a pedagogical level, stating, "They communicate to the viewer, in the language of photography or painting or illustration or commemoration, the qualities, the pleasures or pain, the duties, the kind of past, present, and/or future that is or that is desired" (195). The photographs and visual images used in the posters are instances of visual rhetoric that teach viewers who engage them today. This is an interesting feature and extension of image events as rhetorical theory; at their conception they are constructed as mind bombs, but as time passes and distances the representations, depictions, or artifacts of image events from their contexts they then become potential sources of pedagogy. The things taught by these representations or artifacts inform about the context they were operating in, but also teach future citizens and protestors about agency that they themselves can employ.

The next included poster, in the left center of the flyer, addresses a different theme with an image of two young black boys sitting on a porch. Below them, in the shadow of a step, it states, "GIVE THEM A FUTURE IN MISSISSIPPI." The words immediately invoke an image of the future, always a theme of deliberative rhetoric. The flyer addresses the basic quality of life that black children face in Mississippi. Neither child is wearing shoes, and one of the youths is also shirtless. The two are squinting into the sun as they sit on an unshaded and worn porch. A critic might ask, "Is this photo staged? Did the photographer select these two boys, take their shoes, and then pose the boys on some stranger's porch?" In other words, is it genuine? Are these the "real" living conditions for children in Mississippi? One response is, "Does it matter?" This particular poster asks the viewer to consider the future of the children of Mississippi, asserting that these are the conditions. Although the conditions in the picture are dirty and rough, it is not about the immediate context. Rather, the future is what must be considered, and since these children cannot do anything about it, the viewer must. The image portrays a problem to instill a need to respond.

The composite poster functions as a sort of visual campaign platform. Each of the included posters poses a question or addresses a specific issue that the Freedom Vote undertakes. While each included poster inspires reflection on a particular issue, those issues become more complex as they are connected to each other. The compilation poster both magnifies individual topics and amplifies their interconnectivity and complexity. Rhetorically, the composite poster unifies the individual messages into one visual and interactive platform.

The next two images are digital pictures taken of the actual posters themselves; they are not refocused or enlarged portions of the composite poster analyzed above. While both of these posters are also on the composite poster, a more detailed representation is available due to the higher level of quality the images provide. The poster in figure 4.3 contains a picture of a worker in a field. The viewer is granted an overhead view. The worker appears to be reaching back to place something in his sack. Is it cotton or some other type of crop? It is in fact cotton, meaning it has to be harvested by hand, and that means manual labor. The viewer cannot see the worker's face, which means the individual is not an identifiable person who can be singled out, but instead becomes a symbol of not just field workers in Mississippi but all laborers. He represents all blacks who do manual labor in Mississippi, from factory and industrial workers to house maids and child care providers, anyone who does manual work with his or her hands.

Figure 4.3. Freedom Vote poster "What Does the Future Hold for the Farm Worker?," COFO, 1963.

The poster asks, "WHAT DOES THE FUTURE HOLD FOR THE FARM WORKER?" Questions are an excellent way to get viewers engaged and thinking or self-reflecting. Readers are here asked to consider the future quality of life for people who work in agriculture. "Any iconic photo structures relationships between those in the picture and the public audience; indeed, that rhetorical relationship is the most important appeal in the composition and the primary reason that the images can function as templates for public life" (Hariman and Lucaites 58). Much as the children in the previous poster (and the individuals in the next poster), political action on the part of the viewer is warranted by the image.

The overall layout of the poster is fairly simple. The informative black box is in the bottom right-hand corner, the image of the worker in the upper third, and the rhetorical question at the top. A critic might raise issues with the inefficient use of space. The text at the top cuts off the worker's head, and there is a large space beneath the worker and above the information box that is just a field. However, the vastness of the field may be intentional. The worker's left arm and hand stretch out and are hidden by the plant growth. The worker does appear to be totally surrounded and isolated by the field in which he labors. There seems to be no escape for him, just the alienation of his work, which appears to be endless. His freedom has been replaced by labor.

There is something compelling about this individual worker, though—a sense of disarming ambiguity. He potentially represents not just black farm workers, but all manual laborers across the country, broadening the audience base that the poster can connect with. His hat is not distinguishable, nor his shirt—just a plain button-up with patches over the left shoulder. His bag must have some weight to it; there are stress lines on the left shoulder of his shirt as if the bag is tugging at his body. This is an image of a black body at work, doing manual labor, and the text at the top begs the deliberative question of what the future holds for him. This question invites the viewer to interact with the poster and with the worker, much like the previous poster, by engaging with the worker's current conditions. By acknowledging the rather bleak present state of affairs, the poster challenges the viewer to consider the future.

Another Freedom Vote poster, figure 4.4, also places the viewer in an interesting perspective. This poster portrays a scene in action, stretching out from the top-left corner and covering roughly two-thirds of the poster. In the bottom-right corner is the informative black box. Notice how regardless of the issue or theme addressed in each individual poster, the black box unifies them and provides a call to action—a rhetorical form of agency that promotes agency. The text beneath the picture reads "STOP POLICE BRUTALITY." Although this poster has the least amount of written text, it makes the most compelling rhetorical argument, due to the scene in the image and the viewer's point of view of that scene.

94   The Campaign Image Imagined

Figure 4.4. Freedom Vote poster "Stop Police Brutality," COFO, 1963.

In the foreground, with their backs to the viewer, are two black men. One is standing along the left edge of the photo, head cropped out of the shot, with his hands out of his pockets. The other man is in motion, getting up from the ground. The viewer is unable to see his face as well. But what may matter more are the faces that the viewer *can* see—the faces of the four white men and a German shepherd. The dog is the focal point of the image, occupying the center of the photo. The handler is just in back, talking to an oncoming man as two uniformed police officers approach. The closest uniformed officer has his nightstick in hand as he approaches. The viewer cannot be sure as to how and why the black man in the bottom right of the photo got to the ground, but an act of aggression may have occurred. The photo, in combination with the text, represents the institutional reaction of Mississippi law enforcement to protest activity. The image places in the mind of the viewer a very *indistinct* situation—one that they're hoping every black citizen will recognize and identify with. The text enthymematically engages the viewer, "drawing the audience to participate in its own persuasion by filling in that unexpressed premise" (Blair 41). The image and text make the argument that this is a systematic reaction to black people in Mississippi and suggest that more violence is coming. The man approaching from the right of the frame has his hands on his hips in a nonchalant manner. None of the policemen seem perturbed, nor does the dog appear particularly menacing, summoning Arendt's banality of evil. While it does seem aggressive and defiant, the dog is actually turned away from the viewer. But the situational viewpoint is also compelling: the viewer is put alongside the two black men, as if the viewer is a part of the scene and a potential victim, not just a witness. This poster is about fear, and it visually communicates this emotion to the viewer.

Unpacking the visual arguments contained within each of the individual posters leads the criticism toward pathos, emotional appeals, means of identification, and matters of policy. These campaign posters may be artistic in their presentation, but they still provide useful information. They simply do it in a different, more uniquely visual styling than the campaign's general flyer, which promotes identification through interaction with the visual and written texts. Reverend Ed King remembers, "The Freedom Vote campaign had no money for big billboards, [and] any such signs that might have been erected would soon have been blasted away. We did spread our campaign posters all over the state." King argues that this series of posters was particularly important precisely because only the candidates' names, and not their pictures, appeared on the posters. These posters were therefore less risky for business owners or churches to display, but they still allowed individuals to show their support for the Freedom Vote, another testament to the self-aware reflexivity that Davi Johnson attributes to image events.

While the posters are forms of rhetorical agency themselves, as they evidence the strategic use of visual images and written texts in order to gain cooperation or interaction with an audience, they also hold the potential to promote agency within the viewer. A viewer must examine a poster just to figure out its meaning in the first place before making a further judgment of whether to continue engaging with that particular text. It is up to the viewer as to what level of engagement the texts operate; the deeper the engagement, the more interaction and reflection the viewer undertakes. A viewer could scan the poster, see that it concerned the Freedom Vote, and choose either to ignore it or to stop and further engage the poster, but each individual still must look and read in order to reach a decision. With these posters up in black churches and businesses, they acted as catalysts for political discussion, encouraging discourse about the Freedom Vote and other issues concerning Mississippi.

There does not have to be a right or wrong to the messages put forth by the posters; they are visual texts open for interpretation. "What is important to recognize is that his variability in meaning increases the value of the image" (Hariman and Lucaites 107). Yes, the parties responsible for the posters have an agenda and a preferred reading they would like viewers to glean, but the posters are not bound to that interpretation; they are free to be read or misread by anybody. They are visual texts, rhetorical sources and evidence of the Freedom Vote campaign, and, like the campaign, they are forms of agency that instill further agency in the viewer. The posters give the audience something to do. Yes, they are texts that have been produced, reproduced, and circulated as a response to conditions in Mississippi, but they also provide a call to action and a means for enacting and participating in that call.

What links all the posters and the flyer together are that they make arguments. While some of those arguments are concerned with specific policies and others are concerned with broader issues like equality, assertions are being made. According to Delicath and DeLuca, "image events are best understood as a form of argumentative practice" (371). The Freedom Vote campaign itself is a symbolic argument for the need for change, and the subsequent visual rhetoric is employed to make this argument refine and focus the points of contention the protest was designed to challenge. "Image events communicate not arguments, but argumentative fragments in the form of unstated propositions, indirect and incomplete claims, visual refutation, and implied alternatives" (Delicath and DeLuca 322).

The flyer and posters imply an alternative to race relations and the status quo of segregation. Each poster by itself is one part of the argument the Freedom Vote as a whole attempted to make. Hariman and Lucaites argue that "an image of democratic dissent can become a sign of democracy's vulnerability and inadequate political agency" (170). When viewed comprehensively, the argument fragments disseminated coalesce to create a complex and rich argument challenging segregation.

The posters and flyers also perform another important function for the Freedom Vote as an image event, by reaching out to a disenfranchised citizenry. "Image events broaden the scope of participation in the public sphere to include subaltern counterpublics" (Delicath and DeLuca 324). This feature of image events dovetails directly with the immediate goal of the Freedom Vote to demonstrate that black citizens would vote if given the chance. In this case the subaltern counterpublic are the black citizens of Mississippi, and the Freedom Vote campaign is an opportunity to create a moment for the subaltern counterpublic to participate, to have their voices heard, and to have their wants, needs, and desires expressed.

The visual aspects of the campaign are crucial to understanding the tactical developments that they influenced. The visual artifacts went a long way toward establishing the legitimacy of the Freedom Vote. One of the key characteristics of any campaign is the promotional means utilized to endorse itself. This chapter's visual artifacts demonstrate the savvy manner in which the Freedom Vote campaign was conducted and prove just how real, how powerful, this mock election was.

Chapter Five
FREEDOM IN FULL SWING

October 31 and November 1, 1963, were dangerous days for Yale student Bruce Payne in Mississippi. On two separate occasions he found himself caught in events that could have led to him missing his twenty-second birthday a few days later. One instance involved fists, the other bullets. In both cases, Payne faced violence firsthand as a direct result of his participation in the Freedom Vote. The relationship between violence and agency again proved to be complex and serious for the Mississippi movement.

This chapter explores the final week of the Freedom Vote, starting with Bruce Payne's beating in Port Gibson, engaging subsequent media coverage for critique, and culminating with analyzing the rallies of the final weekend of the campaign. In speeches, oral histories, songs, media coverage, campaign materials, and rallies, the rhetorical themes of violence and agency come to the forefront. What binds these two powerful rhetorical themes together is a distinctly religious discourse. As mentioned in chapter 4, the Freedom Vote campaign platform closely paralleled the liberties outlined by Franklin D. Roosevelt in his "Four Freedoms" speech. The platform planks of votes, justice, jobs, and education continued to dominate campaign rhetoric; when framed through the prisms of violence, agency, and religion, that rhetoric became uniquely powerful.

What distinguishes this chapter from the previous ones is that it examines songs and speeches from rallies as a series of events rather than as isolated rhetorical artifacts. The rallies analyzed in this chapter occurred in Jackson and Greenwood during arguably the most important time of the Freedom Vote campaign—the vote. And it is within this demonstration of agency through voting that the campaign's rhetoric was most passionate.

Before Mississippians started casting actual votes for the Freedom Vote candidates, there had been no way to measure the campaign's impact, aside from the poor media coverage and arrest records. The campaign rhetoric, especially at the local and grassroots levels, tactically evolved to serve the overall strategic goal of the Freedom Vote: to show the world, particularly the federal government, that if given the chance, black Mississippians would vote and would do so in large numbers. The campaign continued to instill and promote agency through actions, policies, speeches, and posters; all tactical rhetoric of the Freedom Vote lent itself toward agency and empowerment.

But *how* did the Freedom Vote organizers communicate this need for agency? What made more than 82,000 black Mississippians cast their votes in an unofficial election? When participation in a "mock" campaign could mean economic or physical consequences, why partake? One possible answer lies in the way that Freedom Vote volunteers and candidates "talked" about agency. They navigated the fear pervading Mississippi's black citizens by framing the telos of agency within the traditions of religious discourse.

David Chappell, in his book *A Stone of Hope: Prophetic Religion and the Death of Jim Crow*, explores the role of religion in the modern civil rights movement. Chappell notes, "The black movement's nonviolent soldiers were driven not by modern liberal faith in human reason, but by older, seemingly more durable prejudices and superstitions that were rooted in Christian and Jewish myth" (3). By appropriating discourse that black Mississippians readily recognized, activists were able to "use religion to inspire solidarity and self-sacrificial devotion to their cause" (Chappell 8). In their edited collection of civil rights speeches, *Rhetoric, Religion, and the Civil Rights Movement, 1954–1965*, Houck and Dixon claim that "the Judeo-Christian religion was the rhetorical hinge on which the movement pivoted" (6). In using religious discourse as a thematic guide to analyze the rallies of the Freedom Vote, "the point is to note not only that religion was used, but to observe how such use has designs on a listener" (Houck and Dixon 13). The tactical use of religious discourse to promote agency among Mississippi blacks proved successful, demonstrated not only by the 82,000 votes cast but also by the continued extension of agency after the Freedom Vote of 1963 with the founding of the Mississippi Freedom Democratic Party (MFDP).

This chapter examines rhetorical artifacts with an eye for the nuanced uses of religious discourse. In this light, stump speeches become civic sermons, campaign songs become hymns of citizenship, and freedom rallies become political revivals. The spiritual and political worlds collide and morph into a unified rhetorical weapon. The Freedom Vote's message then translates into terms easily identifiable for its audience: give your vote to freedom the same way you gave your soul to Jesus.

DON'T STOP FOR GAS

Before leaving New Haven for Mississippi, Bruce Payne felt "privileged to be useful, glad to find an active role in the movement available to a non-southern white like [himself]." Driving down the New Jersey turnpike, Payne was "pleased" that he "would soon be doing, and not just talking."[1] Upon Payne's arrival in Mississippi, Lowenstein and Moses debated where and how Payne would best serve the cause. "Because I had bail pledged, Lowenstein urged that I be sent to Clarksdale, where the situation was tense and arrests seemed likely," Payne recalls, and "nevertheless, Al deferred readily to Bob Moses's decision [that] I should go to Natchez to work with George Greene." Nicolas Bosanquet rode along with Greene and Payne down to Natchez from Jackson on October 29.

The next day, Greene and Payne were driving Ella Jo Baker from Natchez northeast to Vicksburg. Payne remembers pulling off the road into a gas station in Port Gibson. As Payne stood by the fuel pump, four men got out of their cars and demanded that Greene and Baker get out of the car. One of the men, Ernest Avants, accused Payne of "making trouble down in Adams County." Payne responded that he had not, that he was only helping citizens get a chance to vote. "He slugged me in the face," Payne remembers, "and the two others with him joined in slugging and kicking me, occasionally bouncing me off the gas pumps. It was a quiet beating, and not too damaging. I didn't think non-violent resistance prohibited a little discreet ducking, and though these guys hit hard, they clearly meant mainly to intimidate me."

Payne recalls that at the end of his beating, Ella Jo Baker, still in the backseat of the car, told the aggressors how wrong she thought they were. Fortunately, the attackers never turned their attention to her. When the group returned to Jackson, Payne immediately phoned newspapers in New Haven and Washington, DC, where his parents lived.

On Friday, November 1, Greene and Payne were driving near Vicksburg on their way to Fayette to contact a potential polling place. They noticed that they were being followed and decided to evade the pursuer. They were in a rented 1963 Chevy, which was no match in speed for the shiny new 1964 Impala that was trailing them. The two easily were caught on the flat two-lane highway, but when they were forced onto the shoulder of the road, Greene quickly turned the car around and sped off in the opposite direction. Payne remembers:

> The fifth time they caught us, once again northbound, we had managed to get to a section of the highway elevated above the low-lying fields of the Mississippi Delta. Forcing us off this narrower road, the Impala slid to the very edge of the embankment and nearly rolled off it. George said, "We just almost non-violently killed two guys." I laughed, but we seemed trapped, their car slanting past our front end, with too little space for George to manage any quick turns. Avants jumped out of the Impala and ran around it up to the driver side of our car, pointing his revolver at George's head. As he reached for the door, George, who had seen a chance to get

around them by going down the slope, stepped on the gas. We took off. Five or six bullets hit the car. One punctured the left rear tire, fortunately for us, a tubeless. As we sped toward Fayette, we could hear the whistle of escaping air.

When Payne returned to Jackson, Bob Moses asked Payne to fly to DC right away and tell his story to any members of Congress who would listen. Payne did so, and on Monday, November 4, he had lunch with Representative Jeff Cohelan, a California Democrat. Two hours after lunch, Payne found himself sitting in the office of Burke Marshall, assistant attorney general for civil rights.

Payne's work, like that of his fellow collegiate volunteers in Mississippi, functioned at various levels. The first level of rhetorical impact was the actual manpower and time spent working for the Freedom Vote in Mississippi, which impacted the lives of those Payne and other volunteers interacted with during the campaign and triggered empowerment and growth in each individual volunteer. These effects rippled out into the lives of the friends and families of those involved with the Freedom Vote campaign. Also, Payne's physical presence in the Magnolia State led to violent reactions of local white Mississippians, which he then transformed into news coverage. This violence generated powerful rhetorical consequences: media coverage, federal attention, and the increased discontent of locals witnessing yet another episode of violence in their community.

On the night of the shooting, when Payne returned safely to Jackson, Reverend Edwin King spoke with the shaken Yale student. King recalls Payne struggling with disbelief: "None of us on the COFO staff had any questions about whether murder was intended in the affair or not. But the Yale student was now trying to convince himself that they would not have been killed."[2] King remembers, "He asked me, 'Do you think those fellows really intended to kill us? Those bullets did hit the car sort of low.' I assured him, 'In Mississippi it's a dangerous error to confuse good intentions with poor aim.'"

Some campaign workers faced possible death, others just a traffic ticket, but fear and intimidation were daily aspects of life for movement workers in Mississippi. Note the difference in perspective on violence from a native Mississippian like Reverend King compared with that of an outsider like Bruce Payne. For King, the violence is commonplace and expected; for Payne, it is startling and unbelievable.

Other outside volunteers were able to generate media attention for the cause. Norman Thomas appeared in an article that John Herbers wrote for the *New York Times* on the first of November.[3] The headline "Norman Thomas Mocks Mississippi" was followed with the subhead "In Jackson to Back Negro, He Foresees Passports," an allusion to some of Thomas's rhetoric from a speech.[4]

The article focuses not on the candidates or the campaign itself but rather on an outsider brought in to help with the campaign. Herbers quotes Thomas as having declared, "You almost have to have a passport to get into Mississippi." The article quotes Thomas two other times, noting that fifty students from Yale and Stanford were involved with the "mock election." It also reports an attempted arrest of Nicolas Bosenquet on charges of vagrancy and loitering, indicating that Bosenquet had filed a formal complaint with the British embassy in Washington. (Bosenquet was a Yale exchange student from England.)

Ronnie Dugger of the *Washington Post* wrote a story for the paper's November 1 issue headlined "Negro Candidate's Aides Jailed."[5] Again, the focus is not on the actual campaign itself, but rather on the violence and arrests endured by the outsider students helping the campaign. The article reports how two locals physically accosted Ken Klotz and another Yale student in Hattiesburg, breaking Klotz's glasses. City police charged Klotz with assault and battery. The article also reports on Bosenquet, who endured "derisive remarks" from the police attempting to arrest him, such as "he's 'lower than the niggers'" and "bet a white woman wouldn't have him."

These national commercial papers both ascribed to and deviated from the patterns of coverage outlined by the Mississippi local papers in previous chapters. Though the national papers did run longer stories, they were not feature articles and were relegated to the back pages. Pictures accompanying the articles were rare. Though not as pessimistic as the Mississippi papers, the national coverage was not overtly positive in its representation, either. The national papers did not rely solely on UPI or AP wire service stories for their coverage; they could afford to have writers spend time on lower-priority pieces. It is understandable that, due to proximity, the national papers did not report on the Freedom Vote as frequently as the local papers did, but they also chose to focus on the use of northern college students exclusively. What was deemed newsworthy was white-on-white violence.

There was little time—just a few days—left in the campaign, but there was still plenty of work to do. The scheduled days of voting on Saturday the second, Sunday the third, and Monday the fourth were approaching. A series of political rallies, looking more like spiritual revivals, punctuate the final days of the Freedom Vote campaign.

PUSHING FOR THE FINAL WEEKEND

The final drive for the Freedom Vote began on Friday, November 1, 1963, with a large rally in Jackson. Holding the rally in the state's capital ensured big audience numbers and additional media attention in the final weekend of the campaign. Rallies in that time period always included impassioned singing and moving speeches, and this one was no different. Four speeches and a ballad from this rally, which was held at the Masonic Temple on Lynch Street, provide rich texts for the rhetorical historian.[6] The ballad is a particularly moving song by Matt Jones that canonizes Medgar Evers, and the speeches by Al Lowenstein, Reverend Edwin King, Dave Dennis, and Aaron Henry all deal with political agency. The theme of violence is embedded in each of the rhetorical artifacts and is particularly palpable in Dennis's speech. The candidates King and Henry are careful to promote the campaign's platform in their speeches.

The rally is a compelling source of drama and agency in action, particularly when viewed in terms of what Chappell calls "the historical tradition of religious revivals" (87). Comparing Freedom Vote rallies to religious revivals further illuminates the religious discourse used; speeches become sermons, songs become hymns, and the rally becomes a political awakening, a civic conversion.

The rally begins with four songs, opening the evening with "This Little Light of Mine," followed by "Woke Up This Morning with My Mind Set on Freedom," "Everybody Wants Freedom," and finally the solo by Matt Jones, "Keep Your Eyes on the Prize." Songs are powerful rhetorical forms, rich with history and meaning. The songs are distinctly religious, especially "This Little Light of Mine," a personal favorite of activist Fannie Lou Hamer and traditionally a gospel tune. Songs at rallies function similarly to their religious counterparts by recontextualizing concepts, values, and belief systems. In other words, songs also play a rhetorical role in the overall packaging and presentation of a Freedom Vote event.

Dave Dennis assumed the role of master of ceremonies and gave a few introductory remarks about the first speaker of the evening, Al Lowenstein. Lowenstein immediately establishes grounds for identification with his audience through the humorous telling of a personal experience of police intimidation. After leaving a recent planning meeting, Lowenstein remembers, "I got outside, I got into a car and there was my escort, my personal private escort, you've had them too. We've all shared them, we're grateful to them for their solicitude for our well-being, they're always protecting me from you, and I guess they're protecting you from me, and the thing I'd like to have someone to do is to have somebody protecting both of us from them." Lowenstein's statement gets applause from the audience as he blends humor with his personal experience; the "personal private escort" is really local law enforcement officials. Beneath the humor lies a direct link to violence. The joke directly references the intimidating presence of local police and the threat of their violent reaction. Lowenstein's inclusive language—emphasized by words like "we" and "us"—involves his audience members in his reflections, letting them in on his episodes as they relate through similar experiences.

Lowenstein received more laughs from the audience during a tale of how Natchez police mistakenly jailed an Englishman. Lowenstein sets up his punch line by describing how the Englishman (Yale exchange student Nicolas Bosanquet) "got out of a lunch room down in Natchez, Mississippi, was walking into the house [where] he was supposed to sleep, and there were the police, and they took him in and said he was a vagrant. He wasn't a vagrant. He was an Englishman." Lowenstein follows through: "I guess in Natchez the police don't know the difference between vagrants and Englishmen." The joke paid off in audience involvement and interaction; the crowd laughed at the Mississippi law enforcement's inability to differentiate between a transient and a citizen from a foreign country. Lowenstein's use of humor makes his audience comfortable and affords him the opportunity to share news and events from other communities across Mississippi, but, more important, it allows him to ease into serious topics like violence and intimidation.

Lowenstein next tells the audience about his recent arrest and jailing in Clarksdale. Sharing this further bolsters Lowenstein's credibility, as the episode provides evidence of his dedication and willingness to face consequences due to his participation in the Freedom Vote. Lowenstein continues to build identification and trust with his audience by detailing how he, and other outside volunteers, shared physical spaces in Mississippi. Lowenstein argues that the homes, churches, and jails of Mississippi are the best places in the state to find concerned citizens: "They're either in your homes, or in your churches, or in your jails, and we've shared all three with you. We are grateful to you for sharing this part of the process to understand the kind of situation you've had to live in in Mississippi." Lowenstein notes the ironic gathering space of jails as a location to find good people in Mississippi. His language remains inclusive and inviting, even grateful for having gone through hardships similar to those faced by black Mississippians. The anecdote also demonstrates to the audience that outside volunteers undergo an awakening by experiencing Mississippi firsthand.

Lowenstein then shifts his attention to the political system in Mississippi. He speaks directly about the recent creation of a two-party system in Mississippi. Democrats had long controlled the state political apparatus, but Republicans, for the first time, were mounting an attempt to run a candidate for governor. Lowenstein, however, argues that this is not the real reason the two-party system is coming to Mississippi. "The two-party system's coming to Mississippi because Aaron Henry's on the ballot, running in the hearts of the people of this state. *That's your two-party system!*" The crowd erupted at hearing the candidate's name. Lowenstein reframes the discourse around the two-party system in Mississippi to position the Freedom Vote candidates in opposition to both the Republican and Democratic candidates rather than divided along traditional party lines. He argues, "The other party is Aaron Henry and Edwin King and the people here tonight and the people all over Mississippi, who have taken the beatings and the arrests and have not been intimidated and driven out of their homes, and who are going to vote, 250 thousand of them, this coming weekend to show what they feel, and *that's the two-party system in Mississippi!*" Through democratic protest, those involved with the Freedom Vote became uniquely empowered. It was because of the efforts of Henry, King, and all who participated in the Freedom Vote that the political landscape in Mississippi was changing, not because of a Republican presence on the official ballot. Lowenstein compares the social situation in Mississippi to "the anachronism of the Dodo, sitting one man on top of the other," saying "that's not America!" Americans' current behavior of racial oppression is more than just outdated, it is just plain dumb.

Lowenstein briefly mentions how proud he is to be a part of the Freedom Vote, yet he is quick to credit the audience, acknowledging that they bore the brunt and the burden. He argues that he and other campaign workers don't deserve credit from anybody but for a brief period to say as human beings, "We're with you, and as Americans we're proud of you and indebted to you." He mentions his arrival earlier in the summer, and again using humor, he highlights the irony of the situation: "I got to Mississippi on what was United Nations Day all over the United States, and [in] Mississippi, the governor of the State proclaimed it United States Day, which was downright decent of him since it's the only day of the year that they have United States Day in Mississippi." Lowenstein continued to focus on the empowering nature of democratic action: "We're gonna give him the opportunity to have United States Day all year long, because the people of Mississippi are about to vote themselves back into the Union." This is an interesting statement by Lowenstein considering Mississippi had not yet ratified the Thirteenth Amendment, something the state wouldn't do until early in 2013. Lowenstein pays careful attention to democratic practices as rhetorical demonstrations: "They're gonna vote themselves into the tradition of freedom that is America, and they're gonna vote themselves into the full opportunity of being human beings. When they do that, ol' Ross Barnett isn't gonna be governor of anything. He can get into a rocket ship and go up to the moon!" He's telling the audience that they're voting for much more than the candidates. The blending of humor, protest, and empowerment is powerful for an audience in need of all three. Lowenstein's consistent use of humor establishes a link with his audience while he shares information; he uses deliberative rhetoric to forecast the future, a future where black Mississippians can live at their fullest potential as democratic citizens.

The speech concludes with passages of encouragement and empowerment. Lowenstein puts responsibility for the changes to come on the shoulders of his audience. He assures them outside help will come to Mississippi, but he tells them, "It has to start inside of you. If you get discouraged—if you get tired, if you get impatient and you feel 'Lord, how long, I can't wait'—show it here, and we'll come to your help." While at first glance the passage could seem patronizing, it also has an element of encouragement by promising support. The final phrases of Lowenstein's speech promise further support in the audience's journey toward agency, albeit a somewhat circumscribed agency, by assuring them, "You're not ever alone; don't think you are. Don't ever let it seem as if there's no end to what's going on to you, because the end is coming if you'll just keep pressing." Inspirational phrases are an excellent way to conclude the speech, and directs the audience's behavior in a positive and supportive manner.

Lowenstein then introduces the next speaker, Reverend Edwin King. While Lowenstein's introduction contains very little biographical detail about the twenty-seven-year-old candidate, he notes the symbolic significance of King's candidacy. Lowenstein claims King's presence on the ticket represented "the part of the Christian church that stands up in the front lines and defends the kinds of things the Christian church was founded and bound to stand for," and served as a reminder "that the spirit of Jesus Christ is not dead in the world, because it's present in the people." Through King's presence, Lowenstein connects religion and political action and asserts that the two are not mutually exclusive; this strengthens the relationship between religious ideals and their manifestation in the realm of social politics. In other words, it was not a sin to be political. By highlighting King's position in the Christian church, Lowenstein condones the presence of religious actors and religious values in the political arena.

Reverend King's speech emphasizes unity and brotherhood by addressing religious ideals that also correspond with democratic political principles, such as equality, persuading his audience through a fusion of the religious and the political. "Someone says I should talk about a new heaven and a new earth. I was in court a couple of days this week, and I heard our mayor make that remark that he's made before that Jackson is the nicest city this side of heaven." The audience responded with an outburst of laughter; the irony was not lost on them. This prompted King, "And that's just what the people in court did, they laughed at the mayor of the city of Jackson. And a new heaven and a new earth are coming when we can sit in court and laugh at the man who calls himself the mayor of all the people of Jackson. Of course it's really sad that a mayor can think like that. He's confusing good religion and good society both." King next establishes credibility with his audience by reminding them that he has spoken in Jackson before, that he has worked with many of them, and that some of them had "been jailed together." King then addresses the public perception of the Freedom Vote's unique racial constitution: "I think it would really be wonderful if the only unusual thing about our campaign is that two Delta Mississippians are running for Governor and Lt. Governor," where tradition called for a northern and southern representation of the entire state, not just the Delta region. "But it seems that a lot of people think there's something else unusual about our campaign. And we look forward to the day when people won't think about those things, because those things don't really matter." King dismisses the unique racial constitution of the Freedom Vote candidates as the distinctive characteristic. For King, the real exception of the campaign is their distinctly Delta backgrounds. King declares that racial differences "don't really matter," emphasizing unity and brotherhood.

He admits, "I've joined this campaign because it's time for Mississippians to work together to solve the problems of Mississippi." King does not say it is a black problem or a white problem, but rather he positions "the problems of Mississippi" in terms that bond blacks and whites as the state's citizens. King declares, "We have a witness to make for our Christian faith and our democratic ideals, that as we work and as we suffer to bring freedom to Mississippi, we know that we are bringing it to all men in Mississippi." Again, King fuses religion and politics to bolster unity, equality, and brotherhood. King then addresses the public perception of the Freedom Vote: "This campaign has shown, perhaps as nothing else could, the mockery of democracy and the American way of life in this state." King reclaims the labels used by the press and opponents to highlight real hypocrisy: "Some people are using the word[s] 'mock election' to talk about our campaign. We think Mississippi's elections, every one of them, are a mockery of everything that America stands for unless everyone can vote." In this move of rhetorical jujitsu, King claims the "mock election" label and applies it to the traditional election process in Mississippi. King thus elevates the Freedom Vote by arguing that it reveals the hypocritical nature of Mississippi's current conditions.

Freedom must be brought to the teachers and preachers of Mississippi, both white and black, according to King. He tells of the recent jailing of Jackson citizens and ministers from Chicago who attempted to attend religious services together, noting that "apparently [the police] consider visiting a church the most dangerous thing of all, and this may well be because we have found that our religion supports us in the battle in which we are engaged." The hypocrisy of the current system is not confined to the civic realm but is clearly present in the spiritual world as well. King argues that participants in the Freedom Vote do not have to worry about such hypocrisy, though, as their religion supports them. From his perspective, churches denying entrance to their own members is outrageous. "It's a pretty sad state of affairs," King says, and he shares with the crowd events from the previous evening. Norman Thomas had made a quick appearance at a rally in Greenwood the night before. King tells the audience that "some rather prominent Americans had been putting money aside in case Norman Thomas went to prison in Mississippi." King shares with the audience that after the rally, a car full of campaign workers was rammed, chased, and then blocked from leaving town. King also shares the episode faced by Ken Klotz and the other Yale students in Hattiesburg. He concludes, "Other people have had some pretty fantastic charges against them, but we stopped even charging people in this state. If you work on an election for freedom, the police don't even have to have any excuse to arrest you. They just pick you up." Intimidation is systemic in Mississippi, especially if one acts in a manner that challenges the status quo.

The speech becomes more uplifting as it nears the end. King reads from a letter that he says is handwritten by a ninety-five-year-old native Mississippian, P. S. Bowles, the son of former slaves. In the letter, Bowles tells King that his father's master was also his father's father, prompting King to say, "But I tell you when the master is the father, the son has a freer soul than the father." Bowles shares with King episodes from his father's life. Bowles says that it was his father's job to take the master's children off to college every year, and to pick them up at the end of the academic year. Bowles writes, "My father said that at that time he wondered when the slaves would ever have a chance to go to college. But it was beyond the reach of his fondest dream to get the idea that he would ever have a son who in his father's own lifetime would come to be president of that college." King clarifies the transition, "And Oakland College became Alcorn College, and a former white college became a Negro college, and the son of the slave who had worked at the college became president of that college." The transformation is one that is within reach for the audience and parallels the current transformation; what was once distinctly white must now include blacks. Bowles shares this testimony of hope with King, who in turn shares it with his audience, to provide a neighboring context for hope. King concludes, "This is what this campaign is about. This is why I as a minister have joined it. We live in a sick society, but we have to be concerned about all of society." King's personal commitment is focused on religiopolitical salvation for all of Mississippi; he joined because he sees hope in the coming together, healing, and mutual salvation of both blacks and whites.

King establishes a course of action for his audience, but first he notes the ineffectiveness of violence in Mississippi to discourage and prohibit action. "We've been to jail by the thousands in this state in the last two years. They've killed some of us, but now they know, and this is why they're so afraid: brutality and murder do not stop a Christian or a man who has the light of freedom. And we are going to let the light of freedom shine throughout all Mississippi." This passage uses religious ideals to motivate political action; it is an example of religious empowerment of and justification for political agency. King purposefully includes atheists and agnostic points of view as well when uttering "or a man who has the light of freedom." Freedom is not confined to the exclusive jurisdiction of the believer but is a concern for all citizens.

King shares another episode of intimidation with his audience. Earlier that evening, two students had been arrested for trying to attend a music concert in Jackson. Robert Honeysucker, a black music student from Tougaloo, and Nicolas Bosanquet wanted to hear the London Philharmonic Orchestra play. The two were arrested for attempting to integrate a public facility. King assures the audience that "in jail tonight they are singing better music than they could ever hear than that captive audience of people who think they're free but are too blind to see."

King's speech concludes with distinctly religious discourse, examples, and visual metaphors. While King has linked religion and politics throughout his speech, he unifies them into a final empowering declaration:

> Jesus said that when he came, when he went to Nazareth, and began his ministry, that he came to proclaim release to the captives, to break the chains of bondage, to bring sight to the blind. The person who has been blind all his life does not know what the light is. You are not blind. We have the light; we want more light. But perhaps most of the people in this state may be blind, although I think in their souls every person in Mississippi knows what God has to say about brotherhood. And they have to fight their own souls. They have to silence the voice of God speaking in their hearts if they are to live and do the things they do, not to us, but to each other. Part of the mission of Jesus was to proclaim the acceptable year of the Lord. We proclaim that the acceptable year of the Lord is now. And we will light that light of freedom given us by God to shine all over this land. Thank you.[7]

King plays upon sight, in both a literal sense and a symbolic sense. The physical ability to see what is going on in Mississippi is contrasted with blindness and a call for more light, more truth. Symbolically, King associates light with truth, and he uses blindness as a metaphor for ignorance. King scrutinizes white segregationists when he states, "I think in their souls every person in Mississippi knows what God has to say about brotherhood." King highlights the inner tension Mississippi whites must have been experiencing, claiming that they have to censor and deny their thoughts, literally "silence the voice of God," in order to cope with the paradox. King draws parallels between Jesus and the Freedom Vote, illustrating how both are out to free captives in bondage, making Freedom Voters agents of the divine. He links light, as a metaphor for truth, and salvation by proclaiming that the light of freedom will expose injustice throughout the land. King returns his focus to unity as he extends this promise to all humankind throughout the land.

After King's speech, the audience sang the campaign song "When the Vote Comes Rolling In," played to the melody of "When the Saints Go Marching In." Next, Matt Jones performed a powerful solo, "The Ballad of Medgar Evers." Thematically much like Bob Dylan's "A Pawn in Their Game," but on a local scale, Jones's lyrics describe the tragedy of Evers's murder and the deep introspection that the assassination created.[8] Jones's solo was accompanied by only a simple piano part as his voice crescendoed with the emotional swings of the tragic assassination. His voice was operatic and classical, with sweeping intonations and expert vibrato. In the next verse, Jones also connects the Evers murder with the recent bombing in nearby Alabama as he sings, "In Birmingham, Alabama, on Sunday morn, / Some little children died in a church. / Some were injured, and some had died, / And some were badly hurt." The final verse and chorus further link the two events and attempt to give meaning to the tragedies by framing them as ultimate sacrifices in the struggle for freedom: "Medgar has some company with him, though, / Those brave souls from Birmingham. / Like Christ, they died for you and me. / They died for you to be free." Jones includes the audience by reinforcing the significance of redemptive suffering in the final verse. "They died for you to be free, / They died for you to be free. / Like Christ, they died for you and me. / They died for you to be free." As is the case with other movement songs, Jones's ballad educates the listener and inspires action by providing direction for the audience's emotions. It also contextualizes the suffering of the past and present, which was important in combating the general fear and threats of violence facing the campaign. This directly parallels the redemptive suffering alluded to throughout Reverend Ed King's address.

Note that the songs at Freedom Vote rallies were not merely bids for audience participation. Movement songs have direct links to older religious spirituals, playing upon familiar melodies but altering the words to fit current contexts. By improvising songs and changing traditional lyrics, social activists connected to deeply embedded black oral tradition in America. The songs recontextualize the religious themes of suffering, redemption, deliverance, and awakening. Perhaps another important reason for using well-known tunes, and repetition within the songs, was that they would stick in the audience's heads. The presence of the songs also remind that "all protests are mixed media," and are another tool that the campaign can employ (DeLuca, Lawson, and Sun 485).

An impassioned speech by Dave Dennis leads up to the keynote address of the evening from the candidate for governor, Aaron Henry. Dennis says to the audience, "We've come to the stage that usually at most of our mass meetings we call for collection. Tonight, we don't want your money really. Just your participation." The intensity in Dennis's voice escalates as he attempts to motivate his audience to action: "We've had too long people marchin' around a table and givin' a dollar or somethin' like that and goin' home and getting' in bed and sayin' they done their part. We don't need that, because your dollar is not gonna buy a vote tomorrow, Sunday, and Monday." Dennis denounces complacency and mere financial support as inaction. He wants action in the form of voting.

In his speech, Dennis repeats the word "tired" to illustrate the unwillingness to endure injustice any longer. He argues, "We're all tired. We tired of people smilin' at us outta one side of their mouths and cursin' us out the other. We've had just about enough, you see." Dennis cites specific people and activities, claiming, "The young people are tired, the old people are tired. We're tired of you tellin' us day in and day out 'bout the fact you don't want to eat with us, you don't want to worship with us, you don't want to talk with us, but when you want somebody to cook your food, you get my black mammy to come and do it for you, you see." Dennis notes the hypocritical nature of segregation in the everyday relationships between Mississippi blacks and whites, how blacks are good enough to do things *for* whites but not *with* them. Note the personal nature of Dennis's language with the repeated use of the accusative "you" throughout. Where King pointed out religious contradictions, Dennis focuses on cultural contradictions. Dennis is worked up, and his notion of being tired and having "had just about enough" hints at a potential violent backlash on the part of oppressed blacks, and Dennis's zeal reaches its emotional apex: "This is what this movement is. It's a very powerful movement. And this is what the votin' is. It's sort of an expression from the hearts of each and every individual. It's tellin' them, 'I'm tired.' I'm tired, I'm tired, I'm tired. I'm *damn* tired, you see." Dennis frames the action of voting as a form of communication for the audience: if you vote, then you are expressing yourself. But veiled notions of violence rest just beneath the surface. The phrase "I'm damn tired" punctuates a list of the repeated phrase "I'm tired," building the tension to the point where being tired is synonymous with being ready to act out.

Then Dennis shares with the crowd a personal episode he experienced the summer before. He recalls meeting with Governor Ross Barnett, who repeatedly told Dennis, "All we want to do, son, is preserve these here races." Dennis retells his response to Barnett: "And I looked at Mr. Barnett, I became quite angry, and I held up one hand like this, and I told him that no two black people got in bed and made a gray-eyed, bright, kinky-haired nigger like me, you see."

Dennis highlights the hypocrisy of segregation by providing his body as a demonstration of that duplicity. He continues to touch upon this theme of sexual integration: "See, you hate us, you hate us, you hate us, and still you love us, and you love us, and you love us, you see." The repeated use of "you see" at the end of phrases forces the audience to acknowledge the incidents that Dennis is referencing. The tension that Dennis builds creates exigency and promotes agency. Dennis's style is unique from the speakers thus far in the rally; though he is not on the actual ticket, his passion comes through loud and clear. His style is not uplifting like King's but rather prophetic and indignant.

Lowenstein then introduced Aaron Henry of Clarksdale, Mississippi. The gubernatorial candidate's speech fits a more traditional template of a political campaign speech, but the context and the fact that Henry is black make the speech anything but typical. Couched within Henry's speech is a promotion of citizenship through a fusion of traditional political and religious discourses. Henry first thanks Lowenstein for the introduction and informs the crowd that he is "proud of the fact that the friendship that we gained as students has lasted all this time, and I'm sure that Al will be my friend forever, and I certainly intend to be his." Henry shares some of his experiences on the campaign trail with his audience. He addresses the campaign event in Greenville touched upon earlier by Reverend King, where the two ends of the Delta were represented by each candidate. He shares an episode of intimidation from a Hattiesburg rally: "The firemen came into the house, looking around as if they thought there were fire, and they stood inside with their fire regalia to intimidate the crowd. And as we announced to them, there, as we say here tonight, that there certainly is a fire going on, gentlemen, but water won't put it out." Henry eloquently likens the burning spirit of freedom to that of an unquenchable flame. He then tells the crowd about an instance in Biloxi, where rocks were thrown at the windows of a mission where a mass meeting was being held; such instances demonstrate the acknowledgment on the part of white supremacists that their way of life is ending. "They would not be so content upon trying to do us harm if we were not in a position of winning, and of course that's what they realize." This further contextualizes and grounds the violence, giving it an actual place and time. Henry tries to frame that the violence can ultimately be endured because victory is assured in the end.

Henry frames and directs his words to "the kind of people" that he and his audience are: "the poor people." He notes that, to most of the audience, "a Cadillac car is freedom" or "a job in a classroom where we sit for thirty days and have a salary is freedom." In a materialistic society, owning things and products represents success. According to Henry, those things do not matter: "The *main* thing about directing our remarks to the poor people is that we recognize a division among the poor people. And this division, however, finds us divided in this way—that we are divided into poor Negro people and poor white people. That's the only difference." Henry illustrates how segregation and inequality are maintained in Mississippi through propaganda, which promotes racial unrest between a class of people who ought to be working together.

Henry talks about global political figures, noting that "ironically or perhaps coincidentally" the three most important individuals in contemporary global politics have last names that all start with a "K." He first talks about Khrushchev in Soviet Russia, then about Kennedy in the United States, before finally arriving at Martin Luther King Jr. Henry then extends his discussion of King to include the iconic leader's understanding and use of the classical Greek notions of love. Henry explains that the first usage of love is *phileo*, or a type of reciprocal love, pointing out that it is not this usage of love that King strives for: "Certainly we cannot say that on this basis must we love our fellow white brother, because he certainly doesn't act like he loves us." The second notion of love Henry addresses is *eros*, or the sexual yearning for acts of passion. He dismisses this understanding of love, too. It is the third and final notion of love, *agape*, that Henry feels King supports: "And when we arise to love on the *agape* level, we love men, not because we like them, but because God loves them, and that makes a difference. When we arise to love on the *agape* level, we are able to hate the act that a man commits and yet love the man." This understanding of love fits nicely with the religious themes of forgiveness and enduring suffering. This signals to the audience that despite all the problems and issues, the community, the state, and the nation will be able to move forward in a spirit of exoneration, mutual amnesty, and respect of equality.

Henry criticizes the political system in Mississippi next. He first attacks the new two-party system as mere maintenance of the old one-party system. Henry draws the audience's attention to the things that they should be hearing from the other candidates yet go unsaid: "What these two candidates need to be telling us, though, is how much money are we making in Mississippi or how much money are we not making. Why is it that the politicians simply refuse to talk about the problems that affect Mississippi and its people?" By breaking the silence, Henry exposes the audience to the issues that concern their everyday lives and existence. Henry begins each indictment with the words "Why is it," which forces the audience into a state of self-reflection and to draw their own conclusions. "Why is it they never talk about the terrible shacks that many of us live in and have to call home? Why is it that they never discuss the question of a decent wage? Why is it that a worker in Mississippi earns an average of sixty-two dollars and fifty-seven cents a week, when the average wage of this nation is a hundred and two dollars and eighteen cents a week?" He's returning to poverty, a uniting topic for his audience, as it affects both blacks and whites. Exercising an almost Marxist critique, Henry exposes the injustices in economic terms that black Mississippians can relate to from a quality-of-life perspective. It is in terms of sheer livelihood that Henry addresses inequality: "And in the Mississippi Delta, where I come from, over fifty percent of the people earn less than a thousand dollars a year, hardly enough to keep body and soul together. They don't talk about the fact that we generally have no paid vacations, no sick leave, unemployment compensation, nor retirement benefits." These are practical, everyday issues that impact all citizens in the state. Henry uses rhetorical questions to mention the unmentionable; at a thematic level he is speaking truth to silence. "Why is it that none of our politicians say not one word about an income tax that would provide taxation from the more wealthy people and thus provide revenue for the building of better schools, better hospitals, and better roads?" Henry names specific economic policies and practices to highlight economic injustices. This extended passage makes specific critiques about specific policies. This is not some rambling on about general inequities; it is a well-researched and organized analysis of the economic conditions that the poor in Mississippi face. Henry then argues that there are three reasons for the existence and maintenance of this litany of inequalities: "the one-party system," "the existence of the poll tax," and disfranchisement. Henry states, "Our politicians do not care about poor people, black or white, because the politicians themselves are number one; they're usually the plantation owners." He's uniting his audience again, he's giving them a common enemy, and he uses a slavery metaphor. Henry further argues that complacency maintains the status quo: "It's the thundering silence of those that call themselves good. The surest way for evil to triumph is for good men to do nothing." The phrase is not only eloquent, it gives the audience direction. He's using the religious theme of good vs. evil and giving his audience a clear choice: fight the evil or let it triumph.

Henry employs more deliberative rhetoric as he outlines some of the changes he plans to make. The first issue addressed is taxes. Henry plans to abolish the sales tax on items essential to living, such as food. He also pledges to end the "black market tax" on liquor in the state. Henry says he will counter the loss of state funds by employing "a graduated income tax on all families." He even promises a decent minimum wage. In addressing the employment issues in Mississippi, Henry cites federal programs such as the Area Redevelopment Act and the Urban Renewal Program, which the state of Mississippi had refused to participate in. He claims he will also end the "gentlemen's agreements" between factory owners and state officials of hiring whites only.

A major plank in the Freedom Vote platform is the issue of education and Mississippi's school system. Henry argues, "Mississippi has the lowest academic attainment of any state in this nation, and the reason for that is largely because the white person in Mississippi is not really concerned about affording the best education the state can afford to the white children." Instead, Henry argues, they only care that "the white school in a given community is better than the Negro school in that same community." Henry points out that the state was so corrupted by racism that whites were concerned with not the overall quality of education for white children but just that their education was better than that of black students. Education had become a social comparison. Henry demands the integration of public schools: "When we do that, whatever he does for his little blonde-eyed Mary, he's got to do the same thing for my little kinky-headed Rebecca." Henry's use of the feminine gender is not just a coincidence; the referenced Rebecca is his daughter.

Continuing to outline the campaign's platform, Henry talks about justice and asks his audience to think about a moment in history when a white person was ever held accountable for his or her actions against a black person. He argues that one does not have to think long to come up with instances when blacks were killed for crimes allegedly committed against whites. Henry then argues that there should only be two conditions to be able to vote in Mississippi: that an individual is at least twenty-one years old, and that the individual is a citizen of Mississippi. Henry reminds the audience that they never hear of a black man being denied the right "to register to serve his country," and he concludes that the same should be true of voting. Remember, Henry served in the armed forces and has personal experience on his side. Henry repeats the lyrics of a song from the musical *South Pacific* to illustrate that people have to be taught to hate, they have to be socialized to do so.

Henry's speech concludes with the religious themes of sacrifice and endurance. He affirms for his audience that they should not take the hardships they endured for granted, "In these trials and tribulations we have learned well, from the knees of our parents, and from the knees of our grandparents, that in the area of freedom, similar to the days of the early birth of the Christian Church, that had there not been the people who went through these difficulties, there would never have been the victory that we now have today." Henry inserts the audience into a genealogy of sacrifice, and these instances provide grounds for lessons that will eventually pay off.

Henry's final statement strengthens the link between his audience's struggle and the historical narrative of the Christian church. He closes his speech by saying, "That history may so shape events that Caesar may occupy the palace and Christ the cross for a day. But one day, that same Christ will rise up and split history into A.D. and B.C., so that even the birth date of Caesar must be dated by his name. All we have to do is keep on down the freedom road." The analogy is distinctly religious, but it is also rooted in historical fact. In his closing, Henry provides inspiration and action for his audience while again providing a context for white violence. He likens their activities to those of Jesus, and describes how even the mighty Roman emperor Caesar must acknowledge the existence of Christ and his significance. Through the imagery of a divine Second Coming, Henry is able to forecast an inevitably better future. This places his audience on the side of the eventual victors—and eternal justice.

The rally comes to an end as Dennis informs the audience of the next Victory Rally to be held on Monday night. Doris Derby and Matt Jones lead the audience in singing the night's final song, "We Shall Overcome," and then a prayer of benediction formally signals the end of the rally. Nearly every Freedom Vote event ended with "We Shall Overcome." The song is an excellent capstone to a powerful night; it fuses the religious ideals of redemption and salvation through suffering with the localized and personal utterance of the song within a political field of behavior. The important thing is not the song itself but where the song is being sung; it is not at a church, or any other sort of specifically religious space, but rather at a political event.

The rally served to prepare and inspire those in attendance—not only the audience members but the workers and volunteers as well—for the upcoming weekend. Though agency and violence were addressed in various ways, the themes of sacrifice, suffering, and redemption framed the agency and violence in a redemptive manner. Judeo-Christian discourse bound the entire event, transforming a political rally into a religious revival of civic significance. The Freedom Vote leaders overcame the state of fear in Mississippi through this hybrid religiopolitical discourse, driving civic participation through the vehicle of religion. Instead of highlighting the distance between the religious and the civic, the Freedom Vote inverts the relationship to uncover common ground existing between the two.

KEEPING UP THE EFFORT, ON BOTH SIDES

In the few days left in the campaign, there was no shortage of violence and intimidation. A report released by campaign headquarters titled "Events in Mississippi November 1 and 2" summarizes sixteen separate instances.[9] Nicolas Bosanquet and Robert Honeysucker were arrested for attempting to hear the London Philharmonic Orchestra, as previously mentioned in Reverend King's speech. Then four unknown white men beat Yale student Bruce Payne near Natchez. In Tate County, Stanford student Hugh Smith was shot at three times. All these occurrences happened on Friday, the first.

The next day, Rankin County sheriffs interrogated Bob Moses and four campaign workers at the airport as the group tried to obtain rental cars. Patrolmen at the airport also harassed Dave Dennis and Michael Sayer as the two attempted to bring the papers necessary to secure the rental cars. In Natchez, George Greene and Bruce Payne were shot at three times while in their "Freedom Votemobile." Police picked up Jesse Davis in Jackson for allegedly snatching a purse, later dropping him off in a white residential neighborhood where a white mob began to gather until "a Negro motorist came by and fortunately offered him a lift to town." Also in Jackson, police ordered Stanford student Fred Goff out of a black café, telling him, "It's okay to buy a Coke in a nigger café but not to sit in one. If you want to live with niggers, do it outside of Mississippi."

Trouble developed throughout the state that Saturday. Police ordered campaign volunteers Lenora Thurmond and Doris Erskine out of Morton. In Yazoo City, police trailed George Raymond, Theodus Hewitt, and John Lee Watt all day, making campaign work nearly impossible. Outside Rosedale, police stopped John Lewis, Bruce Gordon, and Lawrence DiBivort and escorted the three campaign workers to Mound Bayou, where they told them to stay out of Rosedale. Local police in Belzoni arrested Willie Shaw for "parking too close to a fire hydrant." In Greenwood, five campaign workers—Jane Stembridge, Dorothy Higgins, Dick Fry, Willie Earl James, and Frank Hirsch—were arrested and jailed because their voting booth on a public sidewalk was "set up on private property and [was] disturbing the peace." In Hattiesburg, police interrogated five campaign workers for hours after the group left a federal housing project canvassing for the Freedom Vote. After the interrogation, the campaign workers' car would not start, and they found water in the gas tank. Time and time again, violence and intimidation were the established norm.

Also on Saturday, November 2, the White House received a letter from political figure Norman Thomas detailing his experiences of being rammed in a vehicle with other campaign workers after the rally where he spoke and of rocks being thrown in Belzoni. Thomas tells the president, "I write you this open letter, copies of which I shall send to certain members of Congress and the press, in the belief that what I am adequately reporting has a direct bearing on what you may do by executive power and the legislation Congress is considering for the protection of U.S. citizens." This is another use of knowledge and awareness to stimulate action, this time from a prominent figure in US politics. Thomas writes, "This situation is America's business," further broadening the base of responsibility and therefore increasing the number of people who should get involved. While the campaign constantly tried to connect with the nation and world outside the Magnolia State, the Freedom Vote never failed to address the issues concerning its primary constituency, as evidenced by James Forman's speech at the next rally.

FORMAN'S HISTORY LESSON

A rally in Greenwood on Sunday, November 3, included several speeches worthy of analysis, most notably James Forman's. While the songs, personal testimonies, and scriptures read are worthy of their own analysis, the speeches further establish four themes found throughout the Freedom Vote texts. Reverend Cleveland Jordan's sermon for the evening, James Forman's powerful speech outlining the history of blacks' struggles in America, and the personal testimony of Ivanhoe Donaldson comprise the speech texts. These speeches touch upon, in some manner, one or more of the following rhetorical themes: violence, or the potential for violence; religious ideals (for example, salvation, forgiveness, sacrifice, suffering, love); citizenship and agency; and knowledge and awareness.

The rally opened with the singing of "Freedom Train," and Sam Block spoke briefly about some of the day's events. Reverend Red provided the opening prayer, asking, "How much is on us tonight? Do not leave us, heavenly Father; I don't care how hard the struggle gets or how hard the fight may be, stand on our side." Reverend Red's prayer taps into a divine source for strength.

Reverend Cleveland Jordan then came to the pulpit. He starts his brief speech with an encounter he had had with a local woman who had asked him earlier in the day, "Now what we gonn' do when y'all leave here?" She had mistaken him for an outside agitator. He responded, with a smile, "Well, uh, I live here and gonn' to die here. Ain't a peckerwood in Mississippi can run me away from here. He can kill me but can't run me away from here." With that established, Reverend Jordan switches roles to interrogator: "Now where's that God that you serve? Where is He? These boys didn't bring God when they come here. God been in Mississippi all the time, before these boys were born. Where's that God you got so much confidence in?" Reverend Jordan couches his commitment to stay in Mississippi with religious duty, a duty that does not depend on the aid of outsiders. This connects with Reverend King's revelation of Mississippi Christians' religious contradictions. Reverend Jordan illustrates that people are afraid of the wrong consequences, that they should reconsider and examine their spiritual commitment. He tells the crowd that the woman responded, "Oh, I hadn't thought about that; [I] done forgot God. Now I think about the white man." Reverend Jordan then accused her of being "more scared of the peckerwood than she is God." Reverend Jordan is charging his audience with misplacing their fears and commitment. The episode serves as a lesson in dedication, especially when juxtaposed with his next example.

Reverend Jordan tells a story about a fifteen-year-old girl who was beaten while she was jailed. He says her witness to God is more genuine than that of the old people in attendance. He says, "I been sick of talking about heaven all the time. Don't point me where you ain't been; you may not go there. But tell me how to live here. Here's where you get ready for heaven." Reverend Jordan is reminding his audience to live the Christian way of life here on Earth. He's sick of blacks excusing/ignoring their bad current situations by looking toward heaven and the afterlife instead; he doesn't want them using heaven as an excuse to do nothing any more. He closes his speech with a passage of deliberative rhetoric: "And you gonna be able to tell your children—watch what I say; I may be in my grave, but—these white folks gonna come a day when they won't be able to hire you." Jordan is grounding prophetic discourse in economic possibilities. "If they didn't rob you and underpay you, they couldn't hire you no-how. You workin' for nothing. They ain't always give you the old, tore-up stocking—they gonna have to wear 'em themselves." Reverend Jordan's what-goes-around-comes-around message empowers his audience by forecasting a day when blacks will be financially secure and economically independent from whites. Reverend Jordan's metonymy of an "old, tore-up stocking" represents the financial hardships that blacks have had to endure; he groups security and equality with economic conditions.

When Reverend Jordan left the podium, the audience sang "Keep Your Eyes on the Prize," and then it was James Forman's turn to speak.[10] Forman's speech is a powerful example of how knowledge and awareness can lead individuals to action by critically understanding the links between historical context and contemporary conditions. Forman's speech analyzes the historical struggle of the black body in America, and it is not coincidental that he focuses on physical violence: while attending graduate school at the University of Southern California, Forman was badly beaten in an "altercation" with police officers.[11] Forman opens his speech by telling the audience that he is one of them: "It is always a pleasure, of course, to be in Greenwood, because I get a sort of rejuvenation by being in Greenwood, and being in the Delta, because I'm from the Delta." Forman recalls the first time he heard about Greenwood on the radio, during the first news reports about Emmett Till. He mentions the murder of Reverend Lee in Belzoni, reminding his audience, "There are other Belzonis, and there are other Greenwoods." By mentioning these two murders, Forman shows his audience he has knowledge of the history of violence in the region.

He next recognizes Reverend Johnson for being one of the first in the community to open the doors of his church for the movement. Forman asks the audience to give Johnson a round of applause. For Forman, it becomes a symbol of progress: "He opened up his doors when other churches wouldn't open up their doors. I think it's a tremendous thing, and it's a credit to the hard work of the young people and of you that we are now able to enjoy the facilities of Elks Hall and most of the churches in Greenwood. And this means progress, you see." Forman references the fact that just a year prior the Student Nonviolent Coordinating Committee's (SNCC) efforts had made little headway in the area, but despite those setbacks, SNCC pushed on. "We have taken the first step," Forman says. "We have decided that we want to be free, and that is the first step. You cannot keep a free man in chains. You cannot do it!" Forman is making an argument by comparison, depicting how things had changed. What had started as a few involved individuals was now an entire community participating in the Freedom Vote. He is careful to note that access and accommodation are a big step in mobilizing a community.

Forman brings the theme of his speech into focus by repeating a phrase throughout his nearly forty-minute speech: "And I'd like to take us back tonight because some of us might not understand some of the things we've been through." The last few words in the phrase become more important as Forman moves through his speech. Understanding what they, as speaker and audience and as a community, had been through was a key to empowerment, and they had a large stake in the current conditions. Forman utilizes the themes of suffering and redemptive endurance within a historical reaccounting. He's letting his audience know that he's suffered with them and bringing them together with a common past.

Forman's historical narrative starts on the shores of West Africa. He describes the conditions on slave ships in detailed, visceral language, painting a picture of struggle and hardship. Forman is also careful to shape the historical knowledge of his audience: "So don't let them tell you that we came over here willingly. We didn't! We came over here with guns pointed at our heads and shackles around out feet and on our arms." Forman asks his audience to reclaim their history in their own voice. He demands that they allow no one to construct their history for them; "don't let them tell you" declares their right to seize their own subjective and collective history and encourages the audience to defy unjust authority. Forman challenges public and historical perspectives here, confronting the hegemonic construction of black history in America and the white authority that preserved it. He wants his audience to control their own history—how it is told, and therefore how it is remembered. Forman uses the phrases "guns pointed at our heads and shackles around our feet" as an effective use of metonymy, and it's worth noting that he says "*our* heads" and "*our* feet," making the audience *feel* the experience, placing them there.

Forman notes that twenty slaves were at the settlement in Jamestown and that blacks had been in America just as long as whites—not as an ideal, but a historical fact. He even mentions that many whites came over as indentured servants but were allowed to earn their freedom. He links contemporary economics with history: "And then along came the cotton gin, Eli Whitney. And so that the price of the black bodies became very great because they needed people in the cotton fields." Forman establishes the relationship between capitalism in America and the need for black bodies as sources of cheap labor.

This link between the black body and the economy throughout America's history becomes a theme in Forman's speech. In doing so, Forman is reclaiming the once abject body and the labor that it did for a new type of political labor rooted in citizenship. This is familiar to how Christine Harold and Kevin Michael DeLuca argue that the black community reconfigured the symbolism of Emmett Till's abject body in to a rhetorical impetus for change.[12] Forman argues that it was because of the demand for black bodies that breeding became important in the American South. Forman mentions Crispus Attucks, who "died fighting for this country back in 1787,"[13] and takes his audience through the various wars blacks fought for the nation up to the War of 1812, arguing, "All this time [we] had a price tag over our heads." The economic value of the black body never leaves Forman's attention: "The books will show you that they used to sell the premium price for a male buck was about $1,500. And they didn't give very much for little children, $25 or $30. That's all a black baby was worth in those days." Forman constantly reminds his audience of the economic factors that shaped blacks' standing in America. Laced throughout America's history is violence or the threat of violence to control the black body for whites' economic gain.

Forman is quick to mention, though, that blacks were not complacent about their status. He states, "There were a lot of slave revolts." He provides a few examples of black empowerment for his audience, mentioning Nat Turner, Denmark Vesey,[14] and "a woman called Harriet Tubman who ran an underground railroad from the shores of Maryland, where the Student Nonviolent Coordinating Committee today has a project," adding that his audience "may have heard about Cambridge, Maryland, and Gloria Richardson." Forman informs his audience of past examples of black agency and connects those examples to the contemporary activities of SNCC. He educates, informs, and empowers his audience. This is the sort of empowerment the Freedom Vote was designed to instill in its constituents and demonstrate to the nation.

Forman embraces the white members of his audience by citing abolitionist William Lloyd Garrison as an example of white agency in the struggle for freedom. This brings Forman to the Civil War. He argues, "Negroes fought in that Civil War. It's something necessary for us to understand this, because we're not asking for anything which is not ours. We're not on our knees begging the white man to hand us out any favors." Blacks are sick of being at the bottom—they don't want to feel like beggars, so Forman is showing them that they aren't. Forman claims that blacks deserve power in America, that they've earned it through their sacrifices for the nation. He legitimizes the political agency he is instilling in the crowd by insisting that the country owes them citizenship and the rights that come with it. Equality is a foregone conclusion for Forman; blacks have already paid the price. "Competing social groups will contend over the meanings of bodies," and Forman is helping give black citizens in his audience historical grounds and evidence for their contentions (Harold and DeLuca 267). In a way, the Freedom Vote is designed to reconnect black citizens to the past by empowering them for the future with their already fought-for rights.

The theme of "understanding" and "knowing" what blacks had been through in America forms the organizational structure and impetus for a call to action. Knowing their history was a key step toward empowerment, despite the gruesome nature of the past. "I know it's a horrible story," Forman says, "but we got to know our history, we got to know what we've been through! Because we're not just suffering for the first time today; our forefathers and ancestors have suffered even greater than what we have." This constant relationship between the past and the present is made significant in terms of promoting agency in the audience. "And it seems to me that we have a historical debt to pay to them. They are all in their graves now. They didn't want to be slaves! Don't let anybody tell you that we were happy being slaves." The idea of their paying a debt to their ancestors is significant after Forman just forged such a strong link between the black body and the economy. Forman empowers his audience through knowledge and the reclaiming of history. He does not want the crowd to forget past hardships, because those hardships directly begot what was currently happening in Mississippi. Forman challenges the authority of history:

> And they tell you that we were lazy out in the cotton fields—don't you believe that! Because we've helped to build up this whole Delta of the Mississippi, black hands and black bodies working for $2 and a loaf of bread, not a loaf of bread but a piece of corn bread. Helped to build up Greenwood, and the whole Delta of Mississippi, and not just Mississippi, but the black belts of Alabama, Georgia, South Carolina, North Carolina, Virginia, all across this South. You see, we have built this country. Don't let anybody tell you—not only have we built the country, but we have died in all the wars that this country has ever fought. And yet here we are now, scared to even cast a freedom ballot because of the white man downtown!

Forman wants the audience to have ownership of their own history. There are consequences to the knowledge of the past, and those consequences manifest themselves in the daily lives and behaviors of Mississippi citizens. Forman recontextualizes the past activity of the black body and its relationship to the development of the nation. There is still work for the black body to do, but it is of a different nature for blacks in Mississippi: theirs is the work of entitled citizens.

Forman's narrative marches up through World War II, reminding his audience of the Great Migration of Mississippi blacks north to Chicago. Forman argues that with the move north came new challenges for blacks. Now, they had to be wary of corruption from black politicians: "Up there in the north they got some Uncle Tom politicians, and Reverend Jordan is right, there's no point in everybody coming out here to these meetings, getting shot at, going through all this trouble to elect some Negro who's going to be some Uncle Tom to get all the money for himself." Forman argues for accountability and responsibility on the part of his audience to ensure that their efforts are not wasted on political corruption. This time, his argument for knowledge and awareness centers on blacks monitoring their own communities, combating corruption through surveillance. In a passage promoting efficacy, Forman states, "But don't you let them fool you. If you can come out here night after night to these meetings, you got enough sense to do anything that an eighth grader like Bull Connor in Birmingham, Alabama, [can do]. He ain't got no education, you see." Forman is showing his audience that they already had agency, that they could operate in civic government at that very moment. "It don't take a whole lot of stuff to run that city hall down there, anybody in here can almost run it. Don't let them tell you!" He supports this claim by telling his audience about the African nations that had recently attained sovereignty from their European colonizers. There were blacks sitting in the United Nations, and, by comparison, Mississippi blacks ought to be able to represent themselves, too.

Forman had now brought his audience to recent history, the previous ten years or so. He briefly acknowledges the *Brown* decision in 1954 and focuses on the student sit-ins six years later. He specifically mentions the February 1, 1960, sit-in in Greensboro, North Carolina: "They became free the minute they sat down at the lunch counter. And all of those who have gone down and faced that white man at the courthouse have become free the minute they made that step, because I know what it was like a year ago in Greenwood, and you do too." Knowledge extends into recent history, into the immediate context of the audience. Forman connects directly to the experiences of the audience: "We were saying, 'Child, oh no, I ain't gonna fool with that mess. No, I ain't goin' to no meetings.' And when you came on out, something in you started moving, because you got religion, but you got a different kind of religion. You got a touch of the freedom religion." Forman depicts and promotes agency through related events where freedom and change were results of action. He labels the spirit of their endeavors "freedom religion," combining religious ideals and zealousness with American political ideals, transforming the meetings and rallies into moments of political evangelism. Continuing his religion analogy, he notes a political awakening within those who attended the meetings. He cites specific local examples of freedom religion in the crowd, claiming that the "mantel of freedom" touched Sam Block and Willie Peacock, workers who had missioned in Greenwood for the last fourteen months, converting workers and volunteers into prophets and apostles.

Forman zeroes in on his local audience, returning to episodes of violence similar to the Till and Lee tragedies. He mentions the Burns Photo Shop, where workers had to jump out second-story windows to escape physical beating. He provides more examples of local sacrifice and endurance: "All of you remember, though, the shooting of Jimmy Travis here in Greenwood. All of you remember the time that Block and Peacock got shot at, at the burning of the SNCC office, the shooting in Dewey Greene's home, George Greene's home—all of us remember those things." The close proximity of these events, in both time and physical location, to the audience is unmistakable. The long arc of Forman's historical narrative lands in the current context of his audience members' lives.

Forman turns his attention to the children of the community, using them as the image of future agency for Greenwood blacks: "You got some little kids, five, six years old, sitting there singing freedom songs, and they ain't gonna stand for it. They ain't gonna stand for it, you know what I'm saying? It's impossible to be learning freedom songs and grow up to be a slave!" This is an example of agency and self-reflection inspired through song. Forman argues that the topics and issues contained in the lyrics of the freedom songs educate, inform, and empower the youth.

Forman connects the dots for his audience. He has given them a history lesson, and he begins to tie things together. "You wonder to what avail is it, what does it all mean? Well, it means the more that we struggle, the less our children will have to struggle, you see, and there's even a certain amount of joy and goodness to what we're doing." It was a righteous suffering that blacks were enduring. Forman implores his audience to engage in political activity rather than participate in America's materialistic culture of consumerism. "Because I'd rather be out here in the freedom fight," Forman says, "than sitting at some five- or ten-cent screen watchin' some white folks so-called makin' love. Or at home with my television set watchin' some gangsters shootin' them up, 'Boom, boom, boom.' That's all. It's a corrupt society. And it's gonna be the black man that's gonna help liberate this country." In framing the fight against corruption, Forman lambastes the materialistic lifestyle of contemporary America. "All across this country people are beginning to learn that there's something else to life than a new suit of clothes, a new home, a lamp in the window, or something like that, you know." Forman knows that gaining economic equality is important to his audience, but it's more than material lust that drives them. A change was coming to the American way of life, though Forman did not know just how prophetic this notion was for the general social upheaval and protests that marked the 1960s. There is a more fulfilling lifestyle than buying and owning things, according to Forman, rooted in *doing* and not *having*—agency rather than materialism. For Forman, this "new concept of living" centers on agency and self-actualization.

The remainder of Forman's speech focuses on instilling agency in the individuals in his audience. He tells them that their ballots are important for a couple reasons: their vote would show blacks in other states that there was hope, and their ballots would send a message to the White Citizens' Councils, whose headquarters was right there in Greenwood: "It makes no difference how many times you shoot at a Jimmy Travis, it makes no difference how many Beckwiths you produce [to] kill Medgar Evers, that the masses of the people want to be free." For Forman, the act of participating in the Freedom Vote extended beyond personal agency to communicate to entire communities and groups of people. The Freedom Vote became a political extension that communicated at a great scale; participation in the Freedom Vote sent a symbolic message of equal citizenship.

Forman returns to local people as models of bravery. He tells of the recent shooting that George Greene experienced: "Your boy from Greenwood, Mississippi, fightin' for your freedom, got shot at!" He reminds the crowd of the murder of Mack Charles Parker in Poplarville and that that had not deterred the Freedom Vote workers campaigning there. Forman demands action on the part of the crowd: "Now if these people can do all this, don't tell me we can't go down and cast our ballot. Don't tell me we can't go home tonight and get on the phone for two hours and call up everybody we know." Forman frames his audience's participation as actionable and inevitable. Progress has already been established; there is nothing they can do to stop it, so they might as well play a part in the change.

Forman tells the audience about a final episode of violence that happened in the Winona jail. "Mrs. Hamer from Ruleville, because she wouldn't say 'yes, sir,' they whipped her every time. They brought the guards in there and made the guards whip her. That's right, all this is going on. And what is the difference between now and 350 years ago? Ain't much difference; we still slaves." The history that Forman had been telling his audience was not over; violence and intimidation continued that very day, as evidenced by the beating of Fannie Lou Hamer in Winona.[15] The history of violence is a living one, and knowledge is the key to helping stimulate action to achieve equality. "Freedom is when you know within your soul that you are a man," Forman says. Freedom is a matter of individually recognizing one's own subjectivity, of actualizing one's own existence.

Forman closes his speech by obligating the crowd to act for their children. He argues, "If it takes death because we make a freedom ballot, then let us die. Because if we don't make some supreme sacrifice now, our children are gonna have to suffer." Forman continues to highlight this duty: "It's not right to bring a black child into this world for him to be segregated, when you know you haven't done anything. And remember I'm not talking about the role up in heaven. We got children askin' their parents now, 'Momma, what have you done for freedom?'" Through this obligation a higher goal is attainable. "We owe it to 'em. They didn't ask to be brought into this world. They didn't ask to be brought in here; it was our pleasure that brought 'em in this world. And we oughta do something to get 'em, make 'em better. Don't let us fool ourselves; we got an obligation to our grandchildren. And we got to pay off our debt, and as we pay off the debt, we can go forward singin' 'We Shall Overcome.' Thank you." Forman's deliberative statements direct future action. Forman places responsibility on the shoulders of his audience, a commitment they cannot avoid without causing their children to suffer.

Forman is reclaiming the political economic history of the black body as a means to connect his audience and guide their behavior. By doing so he creates "a temporary nexus around which people could link themselves to each other in a new network, thus reconfiguring their agency in powerful ways" (Harold and DeLuca 278). The audience is to translate this knowledge into action.

After Forman's speech, the crowd sang together "I'm Gonna Sit at the Welcome Table," and then a local youth from Belzoni shared his experiences during the campaign. Ivanhoe Donaldson next gave witness to his own encounter with violence and intimidation. It is important to note how these episodes of witnessing functioned rhetorically. Like familiar religious parables, they inspired others to act by portraying individuals enduring suffering and yet persevering. Donaldson shared with the crowd a recent episode he and Charlie Cobb encountered. The two had been canvassing for only a short time when they ran into trouble. "I'm on the steps talking to this, this ... uh ... elderly man 'bout getting his vote. And then my back is to the ... to the street. And the next thing I know, he's telling me to look out, and this truck pulls right up onto the lawn about an inch from my leg." The threat of violence escalated from there: "This cat opens the door and has a shotgun in his hands and says, 'Nigga, you gotta stop this nonsense. We giving' you all a few damn minutes to get outta town.'" Donaldson's testimony supports Forman's message of the urgent need for empowerment, contextualizing it in terms of proximity and recency. To stop the cycle of violence, blacks must act. Donaldson says, "This stuff's got to stop," and the Freedom Vote represented an avenue for change. He tells the crowd, "Some people down there told us … ya know … soon as this is over with, they're going down to the courthouse and they're gonna register … ya know … because of this election, because of what it's meant to them." Donaldson notes that it was because of the agency afforded by participation in the Freedom Vote that blacks would become political agents, drawing attention to the symbolic power of the Freedom Vote. When Donaldson, the last speaker of the evening, left the podium, the audience sang two final songs, "We'll Never Turn Back" and "We Shall Overcome."

While the rally in Greenwood focused thematically on knowledge, it shared many qualities with the first rally discussed. Through songs and speeches, both promoted unity and togetherness and focused on empowerment through agency, specifically voting. While the presence of religious discourse was not as conspicuous throughout the Greenwood rally, its themes still played an important role.

Some visual clues exist as to what a mass meeting like the Greenwood rally may have looked like. Though the photographs are from a Freedom Vote rally at Hattiesburg, some similarities can be drawn.

The images portray a process,[16] an activity essential to the functioning of healthy democratic societies. The people are voting. They are also protesting. Within the frames, the activity does not seem threatening or challenging to any authority. What makes the action portrayed significant and meaningful is the environment in which the activity is carried out.

The images show the Mississippi Freedom Vote of 1963 in action. In figure 5.1, two women wait in line as another casts her ballot with volunteers looking on. Look closely at the top of the ballot box, there is a Freedom Vote campaign poster. Shift your attention to the elderly woman in the bottom left-hand corner. Bespectacled, wearing a hat and earrings, she waits to exercise the franchise and participate. Does it matter to her that this is a "mock" election? That her vote does not count in the official statewide governor's race? Or does she wait patiently for other reasons? Although her vote is not legitimate in the eyes of the state comptroller, her participation gains legitimacy through other means. Her vote/voting is also an expression of protest, a means of empowering herself. Her demonstration, like the Freedom Vote itself, which may appear simple and harmless at first glance, is a powerful act.

Yes, she is familiarizing herself with a democratic process, and yes, she is letting others know that she wants to participate in that process, but she is also doing more. Hers is a unique act, an exercise in rhetorical agency, in the midst of "one of the most unique voting campaigns in American history."[17]

And these women are not the only ones who took time to learn about and participate in the Freedom Vote. Their actions, along with those of over

Freedom in Full Swing 127

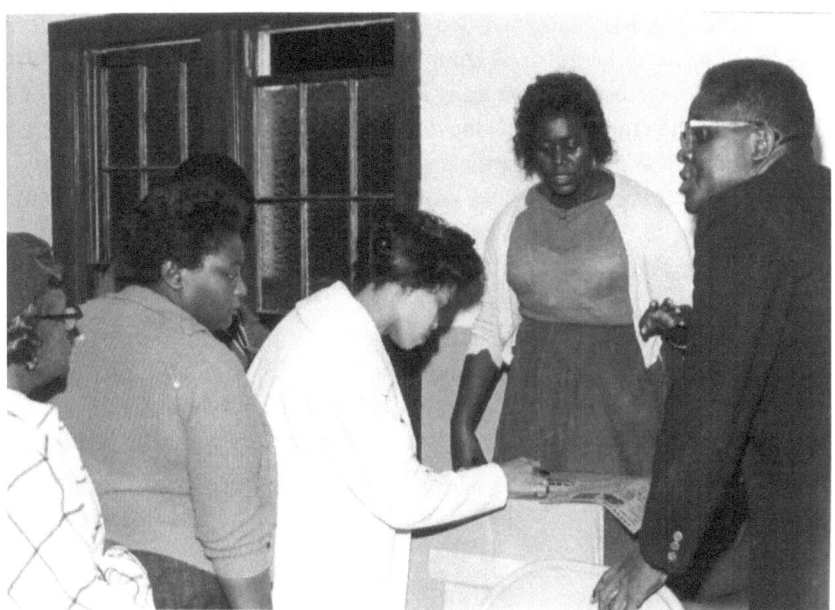

Figure 5.1. Freedom Vote rally, Hattiesburg, 1963, Moncrief Collection, MDAH.

Figure 5.2. Freedom Vote rally, Hattiesburg, 1963, Moncrief Collection, MDAH.

80,000 other Mississippians, revealed just how powerful and real a mock election could prove to be. It is one thing to organize people for protest; it is yet another and altogether different thing to teach and educate them about citizenship while at the same time allowing them to enact those lessons. The captured meetings involved people, regardless of their locations, and, more important, these people gathered together as individuals in a community to participate. The images capture black Mississippians in action, enacting political agency despite the conditions of fear and intimidation.

Instead of witnessing or being delivered, the audience members at these revivals display their faith by participating and voting. At a rally or revival, audience members are converted, awakened, and delivered by exercising the franchise. For the Freedom Vote, one final rally would end the campaign's electioneering, but not its impact on the civil rights movement and national history.

Chapter Six
A RALLY FOR VICTORY, A REVIVAL FOR FREEDOM

This chapter focuses solely on the final event of the Freedom Vote. This final rally, like most Freedom Vote events, is a mix of multiple texts ranging from visual artifacts to songs and speeches. Still working in a close-textual manner of rhetorical history, this chapter critiques a poster/flyer advertising the final rally of the campaign, along with songs and shorter speeches, finally analyzing speeches by Bob Moses and the candidates themselves, Aaron Henry and Reverend Ed King. And like other Freedom Vote events, it comes to represent the very issues that the campaign addressed, namely integrated efforts to work and improve the conditions for Mississippi's black citizens.

A poster advertises the Freedom Vote Rally on November 4, promoting the event as a "Victory Rally." The top of the poster provides information concerning the scene and act of the event; the act, or what is going on, is labeled "Vote Counting" for the "Freedom Vote Victory Rally," and the when of the scene informs the viewer that the act is happening on "Monday Night, November 4, 7:30 pm." Note that the phrase "Victory Rally" is the largest text on the poster; the size of the text frames the perspective of the viewer. The word "Victory" influences how the reader perceives the rest of the poster by framing the event and the overall goal of the Freedom Vote as a success.

Similarly to previous Freedom Vote flyers, this one features portrait shots of the candidates in the middle third of the poster, but this time the two candidates are not separately labeled; they are unitedly referred to as the "Henry-King Ticket." Rather than specifically name each candidate and what office he was running for, the poster bonds the two men together in a single and uniform entity. The word "FREE" appears next to some of the activities planned for the evening. Those who attend can enjoy "entertainment, refreshments, and big band music" at no cost.

The words "see," "hear," and "meet" promise that attendees will experience firsthand the parties responsible for the Freedom Vote. The poster publicly displays when and where the individuals responsible for the Freedom Vote

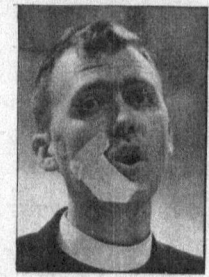

Figure 6.1. Freedom Vote poster "Victory Rally," COFO, 1963.

would gather, sending a clear message to segregationists that their attempts to silence the movement or drive it underground had not worked. The poster details exactly who attendees can anticipate seeing and hearing at the rally. The candidates, Henry and King, are at the top of the two columns. The "VIPs" below them are linked to the organizations that they work for: James Forman and John Lewis of the Student Nonviolent Coordinating Committee (SNCC), James Bevel of the Southern Christian Leadership Conference (SCLC), Mrs. Medgar Evers from the National Association for the Advancement of Colored People (NAACP), and Bob Gore from the Congress of Racial Equality (CORE). Note that all the major civil rights organizations in Mississippi were represented; the list of names symbolizes a united front. The final line of text on the poster rounds out the rest of the scene details, informing the viewer that the event is taking place "At the Masonic Temple in Jackson." The poster is a visual and textual cue to the Freedom Vote's self-assessment, an opportunity that not many image events are afforded.

Like the previous rallies explored, this Freedom Vote Victory Rally comprised songs and speeches, but this time the mood was distinctly euphoric. The rhetoric again centered on the coming together of people, unity through activity, but now that the audience had fulfilled their call to action, the rally had to set the stage for what was to come next for the Freedom Vote participants.

Speeches by Bob Moses, Aaron Henry, and Reverend King recognized the success of the campaign, but they also presented future courses of action. Though it was a victory rally and there were grounds for celebration, the work was still far from over. Religious discourse dominated the speeches and songs, giving the rally a distinct revival feel. Dave Dennis again assumed the role of master of ceremonies, welcoming the crowd and leading them in singing "This Little Light of Mine." The freedom songs continued with "Wade in the Water," followed by "Oh, Freedom" and "Calypso Freedom" before the audience began chanting in unison "Freedom Now!" Dennis declared over the public address system, "If you can't open your mouth and clap your hands along with us, *get out!*" The crowd responded with a deafening roar of applause and cheers.

Dennis then introduced the Freedom Singers and the song leaders for the evening, Willie Peacock, Sam Block, and Cordelle Regan. Another round of songs ensued: "I Woke Up This Morning with Freedom on My Mind," another powerful rendition of "Oh, Freedom," and "Get On Board," performed by the males of the Freedom Singers. Their rendition of "Get On Board" has a distinct sound, similar to Motown recordings in a street-corner or doo-wop style. There are only two verses, and the chorus actually starts the song. A solo singer begins with "get on board" and is answered by the rest of the males with "children, children" in a call-and-response manner: one male sings each verse; the rest of the group joins in for "children, children" and the last line of the chorus, "Let's fight for human rights!"[1] At the end of the song, the singers retarded the chorus down to a virtual halt and playfully improvised with the harmonies. Through the entire song, the audience clapped along with the singers. The rally organizers knew a beautiful fact: music begets audience participation.

Then the evening's advertised speakers made their appearances on stage. Bob Gore from CORE was first to speak. In his brief speech, he rails against the current governor, Ross Barnett, and both the Democratic and Republican Parties for arguing over the effectiveness or ineffectiveness of a two-party system in Mississippi. For Gore, there was no difference between the two parties as long as blacks were systematically denied access to the political process.

James Forman then introduced Sam Block, who led the audience and Freedom Singers in another round of freedom songs: "Freedom Train's A-Coming," "Ain't Scared of Your Jail," "Certainly, Lord," and finally "Wade in the Water." Dave Dennis returned to introduce the next speaker, James Forman. Forman's speech was brief. In it, he asks his audience, "Will you be there?" He asks them if they would be a part when freedom finally came to Mississippi. Forman asserts that Mississippi "needs freedom *now!*"

Forman gave way to Hollis Watkins, who sang a solo version of "Oh, Freedom." What makes this version different from the previous renditions sung that evening is that Watkins improvised the theme for each verse after the first traditional verse of "Oh, freedom, / Oh, freedom, / Oh, freedom, / Over me, over me." He led new verses with "No more segregation," "No more dogs," "Nothing but freedom," and "No more shooting." Watkins got the crowd clapping and singing along with him as the song morphed from a solo to total audience participation; this is symbolic of the participatory nature of the campaign itself.

Dennis then announced to the crowd some of the evening's first election results. So far, 58,300 votes for Henry and King had come in. Dennis introduced the national chairman of SNCC, John Lewis. In his brief address, Lewis declared that there was "a mandate from God to overthrow this system," lending a divine source of credibility to the call for equality. Religion and politics made their presence felt in even the shortest speeches of the evening.

Dennis reclaimed the stage. In his speech, Dennis uses a compelling allegory to compare campaign manager Bob Moses to the biblical Moses, further blending political agency with religious discourse. In telling the story of how the biblical Moses freed the Israelites from the pharaoh, Dennis weaves in ideals and agency relevant to the crowd's daily lives: "And Moses said, 'Trust in the Lord. But the Lord is not gonna deliver you unless you show the Lord that you want freedom yourselves and stand up and hold your heads up high.' The people looked, they said, 'But how can I hold my head up high with a hungry stomach?

How can I hold my head up high when my children are crying?'" Dennis addresses the current conditions of blacks in Mississippi by drawing parallels to the same hardships overcome by the Israelites. He adapts the narrative of the biblical Moses to empower his audience through the Israelites' victory.

Dennis makes the comparison clear by bringing the immediate context of Mississippi into the picture: "We in the state of Mississippi, for years and years, did not really believe that we could do it, but today we find out that we can, and we stand together." The inclusive language unifies the audience and provides context for their struggle. Dennis extends his metaphor to include Bob Moses. He states, "We'll answer the call in the state of Mississippi to another type of Moses, a Moses that we call a modern-day Moses." Dennis reminds his audience that this "modern-day Moses" was one of the first to come to Mississippi, "when no one was in [there] but he and Mr. Medgar Evers." Dennis delays identifying who this "modern-day Moses" is outright for his audience, all the while clearly alluding to campaign manager Bob Moses. Dennis finally introduces the modern-day Moses: "I'm proud to say tonight, as I think all the fellow workers in the house are proud to say, that in our hearts and in our minds, in our everyday life, and within our state, there walks with us a modern-day Moses, Mr. Bob Moses of the Student Nonviolent Coordinating Committee." And with that dramatic extended metaphor as introduction, Bob Moses then took the podium.

Immediately, Moses shifts the focus from himself to some of the volunteers and workers in the crowd. He moves through a list of names including George Greene, Sam Block, Mike Sayer, Willie Peacock, Hollis Watkins, Charlie Cobb, Evelyn Hancock, Claude Weaver, Doris Erskine, and Joyce Ladner before noting, "Well, there were many more, but certainly this is one of the most unique voting campaigns in American history." Moses marks the significance of the rally and the Freedom Vote by saying, "Though we really can't realize it, history is being made right here in Jackson today, and was made all over this state this week." He attempts to frame how the audience preserves, interprets, and gives value to their roles in the Freedom Vote. Moses dismisses the discourse surrounding a two-party system in Mississippi: "There is no sense talking about having a democratic society in Mississippi. It's no sense even about the Republicans talking about having two parties if they get a large enough vote, because in reality what you have is one party right now, and that's the White Citizens' Council." Moses attributes the political inequality to the Citizens' Council, but he suggests the possibility of an alternative: "And if you ever get another party, it will be because young people like these who are standing on the stage from inside and outside Mississippi put their heads and hearts together and work together, and the people outside there in the audience join hands together and forge another party." A real party system for Moses is one that represents all the people of

Mississippi. Moses's call for another party would be answered the next spring with the creation of the Mississippi Freedom Democratic Party (MFDP).

Moses continues to redirect attention away from himself, saying that other Freedom Vote participants "have the real stories to tell." He mentions that George Greene was shot at in Natchez and lists communities where other agents like Greene had been active throughout the state. Moses contends, "Even if they gathered one or two votes, and even if they didn't get any, they went there knocking on doors and telling the people that in 1963 at least a little whisper of freedom was traveling around the state and that the Negroes don't intend for there to be another election in Mississippi without making their voice heard and without making the world understand that whatever goes on in that election, it's not a free election." Moses validates the significance that the agency of the Freedom Vote represents.

After Moses's speech, the Freedom Singers led the audience in "We'll Never Turn Back." Moses quickly introduced Al Lowenstein, who spoke to the importance of the Freedom Vote campaign, framing it in terms of what it meant to the future in Mississippi. The Freedom Vote provided "encouragement for those who believe in freedom," Lowenstein said, applying religious faith to political values. Lowenstein then introduced the first of the keynote speakers, the Freedom Vote candidate for governor, Aaron Henry.

While Henry's speech adheres to some of the traditional functions of a victory speech, it goes beyond those proprietary constraints. Victory and acceptance speeches usually identify and acknowledge the competition, but that was not appropriate for the Freedom Vote Victory Rally considering the competition. Henry opens his speech by remarking that it is difficult to thank everyone who deserves it, but he unites and includes the audience by reminding them, "Tonight all of us are about freedom's business." Henry tells the audience that in a state of "four-hundred-and-thirty-plus thousand Negroes" only around 20,000 were registered to vote, but those days would soon be gone. Note the prophetic undertone of his speech:

> Gone will soon be the days, we hope and pray and work for, when in Mississippi some thirty-seven percent of the people are earning less than three thousand dollars a year. Gone will be the days when some fifty percent of the people in the section of the state where I come from, the Mississippi Delta, earn less than a thousand dollars a year. Gone will be the days when the average worker in Mississippi earns an average of sixty-two dollars and seventeen cents a week. With all of our talk about the right-to-work law, and to balance agriculture with industry, we still have a prevailing condition in our state where the average factory worker earns thirty dollars less per week than the average factory worker all over this nation. Gone will be the days, we hope, when injustice will not reign as king in our state.[2]

The repetition of the phrase "gone will be the days" amplifies the economic injustices he cites by depicting a future without them. In this section of the speech, Henry utters the phrase six times. Accompanying the four above are two addressing equal rights and education. "Gone will be the day, we pray, that we live in an area where we have no rights that our white brother is bound to respect. Gone will be the days when we live in a system that has its educational program geared to remain at the bottom of the list." Henry is promising his audience specific changes that would improve the daily lives of all Mississippians. Henry argues that the keys to stopping inequality are cooperation and integration, because "the only way to keep this white man from discriminating against Negroes is to place the Negro children and the white children in the same classroom together. That's the only thing that's gonna stop 'em." Familiar rhetoric previously employed by Henry appears again: "We've got to hogtie him. We've got to place him in a situation where he cannot discriminate against Negroes. We've got to place him so, for whatever he does for his blonde-head Mary he'll have to do the same thing for my kinky-head Rebecca." Henry's line equating "blonde-head Mary" and "kinky-head Rebecca" is one he has used before to show the two as social equals. Henry rejects the social philosophy of "separate but equal" and contends that public school integration is the only way to force whites to no longer discriminate against blacks, but note the element of force. The phrase "we've got to hogtie him" insists that whites would only make forward progress when forced to do so.

Henry steps back from the campaign rhetoric to list a few individuals he wishes to thank publicly. He says the only regret he has about the closing of the campaign is "the exodus of men like Al Lowenstein." He thanks Mike Sayer, John Lewis, Charlie Evers, and Bob Moses. He reminds the audience that Gene De Alissy and Mike Miller were still in the hospital. Henry notes the accident that the two were in as a starting point: "Perhaps that was the beginning of the intimidation that we have received throughout the campaign. Because since then, men and women have been arrested. They've been cursed out. They've been beaten. They've been shot at. They've had to hide out for their lives. All because the Negroes and the white people who want to be free in Mississippi joined hands and said, 'We gonna be free now!'" Henry marks incidents of violence as moments of empowerment for the people of Mississippi.

The next section of Henry's speech provides special thanks to his campaign committee members. This time he singles out each member by title and which civil rights organization he is associated with: Bob Moses, campaign manager from SNCC; Dave Dennis of CORE, the policy committee chairman for the campaign; Charles Evers from the NAACP, the campaign speaker's bureau chief; and Reverend R. L. T. Smith, financial chairman. Henry also thanks Henry Briggs of Tougaloo and finally Al Lowenstein. Henry acknowledges the sacrifice and work of each individual, and then he provides them as models to his audience. On a more personal note, Henry reflects:

> But I think that, perhaps, the greatest incentive, to me, the greatest drive, the greatest compelling force that has taken me away from the place where I earn a livin' since October sixth, perhaps, is the absence of one of the dearest friends I've ever had. And it's, perhaps, that I feel because he isn't with us that we've got to make up for the fact that he isn't here and, perhaps, work twice as hard. And you know we've said a long time ago that when Medgar Evers fell, he fell the full six feet and two inches of his body forward. And, you know, we'll never have to retrace that six feet and two inches, because he carried us that far down freedom's trail. And we are determined that if it ever comes our time to . . . pay the price, as Medgar paid it, that my five feet and eight inches, and the other dimensions of the rest of us, that when we fall, we too will fall forward and help to carry this Freedom Movement that much further down the road.

Henry turns the murder of Evers into a symbol of sacrifice to give the death purpose. This movement Henry ascribes to Evers's body eternalizes the memory and impact of Evers's life and recognizes Evers as an agent for the cause. It is through this physical sacrifice of the body that the movement symbolically moves forward. Henry here publicly declares his body part of that sacrifice.

Henry takes a moment to mark the solidarity of the four major civil rights organizations that had worked in cooperation on the campaign. He highlights the unity of SNCC, the NAACP, CORE, and the SCLC as key to future success in Mississippi.

Before returning to his campaign rhetoric of the three global leaders whose names start with "K," Henry establishes a place in that global struggle for US blacks. "We know that Mississippi is a part of a whole much greater than Mississippi. Not only is Mississippi a part of the United States, but it's a part of the world, and we, in Mississippi, have got to realize that the image of Mississippi bears also the reflection of his darker brother." Henry is linking Mississippians with others who are fighting for equality around the globe. Mentioning the "darker brother" is an opening for Henry to link the activities and identities of blacks around the world: "The image of Mississippi has to be accountable to such names as Lumumba and Kasa-vubu. And that names like these are going to have more of an impact on world relations than the dance called the Twist and Chubby Checker throwing his hat on America." Henry argues for accountability across the globe for the black race, a unity that should reflect equality. Through this unity, blacks would have a more significant impact on global culture at large, rather than just in the realm of entertainment.

Henry closes his speech with two passages from other campaign speeches, a comparison of Khrushchev, Kennedy, and Martin Luther King Jr. and the examination of the three classical Greek notions of love—*phillia, eros,* and *agape.* Henry reminds the audience, "If we can carry this kind of tenet in our heart, this kind of a desire for love and tranquility and peace, although we are oppressed and fail every day to be free, the next time around victory will be sure." Henry's final passage gives the audience a direction for their emotions. Through this point of view of brotherly love, endurance would lead to success.

Dave Dennis returned to introduce the next speaker, the Freedom Vote candidate for lieutenant governor, Reverend Edwin King. Dennis reminded the audience of the "accident" King had been in during the summer, adding "and it just so happens that the other car involved in the accident was driven by, and belonged to, the son of one of our staunchest segregationists around here in the state of Mississippi." Dennis built King's credibility further by informing the audience that King had been arrested several times for "pray-ins" around Jackson. Dennis let the crowd know that King was from Vicksburg, offering further grounds for identification and proof that local Mississippians could effect change from within their own borders.

As King took the podium, he echoed the call of a gentleman from the crowd: "Freedom, right! That's all that really needs to be said. Freedom!" King first congratulates everyone in attendance. For him, this notion of survival being meaningful is evidenced in the scar on his face. He mentions that even though there were over 200 arrests and beatings throughout the campaign, "no one is dead." King states, "We are helping all the people of Mississippi to see that they are going to have something in common with America and that this is something good, and they will one day thank us." For King, the Freedom Vote showed all citizens of Mississippi that they were a part of democratic America. He hints that the rest of Mississippi owes those involved a debt of gratitude.

King situates the Freedom Vote among a series of events comprising the contemporary struggle for civil rights in Mississippi. King says the Freedom Vote "is the outgrowth of a hundred years of suffering." He cites the activities of the previous two years, noting the library sit-in in Jackson and the arrival of the Freedom Rides. King attributes the Freedom Vote's success in some part to "the non-violent invaders from the East Coast colleges and the West Coast colleges." He establishes the value of the Freedom Vote: "Politics is not even a game for us, and this has certainly not been a game, but they see the handwriting on the wall. They know that very soon we will not be running anything that can be called a 'mock election' and that our candidates will be winning, and this will be the salvation of Mississippi and of our country." While establishing the symbolic meaning of the Freedom Vote campaign, King unknowingly has foreshadowed the creation of the MFDP. He argues, "Aaron and I have shown that Mississippians can cooperate and work together for the good of Mississippi and for their own good we'll continue to do that." For King, the work was not over, but the Freedom Vote marked a step forward in uniting blacks and whites in Mississippi.

In examining the progress symbolized by the rally and campaign itself, King reminds the audience that earlier that summer, many of them had gathered in the Masonic Temple, and "almost at the place where this platform of victory stands" there had been a coffin. Much like they would never forget Evers's funeral, King assures the audience, "We will never forget gathering here for this victory celebration tonight, and the victory in this election is yours." King credits the audience, empowering the crowd by revealing the progress made from a funeral gathering to a political victory rally. He declares, "This is our victory, no matter what the rest of the state does tomorrow. If we didn't believe in segregation, if we didn't believe this separate-but-equal stuff was old hash, we might ask them to put up a separate-but-equal governor's mansion so Aaron and his wife could move in, in January." King attempts to sustain the political agency the Freedom Vote generated by forecasting a political victory in the next governor's election in four years. King simultaneously challenges the hypocritical nature of segregation, noting that by its own ideology, the state of Mississippi owes Aaron Henry a governor's mansion.

King says that there are lots of people he wants to thank, but he specifically acknowledges the involvement of religious organizations and individuals associated with them. He legitimizes the relationship between religion and political activity first, using himself as an example: "Here I am, a minister engaged in political activity, but ministers of the church and dedicated Christians have always engaged in political activity when it was necessary for the salvation of the church itself." King defends the church's presence in politics by designating it crucial for the church's survival. By thanking these specific organizations, King displays the support of an entire social institution. He next thanks the ministers across the state of Mississippi who helped the campaign by allowing meetings or literature in their churches. King specifically notes Reverend R. L. T. Smith's involvement, providing another model for responsible political agency in the form of a traditionally religious figure.

King again acknowledges the presence of students from outside Mississippi. He says their involvement in the Freedom Vote is symbolic of the kind of cooperation needed: "There's something we've shown in this campaign, and I think the *kind* of campaign, with an emphasis on brotherhood and freedom, that we've run has been valuable." King specifically names Jane Stembridge and informs the audience that she was in and out of the Greenwood jail twice that week. He tells the audience that Stembridge is from Georgia, and having recently come from Virginia, her involvement shatters the myth that southerners cannot work together. For King, it is important that the audience realize that the Freedom Vote symbolizes cooperation "not just from Yale students or California students" but from southerners outside Mississippi as well. King concludes with these final remarks:

> What we have begun this summer, what we are celebrating tonight, what people all over this state who've been intimidated and wished they could be with us but have still tried to vote—they are freed even though they were not able to vote in this campaign, they will be voting and be registered voters in the near future. We don't know what the future holds, except we do have our faith in God and we know that, although some of us may suffer, freedom is before all of us. Medgar Evers has his freedom now, and because he does, and because Aaron Henry ran this campaign for governor even after Medgar was murdered this summer, you and I and everyone will soon be free. Thank you.

King extends success even to those anonymous individuals who could not directly participate. The Freedom Vote represents a victory for them as a model for future endeavors. The Freedom Vote then represents the potential for all citizens in the state. King associates the sacrifice put forth in the recent campaign as a testimony of faith that the future holds success and the promising salvation of freedom. Evers, Henry, and the Freedom Vote are now also a part of the legacy for freedom.

The crowd sang one last song together, "We Shall Overcome," which traditionally ended many civil rights meetings and rallies across the South. A band from Hattiesburg, The Blue Gardenias, then played music for the duration of the victory rally. But the political and social activity of the Freedom Vote was not completely finished.

AN OFFICIAL CHALLENGE AND (SOME) MEDIATED SUCCESS

The next day, campaign headquarters issued a news release challenging the results of the official governor's race. Moses is quoted as saying, "Clearly the results of the Freedom Vote indicate that there are at least eighty thousand people who would have voted for Aaron Henry if they had not been disfranchised."[3] The release explains that the Freedom Vote organizers had prepared a suit to oust governor-elect Paul Johnson. Moses further claimed that the 80,000 votes only represented a fraction of the potential votes for Henry due to the impact of private and public intimidation on voter turnout. The work of the "Aaron Henry for Governor" campaign was not over yet, though. Many campaign workers, like George Raymond, Lenore Thurman, and George Greene, were in jail days after the campaign, some for charges stemming from actual campaign canvassing, others for not appropriately cooperating with police officers in trying to bail their fellow workers out.

On November 5 the McComb *Enterprise Journal* and the *Hattiesburg American* published an AP wire story about the Freedom Vote. Though the story ran under different headlines ("Mock Vote Is Called a Success" and "Mock Election Leader Reports 100,000 Votes," respectively), neither paper edited the article from the original AP version. The story credits Al Lowenstein as its source for the number of votes reported and notes, "Some 50 white Yale students participated actively in the campaign." Neither paper ran this positively toned article on its front page.

In the final two days of Freedom Vote coverage, the Mississippi commercial papers ran either a UPI or an AP story on the suit that the Henry campaign was filing with federal authorities in protest of Paul Johnson's win of the official campaign. Both stories ran in two papers; the *Hattiesburg American* and the *Greenwood Commonwealth* published the AP article on November 6, and the *Meridian Star* and the Clarksdale *Press Register* published the UPI story the next day, November 7. Both articles estimate the total votes tallied in the Freedom Vote as between 75,000 and 80,000. It's important to note that in the official state election, Democratic candidate Paul B. Johnson won with a total of 225,456 votes, over the Republican candidate Rubel Phillips, who received 138,515 votes.

The *Clarion-Ledger* from Jackson followed common patterns of coverage concerning the Freedom Vote. Eleven of the thirteen stories run by the *Clarion-Ledger* covering the Freedom Vote were either UPI or AP wire service stories, and only one story made the front page. The *Clarion-Ledger* also tended to run its wire stories a day or two after the other commercial Mississippi papers. Six of its stories included the word "Yale" in the headline, illustrating the paper's focus on the negative activities associated with the students. The longest article about the campaign published by the *Clarion-Ledger* was its first; otherwise, no article ran over six paragraphs long, let alone more than one column of print. The *Clarion-Ledger* never ran a photograph with any of its articles either. The point is not that the *Clarion-Ledger*, or any of the other commercial Mississippi papers, outright lied about the Freedom Vote; it is rather that they failed to adequately represent the Freedom Vote.

The final issue of the *Free Press* to cover the Freedom Vote dates November 9. Again, a powerful photomontage dominates the top of the front page. In the three photos, black citizens can be seen filling out and casting their freedom ballots. The pictures show both men and women, young and old alike, participating. The headline above the photos reads "90,000 Vote for Henry," adding yet another number to the estimated totals. There is another headline across the middle of the front page that reads "Johnson Refused Consent of Governed," further contributing to the very active nature of the events being covered. Instead of articles or stories accompanying the photos and headlines, two extended quotes occupy the rest of the front page. In two columns on the bottom half, beneath the "Johnson Refused" headline, is a printed section of the Mississippi Constitution right next to a section from the Declaration of Independence. By including these excerpts, the *Free Press* connects the events of the Freedom Vote with these political documents and therefore the history and tradition of political activity in America.

Out of Kentucky, the monthly periodical the *Southern Patriot* also gave the Freedom Vote front-page treatment in its November 1963 issue. The headline across the top reads "A New Politics in Mississippi," and the article includes a picture of each candidate. The article begins, "History was made in Mississippi this fall when a Negro and white man joined forces to run for governor and lieutenant governor of this state."[4] The story stretches the length of the far-right column and is accompanied by a block quote from King. The quote, under the caption "No One Free," states: "White people in Mississippi aren't free either. We are prisoners of fear created by the Citizens' Council and the Sovereignty Commission. Our teachers are afraid to speak; our Christian ministers and laymen fear to talk to each other. The 'Freedom Vote' program means freedom for us all." Much like the *Free Press*, but with a broader regional circulation, the *Southern Patriot* affords the Freedom Vote valuable front-page space with photos and quotes set aside to complement the article. The article focuses on the goals of the Freedom Vote and provides brief biographical information about each candidate. There is no mention of northern college students, an indication that their presence was not as significant to the *Southern Patriot* as it was to the more mainstream news outlets. The focus for the *Southern Patriot* is the Freedom Vote and its goals—great publicity for the campaign, and by design in accordance with other image events.

The *Southern Patriot* printed a follow-up story in its next issue in December. This time the article forecasts a lasting political impact of the Freedom Vote on the future. A picture of three Tougaloo co-eds, one white and two black, accompanies the headline "New Political Force Emerging." The article reports that around 85,000 people participated in the vote and assesses the significance of the campaign: "The most lasting thing that came out of the campaign—and this is its historic significance—is that political organization is taking root among Negroes throughout the state. This will continue, organized along congressional district lines, completely outside the old political framework." The foreshadowing of the MFDP is further articulated: "There is the germ of a third party here, but no matter what form the movement takes, it is now a foregone conclusion that Negroes will be running next year in Mississippi for the seat of U.S. Senator Stennis and for the five congressional seats up for election—and in 1966 for Senator Eastland's seat."[5] The accuracy of this deliberative rhetoric is discussed in the next chapter, which deals specifically with Freedom Vote's legacy after its conclusion. Here, it is important to note that the *Southern Patriot* already recognized the significance of the Freedom Vote beyond the immediate events of the campaign. This is evidence that the tactical means and innovations of the Freedom Vote would be extended to achieve strategic goals.

At a national level, the *Chicago Defender* barely mentioned the Freedom Vote. Though traditionally viewed as a newspaper concerned with and sympathetic to the struggle for equality, the *Defender* did not run a single story about the Freedom Vote in its nationally circulated weekly edition. Only three articles about the Freedom Vote appeared in its daily edition. The first article ran in the Wednesday, October 16, issue of the *Daily Defender*. The article is the UPI wire service story previously published by the Mississippi papers. In the *Daily Defender*, the headline reads "Bi-Racial Pair to Seek Top Miss. Office."[6] A second story concerning the Freedom Vote ran in the October 21 issue of the *Daily Defender* with the headline "Yale Students Aid Negro in Governor Race."[7] The article is very short and is located at the top-center of page seven. Neither of the candidates is named in the UPI article, and only Al Lowenstein is mentioned by name.

The final article that the *Defender* ran is a telling one. On the bottom of page six in the November 4 issue, the headline reads "No Hopes of Victory for Negro in Mississippi Governor's Race." The headline immediately sets a pessimistic tone for the article, which covers the official race between Johnson and Phillips and does not even mention Henry or King by name until seven paragraphs into the lengthy article. The article refers to the Freedom Vote as "a mock election" and includes quotes from only Al Lowenstein. The negative tone is hard to overlook. For example, the article states, "A Negro and a white minister, running on a civil rights ticket, are assured of 'election' by Negro voters Sunday—two days before Mississippi's general election Nov. 5. Their success will have only straw vote status."[8] The article fails to mention the campaign's struggles until the end, where it states, "For his activities, Lowenstein has been arrested once, along with a number of Yale and Stanford University students who came to the state to help in the activity." Though the *Chicago Defender* was considered supportive of black efforts to achieve equality, the scarce coverage it affords the Freedom Vote mirrors that of the white mainstream commercial newspapers. It is important to note, however, that since the *Defender* was considered a black newspaper and had a largely black audience, any coverage of the Freedom Vote was valuable, as it at least spread word of the campaign.

Consider, in stark contrast, the coverage that the *Student Voice*, SNCC's sponsored newsletter out of Atlanta, granted the Freedom Vote. The headline across the top of the front page reads "Over 70,000 Cast Freedom Ballots," and is accompanied by the subheading "Henry-King Ticket Tops Mock Election." Photos of each candidate supplement the article, and while the article is not necessarily long, it is not brief either, but longer than the articles in the state papers. The article reports the election results: "There were 78,388 Freedom Votes cast, Henry received 72,869."[9]

The article quotes Bob Moses, John Lewis, and James Forman, who all highlight the significance of the Freedom Vote. The article discusses the campaign's platform, and its only mention of Yale and Stanford students seems almost an afterthought, tucked near the end of the article. The focus is the symbolic meaning of the Freedom Vote and its function as a communicative form of protest and demonstration.

Several magazines and monthly periodicals covered the Freedom Vote in their December issues. Jeannine Herron wrote a piece for the December 7 issue of the *Nation* titled "Underground Election." She begins, "Bullets, beatings, arrests and fines drove the campaign of Aaron Henry, a Negro, for Governor 'underground' as the 1963 gubernatorial campaign neared a climax in Mississippi. The outrageously 'uppity' plan for a mock campaign of unregistered Negro voters to dramatize the flagrant totalitarianism of Southern politics was taken seriously by the white power structure."[10] Herron cites two aspects of the "underground election" that troubled segregationists: the integrated nature of the ticket and the platform of the campaign. Herron reports that the total number of votes cast in the Freedom Vote was near 82,000, and this is important because the actual totals from the Freedom Vote were never officially released. Her number was reported nearly a month after the end of the campaign and rests between the previously reported totals, which ranged from 75,000 to 100,000. Despite having more room to write about the Freedom Vote than the newspapers, Herron falls into the pattern of only reporting what happened to the outside volunteers, with the bulk of her article focusing on beating and shooting incidents involving Bruce Payne (388). Aside from her opening remarks, the story's only mention of Henry is a quote from the Hattiesburg rally, where he told firemen, "There's a fire burning in here, all right, but those firemen will *never* put it out" (389). A story published in the December issue of the *New South* accredited simply to "M. L." follows the same pattern of focusing solely on the northern college students.[11]

Taking this pattern to its extreme is an article from the December 15 issue of *Presbyterian Life* titled "Four Yale University Divinity School Students Describe ... a Week in Mississippi." Granted, the article is anonymously written by four Yale students. However, the fact that this was the only article about the Freedom Vote published in *Presbyterian Life* further demonstrates the press's infatuation with the activities and very presence of the Yale students in Mississippi. The article begins, "We did not go to Mississippi on a freedom ride or to sit-in at lunch counters, to kneel-in at churches, or wade-in at beaches. We merely went to encourage Negroes to vote in a mock protest election."[12] It is interesting to note that through this mass-mediated story, the authors subtly critique the press's coverage of Mississippi, offering instead a counter perspective. It becomes clear as the article progresses that the authors are the Yale Divinity School students who campaigned in Hattiesburg. All the incidents detailed by the story match up with reports of the arrests and jailing of John Else and Ken Klotz. The article encourages readers to get involved: "White Southerners complain that we Northerners do not understand the situation when many of them, who have lived with it all their lives, have never talked to a Negro as an equal. No one is an 'outsider.' The guilt and responsibility is [sic] upon each of us that such situations are allowed to exist within our nation." The article concludes by highlighting the moral imperative for Christians to ameliorate the situation in Mississippi: "Aside from this political rationale, we are called by our Christian heritage to bear the responsibility for one another and to fight against the evils and injustices of the world. Surely *this* evil and injustice are among the most obvious and most urgent in our world today."

A HUMAN SUCCESS STORY

The Freedom Vote's impact extends beyond the generated media coverage and sheer numbers of potential voters. "I returned to Yale," Jim Vaughn wrote a few days after his return to New Haven, "with a conviction that I had a responsibility to convey something of what I saw and experienced in Mississippi to friends who supported the trip but were unable to go, to other personal friends interested in my own participation, and to a wider audience, to whom such information will, I hope, have some relevance in their own participation or interest in the current civil rights struggle, north and south."[13] As a participant-observer Vaughn is reflecting on the strategic success of Freedom Vote tactics. He affirms, "I am convinced that our presence as whites, diligently working side by side with the Negroes in the 'Freedom Movement' is one of the most effective ways of challenging this revolutionary spirit into constructive activity which will, indeed, 'Overcome' someday." Unity and equality were some of the major themes of the Freedom Vote, impacting not just organizers and volunteers but also those casting ballots, the very participants themselves.

Richard Van Wagenen remembers that, upon returning from Mississippi, "the big question everybody asked [him] was 'Did it do any good?'"[14] He argues that there are two aspects to the answer. First, it certainly did *him* good: "I learned that America has a police state within its borders, that the southern Negro is the bravest man in this country, that whatever the legal situation may be the oppression of one race by another is morally reprehensible and to be opposed." Then he reflects on what he deems more important, the potential good he may have done in Mississippi:

> I think I did more good than harm, though my two days represented very little in terms of actual accomplishment. But a lot of people saw a white man talking on equal terms with a colored man for the first time because I was there. A lot of people realized for the first time, perhaps, that there are qualities in a man that transcend pigmentation. A lot of Negroes found that there were whites who felt as they did, who sympathized with their cause. And I helped to provide a vital element in the campaign—publicity.

For Van Wagenen, his participation in Mississippi functioned both at a symbolic level of unity and brotherhood and at a pragmatic level of generating media coverage and awareness. He directly comments on the Freedom Vote's use of the image event tactic of capturing media attention as a means of attaining strategic goals.

This chapter examined the last rally during the final days of the Freedom Vote in order to more completely understand how and why 82,000 people decided to vote despite an atmosphere of intimidation and fear. Examining these events and their rhetorical texts with an eye for religious discourse helps illuminate the answer. This fusion of the political and religious was not coincidental; it was a tactical innovation to overcome obstacles. Chappell argues, "What is remarkable about the civil rights movement, and what makes it most like one of the great historic revivals, is that the enthusiasm moved out of the church and into the streets" (97). The events analyzed in this chapter are a testimony to this claim.

The next chapter explores how the Freedom Vote tactically and symbolically lived on through the next few years of the movement. Though the Freedom Vote was over, it continued to influence the civil rights movement in Mississippi and throughout the country.

Chapter Seven
FROM FREEDOM DAYS TO FEDERAL LAW

This chapter explores the events that the Freedom Vote engendered: the creation of the Mississippi Freedom Democratic Party (MFDP); the Freedom Days in the spring of 1964 throughout the state; the Freedom Summer project; the challenge of the MFDP at the Democratic National Convention in Atlantic City, New Jersey; the Freedom Vote of 1964; and the civil rights legislation of 1964 and 1965.

To say that the 1963 Mississippi Freedom Vote caused the events that followed it is to oversimplify the relationship. There are strong links, however, between the Freedom Vote and the civil rights movement in Mississippi and the nation. Specifically, the Freedom Vote provided a structured model and organized network for future civil rights work as well as tactical developments, such as how to effectively generate publicity through the inclusion of northern whites and promote agency through participation. This chapter illuminates how these developments enabled the events following the Freedom Vote.

One thing that all these moments share is the presence of the MFDP, which owes its origins to the Freedom Vote of 1963. Examining the presence of the MFDP in the events after the Freedom Vote reveals how the organizational structure created by/for the Freedom Vote was important to the success of the movement in Mississippi and across the nation. This chapter manifests the impact that the Freedom Vote had on a series of Freedom Days throughout Mississippi, explores the establishment of the MFDP in the spring of 1964, and examines the lineage from the Freedom Vote to the Freedom Summer project and the MFDP challenge in Atlantic City. The connection between the Freedom Vote of 1963 and the Freedom Vote of 1964 further strengthens the claim put forth in this chapter that the Freedom Vote of 1963 did in fact have an impact on the movement. The Freedom Vote also influenced areas outside the Magnolia State, such as nearby Selma, Alabama, during the spring of 1965. All these events played a part in the passage of the Voting Rights Act of 1965.

The Freedom Vote provided not only a political model and an organizational structure for civil rights activity but also effective tactics for generating publicity. The inclusion of northern whites was a Freedom Vote tactic again employed to raise national awareness of the civil rights events in Mississippi. The Freedom Vote was the first step beyond sit-ins at lunch counters and bus boycotts to directly involve blacks in the democratic process, a powerful strategy that civil rights leaders used again in later events to empower their audience. This raised the stakes from a publicity perspective in that the activity is newsworthy because it illustrates the hypocrisy within a framework of political activity and citizenship. This chapter explores speeches, posters, pamphlets, and coverage from *Life* and *Time* magazines, the *New York Times*, and various other historical and archival sources with a focus on the influence of the Mississippi Freedom Vote of 1963. Again, the Freedom Vote proved to be no small thing.

SPREADING FREEDOM DAYS

After President Kennedy's assassination, civil rights organizations in Mississippi were left with the question, "What now?" Many leaders strongly expressed that northern white students should no longer be part of the movement, especially in the plans and execution of the summer's approaching project (Dittmer 209). The Freedom Summer of 1964 was an attempt to capitalize on the successes of the Freedom Vote. The plan was to educate and register qualified black citizens and again bring national and federal attention to Mississippi. The challenge was exactly how to achieve these goals, and in the manner of a carefully designed and executed image event.

Bob Moses, who was usually quiet during discussions and debates, clearly articulated his perspective on the issue of including white participants and volunteers: "Whiteness is no argument. That's an irrational, racist statement. That's what we're fighting. If no white person can be head of any project, then I don't want to be part of an operation like that" (Dittmer 209). Historian John Dittmer notes the only other staff members supporting Moses were Fannie Lou Hamer and Lawrence Guyot. Those opposed to the use of whites in the summer's project felt that the northern volunteers would take away resources needed in the Student Nonviolent Coordinating Committee's (SNCC) main goal of developing leadership and organizing communities at a local level.

Freedom Summer organizers could not ignore the lessons learned during the Freedom Vote. The involvement of Yale and Stanford University students had generated media publicity, which the Freedom Summer organizers needed to maintain in order to keep up the Freedom Vote momentum. The movement could not afford to stop moving. Guyot came to Hattiesburg on behalf of the Council of Federated Organizations (COFO) and proposed a Freedom Day patterned after the one that had taken place in Selma, Alabama, the previous fall. Doing so would allow local citizens another chance to participate in the movement while the civil rights leaders continued planning and debating Freedom Summer.

Guyot laid out his plans for a massive one-day demonstration. The local county registrar, Theron Lynd, was under scrutiny by the US Supreme Court for not allowing blacks on the voter registration rolls. The demonstration would put additional pressure on Lynd to register local blacks and also would empower local blacks. Guyot's plan received an approving nod from leading organizers. The Freedom Day demonstrators gained rhetorical clout and some moral legitimacy when Guyot brought fifty northern clergymen through the National Council of Churches to Hattiesburg for the demonstration, a clear extension of the tactic employed during the Freedom Vote to attract media publicity and possibly federal attention. It also helped tap into the religious community and continued to use northerners for publicity. As January came to a close, movement leaders and news reporters arrived in Hattiesburg, anticipating a showdown at the Forrest County courthouse.

Historian Howard Zinn remembers his initial exposure to Hattiesburg and the Freedom House that SNCC had rented on Mobile Street (75). "I saw Mrs. Hamer sitting near the doorway. Upstairs, Bob Moses greeted me and took me past the big open parlor area where a meeting was going on planning strategy for the next day." At the Freedom House on January 21, organizers prepared for the evening's mass meeting, reviewed plans for the next day's demonstration, and discussed strategies for potential problems. Preparation sessions were ended early by organizers in order for everyone to attend the rally.

The mass meeting's audience boasted leaders from every civil rights organization working in the state of Mississippi.[1] The makeup of the leaders resembled that of a Freedom Vote rally, invoking again the feel of a religious revival. As explored in previous chapters, Judeo-Christian discourse afforded the activists a palpable vehicle for delivering their message. Civil rights leaders borrowed songs, language, metaphors, and fables from the Judeo-Christian narrative because the audience was familiar, even intimate, with that tradition.

Aaron Henry, who had run on the mock election ticket for governor the previous fall, spoke first, declaring, "The rights we seek are our own." Henry played master of ceremonies and introduced John Lewis of SNCC, who gave a terse speech. Annelle Ponder of the Southern Christian Leadership Conference (SCLC) then spoke about her organization's new citizens' project in the area. The briefest speech of the evening came from Dave Dennis of the Congress of

Racial Equality (CORE), who simply broke into the first verse of "Wade in the Water," eventually giving way to the inspirational singing voice of Fannie Lou Hamer, who brought the hymn to a close. Jack Pratt, a white attorney working for several civil rights organizations, explained portions of the Mississippi State Constitution to aid those attempting to register the next day.

Next, Henry introduced the keynote speaker for the evening, calling her the "mom" of the movement. Ella Jo Baker first started her career in civil rights as a secretary for Roy Wilkins at the National Association for the Advancement of Colored People (NAACP) offices in New York. Martin Luther King Jr. later invited her to take part in organizing the SCLC's efforts in the South, and in 1960 she led the founding meetings of SNCC at Shaw University, her alma mater. Her speech, only eight minutes long, reverberated with a wisdom echoing lifelong experience.

Baker's rhetorical goal is to extend the struggle for equality beyond the issue of race, and she attempts to awaken individual accountability. "I'm not talking about Negroes; I'm talking about people," Baker states. "People cannot be free until they realize that peace—we can talk about peace—that peace is not the absence of war or struggle; it is the presence of justice." This rhetorically savvy phrase not only includes all of humankind but also contains within it the universal value of justice. It is this drive for justice for all that Baker attempts to instill in her audience. She shapes the dilemma as a human capacity rather than just a racial aptitude. Baker extends this general principle beyond mere politics and voting. "People cannot be free until there is enough work in this land to give everybody a job." This declaration received great applause. Baker continues, "Tomorrow, if we were able to vote our full strength and we still voted our full strength, until we recognize that in this country, in a land of great plenty and great wealth, there are millions of people who go to bed hungry every night, that tomorrow, if we were to call up all the able-bodied men in our country who could do some work, we wouldn't have work for them to do."[2] Baker depicts self-reliance and stability not in terms of political or racial means but rather through simple access to employment. She again moves the issues of equality and justice outside the parameters of race. By highlighting poverty as the problem, she's giving blacks a direction for their anger; instead of blaming the color of their skin, which they can't change, they can target poverty, which they can change. It also unites blacks and whites in the cause.

Baker reveals the main focus of her speech in the apex of the address. "Unless we see this thing in its larger perspective, unless we realize that certainly we must sing, we must have the inspiration of song . . . but we also must have the information that comes from lots and lots of study." Baker attempts to forge this link between knowledge and power in her audience's minds: "We must also know that we are, in the final analysis, the only group that can make you free is yourself, because we must free ourselves from all of the things that keep us back." This is the main point of her speech: freedom comes from within. Membership in an organization or inclusion by race does not grant one freedom; people give themselves freedom. Baker emphasizes the importance of self-reliance, wanting her audience to acknowledge the power derived from independent thought and action.

Baker improvises and paraphrases one of her favorite Scripture passages as she nears the conclusion of her speech: "For now we are nearer than when we first believed." This links her back to the religious ideals at the top of her speech. She notes singing is good, but that singing will not change life in Mississippi on its own merit. "I love to hear us sing. I've heard a lot of singing in my day—I've been a part of a lot of singing—but I know, and you must know, that singing alone will not do it for us." She wants more than the spiritual or emotional support of singing freedom songs; she wants progress. For Baker, progress requires more than singing; it takes critical self-reflection on the part of individuals. Members of her audience must recognize their own efficacy and act in their everyday lives.

The first step she is calling for is education. "We are going to have to have these Freedom Schools," Baker continued, "and we are going to have to learn a lot of things in them. We are going to have to be concerned about the kinds of education our children are getting in school." Baker again highlights the link between power and knowledge, the role information plays in the struggle for justice.

In her closing statements, Baker attacks complacency within the white community. "They have been fooled, and they have been fooled by those who told them the 'Big Lie.' The Big Lie was to the effect that they could do what they wanted in Mississippi with the Negro question." Baker calls the complacent attitude of Mississippi whites toward segregation the "Big Lie," a label that reveals the deception that whites have been living under. She again moves beyond Mississippi, saying, "And you know what? The rest of the country for a long time tacitly agreed. That is, they didn't do anything about it." Baker illustrates how the complacent white community failed to grasp its unique ability to fight the hegemonic grip of racism.

A brief instance of prophetic discourse enters Baker's text as she nears the apex. "All of us stand guilty at this moment for having waited so long to lend ourselves to a fight for the freedom, not of Negroes, not of the Negroes of Mississippi, but for the freedom of the American spirit." This indictment is aimed beyond the four walls of the mass meeting to impart a sense of duty and urgency on the nation as a whole. Baker closes her speech by referencing the civil rights staff members in attendance directly, saying, "The freedom which they seek is a larger freedom that encompasses all mankind. And until that day, we will never turn back." Her language is inclusive to the very end, always extending beyond the immediate audience to encompass "all mankind."

There are few wasted words in Baker's simple yet eloquent address, and the tropes within her speech are those present in the rhetoric of the Freedom Vote. She fuses political and religious ideals, always pushing for agency and individual responsibility. In doing so, Baker situates the local movement in a broader context while at the same time illustrating the need for individual action to bring about change.

After Baker's speech, as it neared midnight, Lawrence Guyot provided words of advice and encouragement to the crowd. He shouted "Freedom!" and the audience responded "Now!" The meeting concluded with a prayer of benediction, and then the spectators filed into the dark streets singing "We Shall Overcome."

THE DAY HAS ARRIVED

At 9:30 the next morning the sound of marching feet on wet pavement echoed as two lines of policemen headed toward the courthouse. Historian Howard Zinn stood across the street from the Forrest County Courthouse with John Lewis, as an officer with a bullhorn issued the order to clear all sidewalks and disperse. The picket line included SNCC staff, white clergymen, and local students who stood their ground despite the police presence. One of the police lines moved into a parallel position with the demonstrators picketing on the courthouse steps, again giving the order to disband.

No one moved from the picket line; as planned the night before, the line would stay as long as possible. The police began clearing the sidewalks across the street from the courthouse, and many people simply walked across the street to the steps of the courthouse to join the picket line. Zinn recalls, "There were virtually no white observers." The scene was peaceful and remained peaceful for the duration of the rainy day. Precedent was broken in Mississippi: in the presence of police, a line of black and white demonstrators successfully picketed a public building. In over two-and-a-half years of demonstrations in Mississippi, this was the first time a picket line was never broken up.

Groups of four were even allowed to enter the registrar's office, where TV cameras stayed fixed on the infamous registrar Lynd. In March 1962 the Justice Department reported that Lynd "had never registered a single Negro" but "had allowed 1,836 whites to register without filling out the application or interpreting a section of the state constitution." Earlier in January the Supreme Court threatened to find Lynd guilty of civil contempt if he continued with his discriminatory practices. The protestors again broke precedent as the local blacks entered the office and attempted to register.

By noon twelve local blacks had been permitted to fill out applications, and the courthouse closed for lunch. Through the rain, the picket line stood all afternoon. Police officers occasionally harassed some of the demonstrating black males by asking to see their draft cards, but no violence broke out. The line disbanded at 5:00 that evening, and SNCC staff felt they'd won a "quiet" victory. The victory came not from the reporters or white clergymen present at the courthouse, but rather the impact that the successful demonstration had on local blacks themselves.

Another unprecedented event for the state of Mississippi took place the very next day. The Hattiesburg Municipal Court convened to hear the case against Bob Moses for "obstructing traffic by standing on the sidewalk and refusing to move on when ordered to by a policeman." The charges were one of the two arrests from the previous day's demonstration. Judge Mildred W. Norris presided over the hearing. She entered the chamber and noticed that the crowd was not following the designated segregated seating arrangement. She told the marshals to "please segregate the courtroom." Thus far, every attempt to integrate a courtroom in Mississippi had ended in further incarcerations, but still no one moved.

As marshals began moving the crowd, Zinn raised his hand to be noticed. A marshal asked, "Do you wish to make a statement?" Zinn replied affirmatively, to which Judge Norris stated, "You may make a statement." Rising to his feet, Zinn addressed the judge, "Your Honor, the Supreme Court of the United States has ruled that segregated seating in a courtroom is unconstitutional. Will you abide by that ruling?" Immediately John Pratt, one of Moses's defense attorneys, asked for a recess, which the judge shockingly granted, as judges in Mississippi rarely granted any request from attorneys who represented or supported civil rights volunteers. When Judge Norris reconvened the proceedings, she stated, "We here in Mississippi have had our way of life for hundreds of years, and I obey the laws of Mississippi. I have asked that you sit segregated or leave, or be placed under arrest. We would have appreciated your complying." After a short pause, she continued, "But since you do not, we will allow you to remain as you are, provided you do not create a disturbance." Much to the surprise of the courtroom inhabitants, the trial continued with no mention of the seating issue again. During the trial, Judge Norris fanned herself with a piece of the state's evidence, a small cardboard sign with a picture of two black boys and the words "Freedom Now!" on one side and "Give Them a Future in Mississippi" on the other. This was a unique image in Mississippi's history: the first integrated courtroom watched a white Mississippi judge fan herself with movement propaganda.

The Hattiesburg Freedom Day passed, and soon Moses was out on bail organizing again.[3] What Freedom Day came to represent was extremely significant for local blacks. Hundreds of locals descended upon the Forrest County courthouse and were allowed to publicly express themselves by demonstrating and picketing. Even though few were actually permitted to enter the registrar's office, and only a handful would later find out that their applications passed, the silence was broken. New ground was gained by changing local attitudes. The myth that "everything is just fine for blacks in Mississippi" began changing; the protestors finally debunk this myth by refusing to let whites go on believing it.

By including northern whites, using forms of social protest that enacted agency, and linking religion and politics, civil rights leaders applied many lessons from the Freedom Vote to the Hattiesburg Freedom Day. Even the presence of the word "freedom" in the event name was a direct result of the rhetorical success of the Freedom Vote. The model of the Hattiesburg Freedom Day was replicated in Freedom Days across the state that spring, and the ability to motivate local blacks without any iconic public figures coming to the scene was well noted. The Freedom Day at Hattiesburg capitalized on the energy created by the Freedom Vote just two-and-a-half months earlier.

If any debate still lingered about the use of outside whites to get media attention, the murder of Louis Allen quickly silenced those arguments. A week and a half after the Hattiesburg Freedom Day, Allen was gunned down in front of his house (Dittmer 215). Three years earlier Allen had witnessed state legislator E. H. Hurst murder Herbert Lee, and Allen had faced intimidation ever since he had spoken with officials from the Justice Department about the incident. The harassment got so bad that Allen made plans to move to his brother's house in Milwaukee, arranging to leave Mississippi on the first of February, tragically a day too late. The Federal Bureau of Investigation (FBI) brought no charges after its investigation, and the media was silent (Dittmer 215). The murder of Allen demonstrated to organizational leaders that the news media cared little about Mississippi blacks being shot in their driveways and instead preferred stories involving outside whites.

On February 12 SNCC ran an advertisement in the *New York Times* that highlighted Louis Allen's murder. In the ad, a series of quotes from both blacks and whites accompanies a few brief paragraphs of text. The first of the quotes along the top of the ad states, "No more auction block for me. No More. No More. Many thousands gone," and is labeled "the affirmation of millions of Americans." Compare this with the next quote, "I'd rather serve Nazis than Niggers," which was "the affirmation of a Southern white restaurant owner." Both quotes deal with defiance; the first evokes unity, the second disdain. The paragraphs below the quotes summarize SNCC's work and goals in Mississippi. What makes the ad compelling is its publication on Lincoln's birthday. Does the ad elevate Allen and SNCC to the level of the Great Emancipator? Maybe not, but it does provide a recent context within an overarching legacy concerning freedom.

For opponents of Moses's plan to continue using whites in the upcoming summer project, aka Freedom Summer, Allen's murder brought a distinct change in outlook. One such opponent, Charlie Cobb, later noted, "They wanted things to change, and if it took bringing in a bunch of white kids, OK. Local people were not into all these ideological kinds of things" (Dittmer 219). For Moses, the results of the Freedom Days across the state, the murder of Allen, and the state's recently passed law prohibiting the picketing of state buildings confirmed his observation from the previous summer: "It is impossible to register Negroes in Mississippi" (Dittmer 224). Dave Dennis recalled, "We made sure that we had the children, sons and daughters, some of the very powerful people in the country over there."[4] Parents could prove to be important sources for change, just as much as their children involved in the protests. As Moses and Dennis planned for Freedom Summer, they reasoned, "If there were gonna take some deaths to do it, the death of a white college student would bring on more attention to what was going on than for a black college student getting it." Dennis added, "That's cold, but that was also in another sense speaking the language of this country." The media coverage sparked by violent reactions toward the white college students during the Freedom Vote had exposed the climate of terror in Mississippi to the rest of the nation; Moses and Dennis understood that these high stakes were the only way to generate publicity and move forward. The federal government had yet to use its influential power to address injustice in Mississippi. The movement needed to do something bigger.

ESTABLISHING THE MISSISSIPPI FREEDOM DEMOCRATIC PARTY

The plans for the upcoming Freedom Summer moved forward, and so, too, did the intention to use northern white college volunteers. During the monthly state convention in March, members of COFO formally voted to challenge the seating of the state's delegation at the Democratic National Convention in Atlantic City and also moved to conduct a "Freedom Registration" campaign during the summer (Dittmer 237). The convention members nominated candidates to run in the summer's upcoming congressional primaries, and in order to help accomplish these goals, during April's state convention COFO members established the MFDP.

The creation of the MFDP demonstrated the rhetorical significance of the Freedom Vote, but moved from a "mock election" environment and transplanted directly in confrontation with the established political system. The political organism created by the Freedom Vote was now entering the world of "real" politics. If the Freedom Vote was "practice," then the creation of the MFDP and the decision to use it as a tool to challenge the state's traditionally all-white Democratic Party system were the implementation, which posed very real consequences. The members at COFO's state convention utilized the preexisting network of leadership established by the Freedom Vote, which included project directors at the district, county, city, and even neighborhood levels.

The formation of the MFDP resembled the rhetorical significance found in the Freedom Vote in another manner as well. Both the Freedom Vote and the MFDP represented things that were "greater than the sum of their parts," meaning that the joining of the individuals created something bigger than the mere bodies counted. By combining their individuality, the people involved in the Freedom Vote and the MFDP created something that was rhetorically powerful beyond their own individual capacity to act. The Freedom Vote and the MFDP became forms of constitutive rhetoric, creating a new identity for blacks in Mississippi, complete with formal institutions, policies, and practices. The Freedom Vote and the formation of the MFDP can then be viewed as models of agency for local Mississippi blacks.

White volunteers would play a key role in operating the summer's Freedom Registration campaign, organizing and conducting Freedom Schools in communities across the state. Civil rights leaders also hoped that the presence of northern white college students would attract media attention as it had during the Freedom Vote. But the involvement of outside white volunteers came at a price.

THAT LONG, HOT SUMMER

In the early spring of 1964 Michael and Rita Schwerner arrived in Meridian, Mississippi, to work for CORE in Lauderdale County. Both Schwerners were college graduates and had been actively involved with social work programs back in New York before they were married. Although the two met initial resistance in Meridian, by the beginning of the summer they had several staff members working in their community center, the first of its kind in the state, and their classes boasted high attendance. The CORE staff members overseeing the state were so impressed that they appointed Mickey head of the Fourth District project, a district covering six counties (Dittmer 246). Mickey was the first white organizer to achieve this level of responsibility in Mississippi.

As civil rights organizers continued their preparations through the spring and into the summer, another group in Mississippi was also stepping up its efforts. The Ku Klux Klan bombed or burned nearly thirty-five churches during the Freedom Summer campaign.⁵ White violence was nothing new, but this increase of Klan activity was staggering. Nightriders swept across the state unchecked by law officials. Intimidation was no longer strictly economic. On the night of April 24, 1964, crosses burned in sixty-four of the state's eighty-two counties.⁶

One church bombing proved pivotal for both civil rights organizations and the Klan. The black community of Longdale was eight miles east of Philadelphia, Mississippi, on Highway 16. The members of Mount Zion Methodist Church had allowed Mickey Schwerner to promote voter registration there and had granted him permission to use the church as a Freedom School during the upcoming Freedom Summer project. In response, the White Knights of the Ku Klux Klan burned Mount Zion to the ground on the night of June 16.⁷ Following an evening board meeting, church members encountered the waiting Klansmen. They threatened and beat several elderly members for their participation with the civil rights workers. The Klansmen sent a message to Schwerner and CORE in the form of smoldering ashes.

Mickey Schwerner was not even in Mississippi the night the Klan sent its message. He was with James Chaney in Oxford, Ohio, at an orientation session for volunteers planning on coming to Mississippi for the Freedom Summer project. Chaney was a black Meridian resident who had gotten involved with CORE early in 1964. The twenty-one-year-old quickly became indispensable to the Schwerners and was renowned for his driving skills on Mississippi's back-country roads. Schwerner and Chaney received news of the church's fate, and the two decided to return to Longdale as soon as possible to salvage their fledgling project in Neshoba County. Andrew Goodman, a recent graduate from Queens College who was assigned to the Meridian CORE office for the summer project, joined them as they drove through the night to return to Mississippi. They arrived in Meridian just before nightfall on June 20 and prepared to head into Neshoba County the next day. The trio had planned to view the remains of the church and interview members who had been there the night the Klan burned Mount Zion. They knew they were going into hostile territory and made plans to return by four o'clock in the afternoon.⁸

Even those familiar with Mississippi's violent history toward "outside agitators" have a hard time swallowing the story of Goodman, Chaney, and Schwerner. It is a story of more than just martyrdom; it is a tale that reflects the Mississippi movement's very struggle against oppression. The trio were arrested for a traffic violation on the outskirts of Philadelphia after 3 p.m. and incarcerated in the Neshoba County jail until their release around ten o'clock that night. On their way back from the church, Deputy Cecil Price pulled them over nine miles south of town and handed them over to a Klan mob. The Klan executed the three in a mafia-like gangland style and hid their bodies under a remote dam.

When the trio failed to show up the next day, many civil rights volunteers knew in their hearts what fate had befallen their comrades.[9] Segregationists in the state claimed that the disappearance was a hoax, that Goodman, Chaney, and Schwerner were hiding somewhere up north in order to bring more unsavory media attention to Mississippi. Hoax or no hoax, the federal government finally sprang into action and began a statewide search for the missing civil rights workers involving the FBI, the National Guard, and navy reservists.[10] FBI director J. Edgar Hoover opened an FBI field office in Jackson on July 10 and attended the opening in person.[11]

Two days after Goodman, Chaney, and Schwerner's disappearance, a search team found the charred hull of the station wagon that the trio had been driving when stopped for allegedly speeding.[12] The blue Ford was found in Bogue Chitto Swamp northeast of Philadelphia. The discovery of the burned station wagon fueled theories about the disposal of the bodies of the civil rights workers.

The disappearance of Goodman, Chaney, and Schwerner did not stop Freedom Summer. Northern college students came to the state as proposed and established Freedom Schools and voter registration drives. The Mississippi House and Senate hurried a rash of legislation that essentially hampered any attempts to politically organize disenfranchised Mississippi blacks.[13] Take a moment to compare the experiences of Bruce Payne and Andrew Goodman. Both were middle-class white males from northern colleges, Payne from Yale and Goodman from Queens College, and both men suffered violence at the hands of Mississippi whites—Payne was beaten and shot at, Goodman was murdered. Payne was in Mississippi for less than a week, and Goodman was tragically in the state less than a day before his disappearance. Both volunteers demonstrated a willingness to sacrifice themselves for what they believed in. Their stories also illustrate just how high the stakes were in Mississippi; generating media publicity was not a game of chance but a matter of life and death for some.

Freedom Schools opened their doors on the morning of July 7 and came to represent the insistent principle of flexibility, always able and ready to adapt to the needs of the students and the surrounding community. Staughton Lynd, the mastermind behind the Freedom School's teaching curriculum, had initially planned to open around twenty schools, but by summer's end more than fifty schools held classes.[14] Organizers had anticipated around 1,000 students but ended up instructing over 3,000 children, adults, and elderly. Learning topics ranged from civic politics, to history, to more basic rubric like math and science.

The bodies of Goodman, Chaney, and Schwerner were found fourteen feet and ten inches from the crest of an earthen dam on August 4, 1964. Forty-four days after their disappearance, the FBI exhumed the remains on the Old Jolly Farm, well within sight of the Ferris wheel at the Neshoba County Fair three miles away (Huie 160). Two days later the MFDP held a state convention to select its delegation to challenge the seating of the Mississippi regulars at the Democratic National Convention in Atlantic City.

IS THIS AMERICA?

The challenge to unseat the Mississippi regulars was a direct extension of the Freedom Vote itself and the lessons and tactics it employed. Both shared the goal of demonstrating to local and national audiences that blacks in Mississippi wanted to participate in politics but were being systematically denied access to the process. During the summer, as predicted, blacks were shut out of the all-white county and district primaries that nominated delegates to the state and national Democratic conventions. Mirroring the employment of similar tactics during the Freedom Vote, a parallel convention structure was formed to officially nominate the sixty-four MFDP delegates to the national convention in Atlantic City in late August.

The MFDP's challenge was a direct descendant of the Freedom Vote. Again, the MFDP employed the organizational structure established by the Freedom Vote to generate publicity and promoted agency through the performance of democratic practices that the Freedom Vote had pioneered. During Freedom Summer, the news media had focused on the search for the missing civil rights workers; now, during the MFDP's challenge in Atlantic City, the news focused on the MFDP and the delegates themselves.

In a particularly powerful moment before the convention's Credentials Committee hearings, Fannie Lou Hamer addressed the committee. Though her address was brief, its rhetorical significance was immense. She asked the Credentials Committee, "Is this America, the land of the free and the home of the brave, where we have to sleep with our telephones off the hooks because our lives be threatened daily, because we want to live as decent human beings, in America?" (Dittmer 288). Her message was captured by the lenses of network news cameras, or "the center of the global order" (Hariman and Lucaites 225). What makes her plea so powerful is its direct appeal to political ethos; she is connecting to and taking advantage of American political values. By speaking out to the committee, she demonstrated that any and every American was capable of being a political citizen. She said nothing about her gender, her race, or her socioeconomic standing; it was her status as an American citizen that granted her authority. Committee chairman David Lawrence moved to postpone the committee's decision on seating the MFDP delegates until the next day. Dittmer notes, "Telegrams of support began flooding the convention immediately after Hamer's testimony, and they continued to pour in throughout the night" (288).

While the MFDP's challenge did gain national news attention, it failed in its efforts to earn the MFDP recognition as an official national party and seat all its delegates at the convention. A "compromise" had been negotiated: the committee would offer two at-large seats given to Aaron Henry and Reverend Edwin King. It was ultimately rejected.

The media coverage of not only Hamer's speech before the Credentials Committee but also the MFDP's challenge and Freedom Summer evidence how civil rights leaders had learned to attract media attention using the Freedom Vote's tactics. Like the Freedom Vote, the Freedom Days and Freedom Summer generated media attention, in large part through the presence of northern white volunteers. With the challenge in Atlantic City, the mere presence of the MFDP sparked controversy and therefore publicity.

In all these instances, movement leaders created moments that the news media had to cover. The movement was instituting what DeLuca and Peeples call "image events": "visual philosophical-rhetorical fragments, mind bombs that expand the universe of thinkable thoughts. Image events are dense surfaces meant to provoke in an instant the shock of the familiar made strange" (144). Image events take action against the hegemonic normative by taking advantage of the norm's preferred means of distributing information. Protestors using image events are then able to reach broad audiences through the distributed publicity.

Exploring next the media's coverage of Freedom Summer and MFDP's challenge in Atlantic City provides insight into how and why civil rights leaders in Mississippi clamored for publicity through the national media.

THE MEDIA FINALLY RESPONDS

The late spring and summer of 1964 witnessed an explosion of Mississippi civil rights coverage in the mass media. The main events covered were the Freedom Summer project and the MFDP challenge in Atlantic City. Over the course of these two events, the *New York Times* ran more than 120 stories. A reader could understand what was happening just by following the headlines. The coverage of these two events broke the patterns of coverage previously established by the *Times*: some articles included photographs, some made the front page, and a few were wire stories. But the major difference lies in the sheer volume of coverage that the *Times* afforded these two events. This could be because Freedom Summer and the Atlantic City challenge spanned a much longer period of time than did the Freedom Vote, but it could also be that these incidents represented what the news media deemed worthy of coverage.

The triple homicide of Goodman, Chaney, and Schwerner certainly caught the attention of the news media and the federal government. Between the murder of the civil rights volunteers and other Freedom Summer–related news, the *Times* ran over seventy articles, fourteen of which included photographs. Early coverage of Freedom Summer focused on the Freedom Registration campaign and the Freedom Schools.

On June 23 the news exploded with stories of the murders. Claude Sitton, in "3 in Rights Drive Reported Missing," reported who the missing workers were, where they were from, and why they were in Mississippi. The article also includes a quote from Sheriff Rainey: "If they're missing, they just hid somewhere, trying to get a lot of publicity out of it, I figure."[15] Sheriff Rainey is clearly attempting to discredit the character of the workers by framing their intent as sinister. From here the headlines and images unfold the narrative: another page-one story by Sitton from June 24 is headlined "Tip Leads to Auto" and includes pictures of Goodman, Schwerner, and the chassis of the burned car; then the headline "Hope for 3 Wanes as Dulles Opens Mississippi Talks" accompanied another article by Sitton, again on page one and this time with a larger photograph of the charred car as well as a picture of James Chaney; "President Sends 200 Sailors to Aid Mississippi Hunt" was the title of an article by Tom Wicker on page one from June 26; finally, Sitton titled another page-one story "Mississippi Drags River in Search for Rights Aides" and included a picture from June 28 that shows FBI agents in boats dragging the Pearl River.

Other events surrounding Freedom Summer also slipped into the news due to the buzz surrounding the project. For instance, "CORE to Broaden Mississippi Drive" by Donald Janson ran in the July 5 issue of the *Times*. Yet most of the coverage of Freedom Summer focused on the search for the volunteers. "Hoover to Go to Mississippi Today in Civil Rights Case" made the front page on July 10, followed the next day by another page-one story, this time with a photo of Governor Paul Johnson speaking and J. Edgar Hoover looking on. The *Times*' coverage illuminated the established norm of racial violence and murder in Mississippi for the rest of the nation. The story "A 2nd Body Is Found in the Mississippi" by John Herbers reported the discovery of the bodies, or partial bodies, of Henry Dee and Charles E. Moore. The bodies of these two young men were only found because of the ongoing search for the other three missing volunteers, which raised the question, "How many more bodies were there?"

A page-one story on August 5, "Graves at a Dam" by Claude Sitton, broke the discovery of the missing workers' bodies. Individual pictures of Andrew Goodman, James Chaney, and Michael Schwerner accompanied the story. The next day, another page-one story by Sitton included an overhead picture of the dam and excavation and was titled "Experts Identify Mississippi Bodies as Rights Aides." But the discovery of the bodies did not conclude the coverage. The paper ran several articles about the victims' families, ongoing protests, and even Chaney's funeral service, which garnered two stories: "Speakers Pour Out Bitterness at Chaney Memorial Service" by John Herbers, and an editorial by Claude Sitton, "Tragedy in Mississippi: Deep-Seated Feelings of Negroes Are Reflected in Funeral for Slain Civil Rights Worker." On August 20, in a page-one story by John Herbers titled "Civil Rights Drive Alters Mississippi," Herbers notes, "The summer civil rights project in Mississippi, which ends this week, brought few tangible changes in the social order. But the state has passed through a crisis and will never again be the same."[16] Herbers's summary seems less than bittersweet, but not totally hopeless either.

Coverage continued as the FBI built its case. "2 Indicted by U.S. in Rights Murders" by Herbers on October 3 and Herbers's page-one story from December 5 titled "Most Tied to Klan," which included a photograph of the twenty-one men charged during their arraignment, show that although the search was over, the media and nation were still focused on what was happening in Mississippi. Months after Freedom Summer ended and the murdered volunteers' bodies were found, news coverage kept the nation's attention on the aftermath and consequences of the summer's events.

Life magazine ran three different stories and an editorial on the triple homicide during Freedom Summer. A six-page story ran in the July 3 issue and included more photographs than text.[17] Pictures of the charred car being pulled from the Bogue Chitto Swamp; two different photos of Andrew Goodman during training sessions at Oxford, Ohio, before his fateful journey to Neshoba County; and an aerial shot of searchers dragging rivers and swamplands dominated the story. An editorial titled "Terrible Silence of the Decent" harangues complacent whites across the South, linking the violence against public beach integrationists in St. Augustine, Florida, to the events in Philadelphia, Mississippi.[18] A one-page story from August 14 titled "In a Mississippi Grave, the Three Missing Men"[19] includes little text but presents three pictures: a picture of Rita Schwerner in a CORE office, a picture of deputies and FBI agents unloading a body from an ambulance, and an overhead shot of the excavation area. The images function as visual evidence of the official investigation into the murders of the civil rights workers, making the government appear as an active and concerned player in the crisis.

One of the more iconic photos concerning the murders of Goodman, Chaney, and Schwerner is printed across two pages in the December 18 issue of *Life* magazine. This picture portrays Sheriff Lawrence Rainey and Deputy Cecil Price smiling and enjoying a fresh mouthful of chewing tobacco, seated and waiting as defendants in the court trial. Price is holding a bag of Red Man tobacco, and the other defendants seated behind the two lawmen are also grinning ear to ear. None of the men in the photo appear the least bit concerned that they are being charged. The picture portrays an environment of impunity for racist whites. What little coverage *Life* did provide was important because the magazine was a popular mainstream periodical, meaning that the news and stories contained therein could reach a broad public audience, the very type of audience with whom civil rights leaders were trying to communicate.

The pattern holds true to some extent for the coverage generated by the MFDP's challenge at the Democratic National Convention in Atlantic City. This event did not win as much attention as Freedom Summer and the search for the missing volunteers had won, but the movement in Mississippi was still trying to bring attention to the inequality and injustice there. The *New York Times* ran over fifty stories on the Atlantic City challenge, affording the MFDP plenty of face time in the national media. Only five pictures ran with the stories this time, but again the volume and content of the coverage indicate that civil rights organizations and leaders in Mississippi had learned how to generate publicity.

Again, a reader can follow the headlines to visualize how the MFDP challenge unfolded. Early coverage of the MFDP focused on the summer project, but as coverage of the Freedom Summer activities became more in-depth, so too did the plans for the Atlantic City challenge. "California Democrats Join Drive to Unseat Mississippi Delegates" by Lawrence Davies reported on June 28 a resolution passed by the California delegation to officially support and recognize the MFDP. The story notes that the Wisconsin, Massachusetts, and District of Columbia delegations had already endorsed similar resolutions.[20] On July 20 Sitton's page-one story warns that "Democrats Face Mississippi Split," and on the next day another Sitton headline reads "Mississippi Freedom Party Bids for Democratic Convention Role."[21] The MFDP challenge won the support of Martin Luther King Jr., who had a tendency to generate news coverage, as evidenced by two stories: "Dr. King Starts Mississippi Tour" and "Dr. King Speaks to Negro Group at Philadelphia, Miss., Rally," both by John Herbers.[22] Both stories mention the ongoing search for the missing volunteers but also focus on the "freedom registration" campaign.

Much like the coverage of the missing civil rights workers, coverage of civil rights activities by Mississippi organizations was more detailed than ever. An article titled "1952 Ruling Is Key in Delegate Fight" from July 27 reported the technical process of a "loyalty oath" that the Democratic Party had initiated after the Dixiecrat walkout during the 1948 convention.[23] This "loyalty oath" clause is the loophole that the MFDP was looking for in order to challenge the seating of the Democratic Party regulars. As the late August convention approached, the frequency of coverage intensified. From August 7 to August 22 the *Times* ran twenty-one stories on the MFDP's attempt to unseat the Mississippi regulars. On the twenty-third the front-page story, "Mississippi Factions Clash before Panel" by E. W. Kenworthy, included two photographs from the Credentials Committee, one of E. K. Collins speaking on behalf of the regular Mississippi Democrats, and the other of Aaron Henry.[24] Publicity like this helped to legitimize the status of the MFDP by depicting the organization and its cause as worthy of media attention.

The next day a page-seventeen article titled "Mississippian Relates Struggle of Negro in Voter Registration" by Nan Robertson detailed the testimony of Fannie Lou Hamer and included a picture of Hamer.[25] The story provides a brief biographical sketch of Hamer but focuses mainly on her testimony, quoting her extensively throughout. Don't forget that President Johnson attempted to change the topic of discussion by calling a press conference to divert attention from Hamer's testimony. Watch the Henry Hampton series *Eyes on the Prize* and the evidence is there; she was silenced by the White House. The article and Hamer's televised address functioned as a sort of coming-out party for Hamer at the national level. People within the movement were certainly familiar with Hamer, but now she was being introduced to a captive national audience. While the coverage of the missing workers focused on the racial violence in Mississippi, the MFDP and Hamer's address generated a different kind of publicity. The MFDP and Hamer represented a proactive, rather than reactive, framework from Mississippi leaders to stop racial violence and inequality in Mississippi, and they brought media coverage that reported what civil rights organizations were doing rather than what had been done to them.

Though coverage of the Atlantic City challenge died down during the last week of August, several stories ran after the Credentials Committee hearing. "Mississippi Seats Taken by Negroes," "TV: A Bizarre Spectacular from Atlantic City," and "Johnson Criticized by Freedom Party" were some of the final reports on the MFDP challenge.[26] *Time* also covered the events in Atlantic City. In the August 7 issue, a story titled "The Big Chairman Up Yonder" claimed that the organizers of the Democratic National Convention in Atlantic City would have to deal with the MFDP in one way or another or risk upsetting the pageantry surrounding Johnson's nomination.[27] The September 4 story "Trying to Paper It Over" reported that the majority of Democratic southern senators and governors stayed away from the national convention because of the controversy surrounding the MFDP. *Time*'s coverage, much like *Life*'s coverage of the missing civil rights workers, provided the MFDP with a broader public audience due to the periodical's national mainstream circulation.

Freedom Summer and the Atlantic City challenge captured more media attention than any other Mississippi civil rights event, but their success was not entirely their own. The Freedom Vote had created the political model and had established the leadership network that proved invaluable to the MFDP. The use of white volunteers during Freedom Summer was a tactical development from the Freedom Vote that continued to bring results. Both Freedom Summer and the MFDP's challenge, like the Freedom Vote of 1963, empowered black Mississippians by providing them with opportunities to directly participate in democratic political processes, opportunities that progressed from a "mock election" to "real world" circumstances. The engendering did not stop there; MFDP organizers were ready to release a sequel.

FREEDOM VOTE II, WITH AN INSTRUCTION MANUAL

One of the final events directly descended from the Freedom Vote of 1963 is the Freedom Vote of 1964. This time the candidates were running for congressional seats but again were denied placement on the official state ballots and so ran a parallel election. The MFDP created a twelve-page "Freedom Primer" that was used to inform potential voters about the campaign and the candidates.[28] The primer provides background information regarding why the campaign was necessary, who the candidates were, and what the reader could do to help change things in Mississippi, all in the form of a story with illustrations. The use of pictures in the primer allowed the Freedom Vote organizers to reach illiterate citizens.

The Freedom Primer is another example of how campaign organizers empowered their audience through both traditional and visual texts. The primer defines just what the Freedom Vote was and why it was necessary, and it provides historical information on the 1890 changes to the state constitution and how those changes impacted blacks in Mississippi. This empowers readers by demonstrating that laws are a man-made institution and therefore can be changed.

The primer even covers the Freedom Vote of 1963. Highlighting the significance of the previous fall's Freedom Vote, the primer states, "The 1963 Freedom Vote was important in another way, too. Because after the Freedom Vote many people felt they wanted to keep on voting and running their own candidates. So they came together in Jackson in January 1964 and they started the FREEDOM DEMOCRATIC PARTY."[29] This means that success on the part of the current campaign is a foregone conclusion. The primer then informs the reader who that year's Freedom Vote candidates were: Aaron Henry for US Senate, Fannie Lou Hamer for a representative seat in the Second Congressional District, Annie Devine of Canton also for a congressional representative seat, and Victoria Gray of Hattiesburg for the final congressional seat. The MFDP was now adding women to the position of candidates, a powerful message of inclusion and equality.

The final page of the Freedom Primer contains a powerful visual argument. In the illustration, blacks line up outside a building labeled "court house." The sign out front reads "Register and Vote." By depicting black citizens outside the courthouse engaged in the very activity that the Freedom Vote was attempting to persuade participants to join, the argument put forth by the Freedom Primer is complete. This final illustration is a clear call to action.

Like the MFDP challenge and Freedom Summer, the Freedom Vote of 1964 employed the social network, political organization, publicity tactics, and methods of empowerment established by the Freedom Vote of 1963. Even one of the candidates was the same: Aaron Henry was running again. While the Freedom Vote of 1964 generated only about a quarter of the total votes gathered in the previous fall's campaign, it did draw more news coverage from major outlets. The story "The Senate Races" from the October 16 issue of *Time* briefly mentions the MFDP's campaign against three-term Democrat John C. Stennis.[30] The *New York Times* also ran a few stories: "Freedom Democrats Renew Mississippi Ballot Appeal," "Mississippi Seizes 5 in a 'Freedom Vote,'" and "Negroes Holding a Mock Election in Mississippi."[31]

Unlike their the coverage of the Freedom Vote of 1963, the news media also printed follow-up stories after the conclusion of the Freedom Vote in 1964. The headline "Mississippi Seats Under Challenge" from the *New York Times* on December 7 shows how the MFDP was able to fuse lessons learned from the Freedom Vote of 1963 and the Atlantic City challenge by generating media coverage and attention. The Freedom Vote campaigns illustrated that blacks in Mississippi wanted to and would participate in the political process, made more significant by the subsequent challenge of the officially elected white representatives. The tactics from the Freedom Vote of 1963 and the Atlantic City challenge combined to create a strategy of confrontation that drew national attention to the hypocrisy, inequality, and injustice in Mississippi while empowering black Mississippians.

The tactic of challenging the status quo was used again after the Freedom Vote of 1964. Taking a page from the Freedom Vote of 1963, the MFDP organized a legal challenge against the state of Mississippi. The legal challenge used the same argument as before: because of the laws and policies of Mississippi's state government, the "elected" officials did not represent the citizenry of Mississippi. Henry and King challenged the governor, the MFDP challenged the Democratic Party, and now three women from Mississippi were requesting seats in the US House of Representatives. Unlike before, this challenge brought with it a legal team and more sustained publicity.[32] The *New York Times* of December 6, 1964, reported that the MFDP had chosen Victoria Gray, Annie Devine, and Fannie Lou Hamer to fill seats held by Representatives William M. Calmer, William A. Winstead, and Jamie L. Whitten.[33] A few days later, an advertisement depicted Hamer sitting with the American flag in her arms, with the simple yet powerful question, "Where are 'the good men'?" The image contextualizes Hamer as a citizen and therefore as a legitimate political agent. Similar to the ad that ran earlier in the spring, a few paragraphs of text provide contextual background. This time the narration connects the challenge in Atlantic City with the current challenge and outlines the goals of the MFDP. This provides a very public face (Hamer's) for the nation to attach to the organization, and provides a political manifesto of the MFDP as well. When a civil rights organization could not generate publicity, it had to buy it. The three challengers were actually forbidden access to the floor of the House of Representatives on January 4, but in a roll-call vote, Democrats mustered a third of the House to vote in favor of not seating the "official" representatives.[34] The journey had taken the challengers from the dusty roads of Sunflower, Forrest, and Madison Counties to the halls of Congress.

The news coverage of the 1964 Freedom Vote candidates' challenge of the "official" candidates extended through the winter and into the spring and summer of 1965, with a few stories every month reporting their progress (or lack thereof). Dominating the nation's attention, however, were the efforts of Martin Luther King Jr. in Selma, Alabama. The movement in Mississippi, the MFDP included, would not regain the public limelight until midsummer of 1965, when marches and demonstrations in Jackson again protested the legitimacy of the "official" Mississippi congressional representatives.[35]

SELMA AND THE VOTING RIGHTS ACT OF 1965

Selma in the spring of 1965 brought another impetus for the passage of the Civil Rights Act of 1965. Dittmer argues, "The demonstrations in Selma, Alabama, that spring, culminating in the march to Montgomery led by Dr. Martin Luther King, had all but ensured passage of a voting rights law that included provision to send federal registrars into counties with a history of discrimination against black voters" (344). The March 19 issue of *Life* featured an eight-page photo essay titled "Selma: Beatings Start the Killing Season."[36] The photos are famous for their depiction of Alabama state troopers beating marchers to the ground. Other pictures provide evidence of a publicity-generating tactic employed by the Freedom Vote: the presence of outside whites. In the series of photos, a northern governor's wife marches among the protestors and embraces Martin Luther King Jr. Another compelling photo shows Reverend James Reeb, a Unitarian Minister from Boston, splayed on a gurney, receiving medical attention. Reverend Reeb died from wounds he received from a white man who clubbed him from behind. The whites supporting King in Selma (just as they had in the Freedom Vote of 1963, Freedom Summer, the Atlantic City challenge by the MFDP, and the Freedom Vote of 1964) helped gather the much-needed attention of the nation to exact pressure on Congress and the president to pass civil rights legislation with real teeth.

Another moment that facilitated the passage of the voting rights legislation is President Johnson's March 15 address to a joint session of Congress. Rhetorical critic Garth E. Pauley argues that Johnson's address is "a speech that stands as his greatest oratorical triumph" (14). Pauley notes:

> The president's March 15 speech was his first sustained response to the crisis and his first statement that satisfied many citizens' desire for a tough, explicit public message. The speech also expressed his commitment to ensuring that Congress enacted a meaningful voting rights statute, a commitment that some had previously questioned, though Johnson had been working behind closed doors since the summer of 1964 to develop a legislative solution to the problem of voter discrimination against African Americans. (14–15)

In a speech televised to seventy million national viewers, the president publicly announced his intention to propose the appropriate legislation, demonstrate the need of such legislation, outline the features of the bill, and request Congress's speedy cooperation (Pauley 15).

The purpose of the act is clear, as indicated by an article published in the *Duke Law Journal*: "To correct the failings of prior legislation, the Voting Rights Act of 1965 presents a single, unified program to achieve voting equality" ("Voting Rights Act of 1965" 463). The Voting Rights Act of 1965 (VRA) set up an administrative process independent from the judiciary process and provided a "triggering formula" that assured immediate action on the part of the federal government in cases of voter discrimination. The most important aspect of the VRA is the automatic remedies that the "triggering formula" initiated: "Certain remedies automatically arise upon the coincidence of (1) the use of a voting test by any state or political subdivision on November 1, 1964, and

(2) either a total registration on November 1, 1964, of less than fifty percent of those of voting age or a total participation in the 1964 presidential election of less than fifty percent of those of voting age" ("Voting Rights Act of 1965" 469). Wherever these conditions existed, the attorney general could instate federal registrars and examiners to physically oversee the registration and voting process. The VRA also prohibited any state alterations of voter registration qualifications without first gaining approval from the attorney general or, for the District of Columbia, the district court ("Voting Rights Act of 1965" 470).

The VRA prevented the possibility of avoidance on the part of the traditional southern political power structure. The remedies triggered by the voting formulas were automatic and did not require any court or judge to review possible acts of discrimination. The VRA also sped up the litigation process by requiring the use of the district court of the District of Columbia for all declaratory judgment actions, which ensured a quicker review of applications for appeal. A common tactic for southern federal judges was to "defer" providing their judgments on cases for months if not years. The VRA also made interfering with another individual's right to vote a felony (Colby 129).

Wayne Santoro affirms, "The most comprehensive response to enfranchise Southern blacks took place with the Voting Rights Act of 1965" (1393). The VRA's impact is indisputable: in 1965 only 28,500 blacks were registered to vote in Mississippi, roughly 6.5 percent of the state's eligible black population; in 1968 that number jumped to 250,777, close to 60 percent of the state's black voters, and by 1984, 406,000 blacks were registered (Santoro 1390). Not only had the number of voters increased but so too had the number of voter discrimination cases tried by the federal courts: between 1965 and 1984, federal courts heard seventy-one Mississippi VRA suits (Santoro 1396).

The Freedom Vote's legacy lived on well after the last vote was cast that fateful fall of 1963 through the strategies and tactics developed initially for its own campaign—using northern whites and enacting public performances of agentic citizenship. In other words, protestors produced image events designed to portray and promote empowerment. The significant increases in media attention and voter registrations also provide evidence that the tactics being deployed were working. The epilogue examines how the legacy of the Freedom Vote is still prominent in the current political climate, and still teaching lessons today.

Epilogue
KEEPING THE FAITH

In July 2006 President George W. Bush signed the Fannie Lou Hamer, Rosa Parks, and Coretta Scott King Voting Rights Act Reauthorization and Amendments Act, ensuring that the pivotal legislation enacted four decades earlier continued to guarantee qualified citizens the right to vote. In attendance to witness the signing that day were family members of the three civil rights icons for whom the bill was named.[1] The Freedom Vote of 1963 was represented that day not only through its connection with the 1965 Voting Rights Act but also in the presence of Hamer's family.

The 1963 Freedom Vote was no small thing. The Freedom Vote was a successful response to an environment of fear and inequality. From a rhetorical perspective, this study demonstrates that the Freedom Vote was ultimately a success but not an end-all solution. Despite not attaining the desired 200,000 votes, the Freedom Vote proved that blacks in Mississippi would vote if given the opportunity. The way the Freedom Vote balanced both immediate and long-term goals was remarkable: 82,000 votes represented a powerful voting bloc ready to influence future elections.

Freedom Vote organizer Lawrence Guyot notes how the campaign worked to educate blacks about their voting legacy: "We all knew in Mississippi about the days after the Civil War, where black men voted for black candidates. We wanted to reconnect Mississippians with their voting heritage."[2] For Guyot, the Freedom Vote's success was in how it reconnected blacks to their voting roots; it was successful because "it was mobile, politically agile, and worked at the local level." The genius of the campaign lies in how it educated its constituency through participation, instructing citizenship through involvement. Guyot reminds us that "you can't teach courage," but you can give someone a reason and opportunity to be courageous. The Freedom Vote empowered Mississippi blacks through education, organization, and communication, giving them the opportunity to stand up for themselves and change the conditions in Mississippi.

In a memo to the national offices of the Congress of Racial Equality (CORE), Dave Dennis recognized what had been accomplished: "This is the first time that Mississippi has been organized to such an extent. We just cannot afford to let it fall back. We must take advantage of our present accomplishments."[3] Dennis outlines several potential programs immediately needed in Mississippi, from a community center with a library to classes covering health issues. The basic concept that links all the programs together is their emphasis on education through participation. What Dennis and others concluded from the Freedom Vote is that the opportunity to vote was important, but the ability to do so with a purpose was equally as important. What good was the right to vote if you didn't know what you were voting for and why you were voting?

What is missing from the narrative in this project is the sustained presence of John Dittmer's "local people." Yes, Fannie Lou Hamer, Reverend Edwin King, and Aaron Henry are all native Mississippians, but they are also extraordinary leaders. Future research in this area must continue to strive to include the perspectives of those at the base of local communities; the focus needs to be taken to another level of pragmatics at the community level.

Examining how the Freedom Vote addressed locals' fears and allowed them to cast ballots exposes a compelling relationship between rhetoric and agency. It was not enough for the Freedom Vote to get blacks to vote; equally important was the candidates for whom they were voting. If blacks in Mississippi voted for candidates who maintained the segregationists' status quo, then obtaining the right to vote was a token and empty victory. Getting blacks to vote for the Freedom Vote candidates made the act of voting that much more powerful. Black Mississippians could not be satisfied with the mere act of voting; they, like all American voters, had a responsibility to use that right to vote for candidates that best represented their interests. The ballots cast in the Freedom Vote then became more than mere votes—they became votes for recognition and change.

As a matter of policy, the state of Mississippi does not keep racial records of voter registration, but there are other numbers and events that evidence the lingering effects of the Freedom Vote. In Mississippi, a state of just under three million people, 37 percent of the population is black—the highest percentage in the nation. According to the report *Black Elected Officials: A Statistical Summary 2000*, Mississippi has the largest number of elected black officials, 897.[4] This is Mississippi, not Texas or California or New York, all states where the black population soars into the millions, but a state with a past of racial violence and black suppression. According to the US Census Bureau, the state has just over one-and-a-half million registered voters, so for a state with such a small registered voting base to have that many black elected officials is significant, especially given the history of violence and intimidation.[5] The state legislature's web page boasts that 25 percent of the state's House of Representatives are black.[6] These numbers indicate a significant presence of black elected officials serving in public office, and at a rate much higher than any other state in the union.

Epilogue: Keeping the Faith

The 2008 Democratic Party primary in Mississippi also yielded interesting results. Then-senator Barack Obama won the state's primary with 255,809 votes, 61 percent of the overall ballots cast.[7] Based on exit polls, 70 percent of the voters who picked Obama were black. This means that a black candidate won the Democratic primary in 2008 based largely on the black vote. Sound familiar? This is exactly what the Freedom Vote organizers had attempted to illustrate forty-five years earlier—that, if given the chance, blacks in Mississippi would vote, and do so in significant numbers, numbers that were large enough to influence the outcome of an election.

On August 28, 1963, just a few months before the Freedom Vote, Martin Luther King Jr. delivered his famous "I Have a Dream" speech. The Democratic National Convention officially granted Obama the presidential nomination on August 28, 2008. This is an infamous date for Mississippi and civil rights: fifty-three years to the day Emmett Till was murdered. As discussed in the previous chapter, the Democratic National Convention has a unique history in Mississippi with the challenge brought against it more than fifty years ago. Along with the tragedies and struggles associated with the days of August past, the moments of hope should also be recognized. Hopefully the legacies and impact of these historic events will not be lost.

The last few presidential elections demonstrate the continued importance of groups of voters in American politics. In 2008 a youth movement helped Obama win the White House with not only their record turnout numbers but also their use of social media to mobilize voters and resources. Then, in 2012, the country saw several states and local governments amend their voting laws, often putting in place restrictions that denied minorities access to the ballot. Yet despite these restrictions, minority voter turnout in the election far exceeded predictions. This proves that the way to win elections in America is not to restrict citizens' access to the franchise but rather to expand that right. Then there's the 2016 presidential election, further evidence that voting still matters, and adding further complexity to issues surrounding voting.

Racism is still a part of the American experience. Though overt displays of racial hatred like cross burning and spectacle lynching are no longer commonplace, they have been replaced with "softer" forms of racism that often go undiscussed. Issues like urban city illiteracy, college graduation rates of blacks, the federal government's response to Hurricane Katrina, economic policies, racial profiling, and the shockingly high incarceration rates of black males in America indicate that the dream may still be deferred. The present discourse around race in America must continue to expand the concept of what comprises civil rights. The Freedom Vote can offer this discussion lessons learned, tactics for success, and effective rhetorical invention. The 1963

Freedom Vote is a great reminder to seriously consider what we do with our right to vote today.

Looking at Occupy Wall Street, Arab Spring movements, protests in Hong Kong, and the reactions to the legal decisions concerning the deaths of Trayvon Martin, Michael Brown, and Eric Garner, we can see the Freedom Vote alive and well, still influencing the art of protest and the voices of dissent. The use of collective individuality to confront social injustice is not going away with the advent of digital technologies; rather, the nature of protest is the same, but the tools are changing. DeLuca, Lawson, and Sun remind us, "For centuries, all social protests have involved bodies and media. Activists always use the tools at hand" (485). Look no further than #blacklivesmatter.

If this examination of the Freedom Vote proves anything, it is that current, and, more important, future forms of protest would be wise to study the not-so-distant past. The key characteristics of contemporary protest (direct action participation; use of mass media, both traditional and social; and working panorganizationally) find their roots in the civil rights movement, and more specifically the 1963 Mississippi Freedom Vote. It is up to us as citizens, not the institutions in our society, to make the world a better place; with that understanding, the distance between dirt roads in the Mississippi Delta to Tahrir Square, or from Hong Kong to Ferguson, does not seem so far after all.

NOTES

PROLOGUE: THE HARBINGER

1. Robert (Bob) Moses was the campaign manager for the Mississippi Freedom Vote of 1963. This quote is taken from a speech given in Jackson, Mississippi, on November 4. The speech is from the Moses Moon collection, an archived series of audio recordings from 1963 and 1964, housed at the National Museum of American History in Washington, DC.

2. In *Freedom Summer: The Savage Season of 1964 That Made Mississippi Burn and Made America a Democracy* (New York: Penguin, 2010), Watson establishes the importance of Freedom Summer at a national level.

3. Little has been written specifically about the Freedom Vote. Both historically and rhetorically, scholars seem to have passed over the event, treating it more as a footnote. There is literally no research concerning the Freedom Vote from a perspective rooted in the communication discipline, let alone rhetorical studies. From inside the field of communication, the American civil rights movement and other topics such as black rhetoric have been studied, but no focused, detailed analysis of either the Freedom Vote or the rhetorical artifacts contained therein exists.

4. From his speech at the Freedom Vote Victory Rally, November 4, 1963.

5. Taylor Branch, *Parting the Waters: America in the King Years 1954-1963* (New York: Touchstone, 1988), 920; Taylor Branch, *Pillar of Fire: America in the King Years 1963-1965* (New York: Touchstone, 1998), 123; John Dittmer, *Local People: The Struggle for Civil Rights in Mississippi* (Urbana: University of Illinois Press, 1994), 200-201; Charles Payne, *I've Got the Light of Freedom* (Berkeley: University of California Press, 1995), 294-295; Frank R. Parker, *Black Votes Count: Political Empowerment in Mississippi after 1965* (Chapel Hill: University of North Carolina Press, 1990), 24; Mildred P. Walter, *Mississippi Challenge* (New York: Bradbury Press, 1992), 121. The scant extant literature on the Freedom Vote comes distinctly from the field of history. In John Dittmer's *Local People*, considered by many in the field to be *the* source for movement history and organization in Mississippi, the Freedom Vote receives seven pages. In Branch's two volumes, *Pillar of Fire* and *Parting the Waters*, and Payne's *I've Got the Light of Freedom*, the Freedom Vote is relegated a few transitory paragraphs. To date, Joseph Sinsheimer's "The Freedom Vote of 1963: New Strategies of Racial Protest in Mississippi," *Journal of Southern History* 55 (1989): 217-244, is the sole piece of academic work that focuses on the Freedom Vote. In less than thirty pages, Sinsheimer points out seven meaningful developments. First, he argues that the Freedom Vote illustrated that if blacks in Mississippi were given the chance, they not only would participate in political activities but would do so in large numbers. This first observation though, is not exclusively Sinsheimer's, as pointed out by the agreement with Branch, Dittmer, and Payne. In terms of organizational significance, the Freedom Vote accomplished four other goals: it unified the civil rights movement organizations at work within the state; it got those organizations working on a statewide level rather than in isolated pockets of community work; it literally integrated

those efforts; and rather than working on guaranteeing individual freedoms, the focus of the campaign instead centered on collective advancement. In addition, one of the more significant developments brought forth by the Freedom Vote was the amount of publicity generated by the northern white college students brought in to help with the campaign.

6. I explain the terms "rhetorical agency" and "image event" in more detail later, but for now "rhetorical agency" refers to the persuasive means by which people attempt to enact change, and "image events" are deliberately staged public spectacles meant to get media attention.

7. David Dennis, "Mississippi—A Pregnant State in Need of an Abortion," memo from the field secretary, SNCC papers, Reel 66. This memo functioned like a field report and provides the perspective of a participant/observer.

CHAPTER ONE: *INVENTIO*

1. Revels, Bruce, and Brooke represent three of the ten blacks ever to serve in the US Senate. Before 2008 there had only been a total of five, including former president Barack Obama.

2. C. Vann Woodward's *The Strange Career of Jim Crow* is an excellent source to familiarize readers with the background and environment of race relations in twentieth-century America.

3. For more on these figures (in the order they appear in the sentence), see Louis R. Harlan, *Booker T. Washington: The Making of a Black Political Leader, 1856–1901* (New York: Oxford University Press, 1972); Louis R. Harlan, *Booker T. Washington: The Wizard of Tuskegee, 1901–1915* (New York: Oxford University Press, 1983); David L. Lewis, *W. E. B. Du Bois: Biography of a Race, 1868–1919* (New York: Henry Holt, 1993); David L. Lewis, *W. E. B. Du Bois: The Fight for Equality and the American Century, 1919–1963* (New York: Henry Holt, 2000); E. David Cronon, *Black Moses: The Story of Marcus Garvey and the United Negro Improvement Association* (Madison: University of Wisconsin Press, 1965); Tony Martin, *Race First: The Ideological and Organizational Struggles of Marcus Garvey and the Universal Negro Improvement Association* (Dover, MA: Majority Press, 1976); Patricia A. Schechter, *Ida B. Wells-Barnett & American Reform 1880–1930* (Chapel Hill: University of North Carolina Press, 2001); and Joyce Ann Hanson, *Mary McLeod Bethune & Black Women's Political Activism* (Columbia: University of Missouri Press, 2003).

4. Jeanette Keith's *Rich Man's War, Poor Man's Fight: Race, Class, and Power in the Rural South during the First World War* (Chapel Hill: University of North Carolina Press, 2004) provides a critical perspective examining class and social status.

5. John Dittmer begins *Local People* by retelling the unsuccessful effort of Medgar W. Evers and other veterans attempting to vote in the 1946 Mississippi Democratic primary.

6. Lewis gets his excerpt of Bilbo's speech from a report filed with the US Congress Special Committee to Investigate Senatorial Campaign Expenditures.

7. The source of these statistics comes from page 12 of the report filed to the Special Committee to Investigate Campaign Expenditures.

8. Lewis provides a table on page 333 of his article detailing the results from eight of the twenty-two counties investigated by the special committee. Those counties include Adams, Harrison, Hinds, Lauderdale, Leflore, Marshall, Washington, and Winston.

9. Paul D. Scott, David R. Goldfield, Sally G. McMillen, and Elizabeth Hayes Turner, eds., *Major Problems in the History of the American South*, 2nd ed. (New York: Houghton Mifflin, 1999), 355.

10. Michael S. Mayer, "With Much Deliberation and Some Speed: Eisenhower and the *Brown* Decision," *Journal of Southern History* 52 (1986): 43–76.

11. Lewis gets his information from a reprinting of the Citizens' Councils letter in the October 1, 1954, edition of *Southern School News*.

12. There is not enough room in this work to fully detail the influence and workings of the Sovereignty Commission. For a thorough discussion of the organization, see Yasuhiro Katagiri, *The Mississippi State Sovereignty Commission: Civil Rights and States' Rights* (Jackson: University Press of Mississippi, 2001).

13. Several sources can be found that focus on the Till story. Stephen J. Whitfield's *A Death in the Delta* (Baltimore: Johns Hopkins University Press, 1988) is the first scholarly work to cover the case. Whitfield uses an unpublished master's thesis by Hugh Stephen Whitaker from Florida State University, 1963. Whitaker is a native of Tallahatchie County and had unhindered access to the jury members and trial lawyers for the defense and prosecution. William Bradford Huie's "The Shocking Story of Approved Killing in Mississippi" (*Look*, January 24, 1956, 46–49) and "What's Happened to the Emmett Till Killers" (*Look*, January 22, 1957, 63–68) published the confession of Milam and Bryant to killing Till and covered the local community's reaction a year after the trial. Both articles were later republished in an early (and out-of-print) collection of Huie's work, *Wolf Whistle: And Other Stories*. A concise retelling of the Till story that remains true to the magnitude of the case can be found in the introduction to Paul Hendrickson's *Sons of Mississippi* (New York: Alfred A. Knopf, 2003). Mamie Till-Mobley, Emmett Till's mother, coauthored a book with Christopher Benson on her account of the time surrounding her son's abduction. In the text of *Death of Innocence: The Story of the Hate Crime That Changed America* (New York: Random House, 2003), she describes examining her son's body at the morgue, moving slowly from Emmett's feet to his head. The mother's identification of the body is particularly moving and powerful. See also Devery S. Anderson, *The Boy Who Never Died: The Murder That Shocked the World and Propelled the Civil Rights Movement* (Jackson: University Press of Mississippi, 2015).

14. Davis W. Houck and Matthew A. Grindy discuss the role that local and regional newspapers played in influencing the jurors' perceptions, affecting local audiences, and framing the character and identity of Till in *Emmett Till and the Mississippi Press* (Jackson: University Press of Mississippi, 2010).

15. Eric Burner's *And Gently He Shall Lead Them: Robert Parris Moses and Civil Rights in Mississippi* (New York: New York University Press, 1994) is an excellent biography of Bob Moses and his involvement with the struggle for civil rights.

16. Microfilm, "Press Release," CORE papers, Dave Dennis section, reels 9, 21, and 25.

17. William Doyle's *An American Insurrection: James Oxford and the Battle of Oxford, Mississippi, 1962* (New York: Anchor, 2001) is an excellent source covering James Meredith's integration of the University of Mississippi.

18. Microfilm, "Press Release," CORE papers, Dave Dennis section. The list goes back to January 1961, where in Greenville, George Mayfield and Percy Lee Simmons received gunshot wounds as two whites riding by on a motorcycle fired into the crowd of a rally. The list contains some of the more infamous and tragic moments of the struggle for civil rights in Mississippi: the beating of Bob Moses by Billy Jack Caston in Amite County in late August 1961; the murder of Herbert Lee by state representative E. H. Hurst in September 1961, near Liberty; violent reactions to the arrival of Freedom Riders in Jackson; the murder of Corporal Roman Ducksworth by Officer Bill Kelly in April 1962 near Taylorsville; a Molotov cocktail thrown into the home of Dr. James L. Allen, vice chairman of the Mississippi Advisory Committee to the US Commission on Civil Rights, in October 1962; the murder of Sylvester Maxwell in Canton in January 1963; four acts of arson on black-owned businesses in Greenwood, all on the same night in February 1963.

The list also includes many more random acts of violence and intimidation from local whites, such as firing guns into the homes and businesses of blacks, egging demonstrators, or even firing blacks from city and county jobs.

19. Ibid.

20. A lot of the rhetoric employed by the Union during the Civil War was grounded in human rights, a powerful warrant echoed in the civil rights movement.

CHAPTER TWO: THE SUMMER BEFORE THE LONG, HOT SUMMER

1. "Negro Is Beaten and Kicked at Lunch Counter in Mississippi's Capital," *New York Times* May 29, 1963, 1. The photos are accompanied with a story by Jack Langguth, "3 in Sit-In Beaten at Jackson Store."

2. Victoria Gallagher and Kenneth S. Zagacki, "Visibility and Rhetoric: The Power of Visual Images in Norman Rockwell's Depictions of Civil Rights," *Quarterly Journal of Speech* 91 (2005): 175–200; Victoria Gallagher and Kenneth S. Zagacki, "Visibility and Rhetoric: Epiphanies and Transformations in the *Life* Photographs of the Selma Marches of 1965," *Rhetoric Society Quarterly* 37 (2007): 113–135.

3. In April 1959 Mack Parker awaited trial for allegedly raping a white woman, and in 1959 that was all the justification some of the good white people of Poplarville needed. A white mob took Parker from his jail cell, beat him badly, and, after driving to the Louisiana border, shot Parker in the chest twice before dumping his body in the Pearl River.

4. M. J. O'Brien, *We Shall Not Be Moved: The Jackson Woolworth's Sit-In and the Movement It Inspired* (Jackson: University Press of Mississippi, 2013). This work is an extensive and detailed look at the protest activity in Jackson during the spring and summer of 1963. At the center of O'Brien's work is the Blackwell photography, which makes the historical narrative immediately and intimately relatable via the visual artifact

5. Martin Berger, *Seeing through Race: A Reinterpretation of Civil Rights Photography* (Berkeley: University of California Press, 2011); Branch, *Parting the Waters*; Dittmer, *Local People*; and Steven Kasher, *The Civil Rights Movement: A Photographic History, 1954–68* (New York: Abbeville Press, 1996), are just a few of the works that reprint the photograph.

6. Branch even uses this argument in his caption of the photo.

7. Moody, *Coming of Age in Mississippi*, 290.

8. John Salter's online blog, *Lair of Hunterbear* (blog), www.hunterbear.org, is a great personal account of a life spent protesting for social justice.

9. For a more sustained examination of the Jackson Movement, see O'Brien's *We Shall Not Be Moved*.

10. Accessed from americanrhetoric.com.

11. William H. Chafe's *Never Stop Running: Allard Lowenstein and the Struggle to Save American Liberalism* (New York: Basic Books, 1993) and Richard Cummings's *The Pied Piper Allard K. Lowenstein and the Liberal Dream* (New York: Grove Press, 1985) both confirm that Lowenstein was a major influence on the "liberal consensus" of the 1960s. Chafe and Cummings both argue that the social democratic policies of Franklin Roosevelt greatly influenced Lowenstein's outlook on America's potential. Born in 1929 in Newark, New Jersey, Lowenstein attended the University of North Carolina at Chapel Hill (UNC), despite the fact that his father was on the faculty at Columbia. Lowenstein was very active after his graduation from UNC,

bouncing around the country and participating in various political campaigns, even serving as president of the National Student Association. He received a law degree from Yale and worked for the United Nations. Lowenstein published a book in 1962, *Brutal Mandate*, about his time spent in South Africa.

12. There is a version of the speech in Clayborne Carson, David G. Garrow, Gerald Gill, Vincent Harding, and Darlene Clark Hine, gen. eds., *The Eyes on the Prize Civil Rights Reader* (New York: Penguin, 1991), 163–165.

13. Davis W. Houck and David E. Dixon, eds., *Rhetoric, Religion, and the Civil Rights Movement: 1954–1965* (Waco, TX: Baylor University Press, 2006), 586. This is an anthology of civil rights speeches that focuses on orators who used religious ideals and themes in their rhetorical addresses.

14. The following speech and subsequent quotes are from a speech Allard Lowenstein gave at several universities across the country called "Mississippi: A Foreign Country in Our Midst?"

CHAPTER THREE: ORGANIZING, RECRUITING, AND CANVASSING

1. Upon returning to Yale after their trip to Mississippi, many Yale divinity students wrote essays chronicling their experiences. Jim Vaughn's essay reads like a personal diary of his days in Mississippi and is available at the Yale University Divinity Library Special Collections in New Haven, CT.

2. The archived SNCC papers and documents are an extensive collection cataloging the organization's history and activity. Access to the collection for this project was permitted through the microfilm holdings at Strozier Library at Florida State University, Tallahassee. Most of the SNCC documents cited throughout this project come from the portion of the SNCC papers organized under Mississippi activities. The document cited here is a news release.

3. Microfilm, "The Freedom Ballot" memo, SNCC papers, 1.

4. Ibid., 1–2.

5. Three excellent sources concerning *UCC v. FCC* and the decision's impact are Kay Mills, *Changing Channels: The Civil Rights Case That Transformed Television* (Jackson: University Press of Mississippi, 2004); Steven D. Classen, *Watching Jim Crow: The Struggle over Mississippi TV, 1955–1969* (Durham, NC: Duke University Press, 2004); and William H. Lawson and Jennifer Proffitt, "Standing as Empowering and Limiting: A Rhetorical Analysis of *Office of Communication of the United Church of Christ v. Federal Communications Commission (1966),*" *Communication Law Review* 9 (2009): 36–47.

6. Microfilm, "Itinerary," SNCC papers.

7. Cover letter to mission statement, from the Freedom Vote subject file at the Mississippi Department of Archives and History, in the Special Collection Section of the Manuscript Collection.

8. "Planning Details for Freedom Vote of Governor," from the Aaron Henry section of the CORE papers. Like the SNCC papers, the CORE papers were also accessed via microfilm from Strozier Library at Florida State University, Tallahassee.

9. Chapters 17, 20, and 21, respectively.

10. "Aaron Henry May Run for Governor," *Delta Democrat-Times*, October 13, 1963, 2. All Mississippi papers were acquired at the Mississippi Department of Archives and History in the microfilm holdings.

11. "Aaron Henry Being Run for Governor by NAACP," *Clarion-Ledger*, October 13, 1963, 15.

12. This quote is from a manuscript entitled "Mississippi Freedom Vote—Fall of 1963" and is the personal memoir of Reverend Ed King reflecting upon his experiences during the Freedom Vote. The manuscript is, as of yet, unpublished. Reverend King has graciously provided me with a copy. This excerpt is from page 28.

13. "Henry to Speak Here," *Delta Democrat-Times*, October 14, 1963, 8.

14. "Henry Announces for Governor," *Delta Democrat-Times*, October 15, 1963, 2.

15. "Negro Is Candidate but Doesn't Expect to Get Many Votes," *Meridian Star*, October 15, 1963, 3.

16. "Negro Says He's Running for Mississippi Governor" is the headline for the UPI story in the *Clarksdale Press Register*, which placed the article on page 8 of the October 15 issue. The *Jackson Daily News* also ran the UPI story, but with the headline "Henry Will Be 'Write-In' Candidate," and put the article on page 9. Both papers ran the story with Henry's pessimistic prediction. It is unlikely that Henry would issue such a statement, especially considering the already hostile nature of the Mississippi news media, but that does not stop the news media machine from circulating the statement. Once a statement, true or false, appears in a newspaper, it inserts itself into the public discourse, thereby gaining legitimacy simply through its presence.

17. "Aaron Henry Is Running for Governor," *Jackson Advocate*, October 19, 1963, 8.

18. "Write-In Drive Started," *New York Times*, October 15, 1963, 32. All articles from the *New York Times* were accessed through the paper's online historical archive.

19. "733 Vote for Freedom," *Mississippi Free Press*, August 10, 1963, 1. All copies of the *Free Press* were obtained through the microfilm collection at the Mississippi Department of Archives and History.

20. "Negroes to File Freedom Votes," *Mississippi Free Press*, August 24, 1963, 1.

21. *Mississippi Free Press*, August 31, 1963, 1.

22. "200,000 Negroes to Vote," *Mississippi Free Press*, September 21, 1963, 1.

23. "Convention to Set Off Mighty Freedom Vote," *Mississippi Free Press*, October 5, 1963, 1.

24. "'We Shall VOTE FOR FREEDOM,'" *Mississippi Free Press*, October 12, 1963, 1.

25. The *Yale Daily News* is a daily paper, and in 1963 it did not run any issues on the weekends. From October 17 to November 9 the *Daily News* ran a front-page story covering the Freedom Vote, often with photographs or images from campaign materials. Stories mainly reported on students' activities during the campaign and detailed the jailings and beatings some students endured. One of the Yale students in Jackson, Jon Van Dyke, conducted an interview with Governor Ross Barnett, which was published in the October 22 issue of the *Daily News*. This shows the range of coverage the *Daily News* provided, further evidenced by the editorial exchange from October 28 to 30 between southern Yale students and northern Yale students over the utility and purpose of student involvement with the Freedom Vote. Also of interest, starting on October 21 and running for five more issues, the *Daily News* reprinted the "Report on Mississippi Issued by the Mississippi Advisory Committee to the United States Commission on Civil Rights" in its editorial pages. The report summarizes and provides some of the testimony of over 150 complaints of alleged denial of equal protection of the law. The presence of the Freedom Vote and its coverage in the *Daily News* is important because it was a means of mobilizing resources outside Mississippi, and it acted rhetorically as a catalyst for involvement, if not by pushing to students to actually go to Mississippi then by stimulating activity like fund-raising on campus, which helped support the movement in other ways.

26. Richard Van Wagenen, "Mississippi Talk," Manuscripts and Archives, Yale University Library, Jodi Wilgore Collection, Box 4. This is an excerpt from a prepared speech that Van Wagenen gave to high school students after he returned from Mississippi.

27. From an interview with the author, August 2006.
28. Letter from Bob Moses to Al Lowenstein, Southern Historical Collection, Manuscripts Department Library of the University of North Carolina at Chapel Hill, Lowenstein papers, Section 2.14. The letter is an emotional and logical appeal for volunteers and resources.
29. This letter is also from the Lowenstein papers.
30. "Fish Fry Fundraiser Flyer," Manuscript and Archives, Yale University Library, Jodi Wilgore Collection, Box 4.
31. Microfilm, "Letter to Ministers," CORE papers.
32. Jim Vaughan, "Reflections Resulting from Participation in Freedom Vote Campaign," Yale University Divinity Library Special Collections.
33. Frank Basler, interview with the author, August 2006.
34. "Police Hold 14 Negro Leaflet Distributors," *Enterprise Journal* (Natchez, MS), October 23, 1963.
35. Report by Joan Bowman to SNCC headquarters in Atlanta, Joseph A. Sinsheimer papers, Rare Book and Manuscript Library, Duke University.
36. Statement by Nelson A. Soltman, October 24, 1963, SNCC papers, microfilm.
37. Report by Donald White, October 26, 1963, CORE papers, microfilm.
38. Press release, October 26, 1963, CORE papers, microfilm.
39. Press release, October 27, 1963, CORE papers, microfilm.
40. Letter from Al Lowenstein to Department of Justice, CORE papers, microfilm.
41. Letter from Jonathan Middlebrook to editor of *Berksire Eagle*, CORE papers, microfilm.
42. Letter from Kenneth Klotz to Senator Birch Bayh of Indiana, October 28, 1963, CORE papers, microfilm.
43. "Summary of Events, October 22 to 28," Joseph A. Sinsheimer papers, Rare Book and Manuscript Library, Duke University.
44. Robert E. Baker, "Miss. Negroes Plan 'Private' Election," *Washington Post*, October 27, 1963. This article was found in Box 1 of the "Freedom Vote" subject file at the Mississippi Department of Archives and History in the Special Collections Section of the Manuscript Collection.
45. Telegram from Freedom Vote campaign board members to President Kennedy, CORE papers, microfilm.

CHAPTER FOUR: THE CAMPAIGN IMAGE IMAGINED

1. Robert Hariman and John Louis Lucaites, *No Caption Needed: Iconic Photographs, Public Culture, and Liberal Democracy* (Chicago: University of Chicago Press, 2007), 27. This book is a must-read for those interested in analyzing our visual culture, from texts to performances.
2. There is obviously a lot more to this "accident" and is representative of other narratives and events from the movement we lose as we lose members and volunteers of the movement. Online citation from a tribute page dedicated to John R. Salter, http://www.hunterbear.org/special_tribute_page_for_hunter.htm.
3. Franklin D. Roosevelt's "Four Freedoms" speech is available online at americanrhetoric.com. It ranks in the top fifty speeches of the twentieth century.
4. This is one of eight images that Leigh Raiford analyzes in "'Come Let Us Build a New World Together': SNCC and Photography of the Civil Rights Movement," *American Quarterly* (2007): 1129–1157. It is on page 1143 of her article, and the only image also used by the Freedom Vote.

CHAPTER FIVE: FREEDOM IN FULL SWING

1. While teaching at Duke University, Bruce Payne wrote an unpublished memoir, "Non-Violence and the Politics of Change," about his near-death experiences in Mississippi. The author would like to thank Mr. Payne for providing a copy of this text.

2. King, "Mississippi Freedom Vote—Fall of 1963," 93.

3. Norman Thomas was a minister who at the time had run for president of the United States as a candidate for the Socialist Party of America.

4. John Herbers, "Norman Thomas Mocks Mississippi," *New York Times*, November 1, 1963.

5. Ronnie Dugger, "Negro Candidate's Aides Jailed," *Washington Post*, November 1, 1963. This article was found in Box 1 of the "Freedom Vote" subject file at the Mississippi Department of Archives and History in the Special Collections Section of the Manuscript Collection.

6. All four speeches and the song are transcribed from audiotapes from the Moses Moon collection housed at the National Museum of American History. Like the two rallies that follow this one, the entire event is captured on audiotape, and the proceedings of the event can be accurately transcribed.

7. From the Moses Moon collection, National Museum of American History.

8. Matt Jones, "Ballad of Medgar Evers" (song, Freedom Vote rally at Masonic Temple, Jackson, Mississippi, October 31, 1963), Moses Moon collection, National Museum of American History.

9. Mississippi Department of Archives and History, Freedom Vote subject file.

10. James Forman was born on October 4, 1928. He was raised primarily in Chicago but did have family ties in Mississippi. Forman served in the air force during the Korean War, stationed in Japan. He played a vital leadership role for SNCC during the 1960s, serving as the executive secretary. His book *The Making of Black Revolutionaries: A Personal Account* (Seattle: Open Hand Publishing, 1985) provides an insider's perspective on the major events of the civil rights movement during the 1960s.

11. Forman retells this encounter in the opening chapter of his book *The Making of Black Revolutionaries*.

12. Christine Harold and Kevin Michael DeLuca, "Behold the Corpse: Violent Images and the Case of Emmett Till," *Rhetoric & Public Affairs* 8 (2005): 263–286.

13. Attucks was one of five who died in the Boston Massacre, which was on March 5, 1770.

14. Forman's referencing of Turner and Vesey is not coincidental. Both planned slave revolts in the early 1800s, Turner in Virginia and Vesey in South Carolina. Turner's revolt was the largest in US history; Vesey was executed before his took place because word of the revolt leaked. In the beginning of his book *The Making of Black Revolutionaries*, Forman writes, "WE ARE NOT born revolutionary. Revolutionaries are forged through constant struggle and the study of revolutionary ideas and experiences."

15. For more details on the later court case concerning this event, see William H. Lawson and Scott A. Smith, "Defeat in Decision, Victory in Action: A Critical Legal Rhetoric Reading of *U.S. v. Patridge et al.* (1963)," *Communication Law Review* 12 (2012): 11–28.

16. The two photographs are from the Moncrief Collection housed at the Mississippi Department of Archives and History in Jackson.

17. Excerpt from the Bob Moses quote on page 2. The entire speech will be analyzed in the following chapter.

CHAPTER SIX: A RALLY FOR VICTORY, A REVIVAL FOR FREEDOM

1. Freedom Singers, "Get on Board!" (song, Freedom Vote Victory Rally, Jackson, MS, November 4, 1963), Moses Moon collection, National Museum of American History.
2. Aaron Henry (speech, Freedom Vote Victory Rally, Jackson, MS, November 4, 1963), Moses Moon collection, National Museum of American History. The entire rally was recorded and is archived with the Moses Moon collection. The event and all speeches in this chapter were transcribed directly from those audiotapes.
3. Microfilm, Press Release, CORE papers, Aaron Henry section.
4. "A New Politics in Mississippi," *Southern Patriot*, November 1963, 1. This issue of the *Southern Patriot* is from the microfilm collection at Strozier Library at Florida State University, Tallahassee.
5. *Southern Patriot*, December 1963.
6. "Bi-Racial Pair to Seek Top Miss. Office," *Chicago Daily Defender*, October 16, 1963. All copies of the *Chicago Defender* are from the microfilm collection at Florida State University, Tallahassee.
7. "Yale Students Aid Negro in Governor Race," *Chicago Daily Defender*, October 21, 1963.
8. "No Hopes of Victory for Negro in Mississippi Governor's Race," *Chicago Daily Defender*, November 4, 1963.
9. "Henry-King Ticket Tops Mock Election," *Student Voice* 4 (November 11, 1963): 1. This copy of the *Student Voice* was obtained through the SNCC papers on microfilm at Strozier Library, Florida State University, Tallahassee.
10. Jeannine Herron, "Underground Election," *Nation*, December 7, 1963, 387, Joseph A. Sinsheimer papers, Rare Book and Manuscript Library, Duke University.
11. M. L., "The Mississippi Freedom Vote," *New South*, December 1963, 10–13, Joseph A. Sinsheimer papers, Rare Book and Manuscript Library, Duke University.
12. "Four Yale University Divinity School Students Describe . . . a Week in Mississippi," *Presbyterian Life*, December 15, 1963, 26, Joseph A. Sinsheimer papers, Rare Book and Manuscript Library, Duke University.
13. Jim Vaughan, "Reflections Resulting from Participation in Freedom Vote Campaign," Yale University Divinity Library Special Collections in New Haven.
14. Van Wagenen, "Mississippi Talk."

CHAPTER SEVEN: FROM FREEDOM DAYS TO FEDERAL LAW

1. All excerpts of speeches are from the Moses Moon collection at the National Museum of American History. The collection is audiotape recordings of rallies and mass meetings in the South from early 1963 through the summer of 1964.
2. Ella Baker (speech, Hattiesburg Freedom Rally, Hattiesburg, MS, January 20, 1964), Moses Moon collection, National Museum of American History.
3. Branch, *Pillar of Fire*, 214–220.
4. Dave Dennis oral history in *My Soul Is Rested: Movement Days in the Deep South Remembered*, ed. Howell Raines (New York: G. P. Putnam's Sons, 1977), 274.

5. Clayborne Carson, *In Struggle: SNCC and the Black Awakening of the 1960s* (Cambridge, MA: Harvard University Press, 1981).

6. Claude Sitton, "Mississippi Is Gripped by Fear of Violence in Civil Rights Drive," *New York Times*, May 30, 1964.

7. Dittmer, *Local People*, 247. The burning of Mount Zion was reported as a side note in the article "Mississippi Tense Over Voter Drive," *New York Times*, June 21, 1964.

8. R. W. Apple, "2 of Missing Men Feared for Lives," *New York Times*, June 25, 1964. James Chaney had remarked to Sue Brown at the Meridian office that "there's likely to be trouble."

9. Claude Sitton broke the story for the *New York Times* on June 23, 1964, in his piece "3 in Rights Drive Reported Missing." The article appeared on the front page and even included a quote from Deputy Price: "I told them to leave the county."

10. Claude Sitton, "Mississippi Drags River in Search for Rights Aides," *New York Times*, June 28, 1964. More details about the ongoing search effort appear in Sitton's "400 Sailors Hunt 3 in Mississippi," *New York Times*, July 1, 1964.

11. Dittmer, *Local People*, 250. An article titled "Hoover to Go to Mississippi Today in Civil Rights Case" with no author's name in the *New York Times* claims that the field office would be the largest that the FBI had in the South.

12. Claude Sitton, "Tip Leads to Auto," *New York Times*, June 24, 1964.

13. John Rachal, "'The Long, Hot Summer': The Mississippi Response to Freedom Summer, 1964," *Journal of Negro History* 34 (1992): 320. Legislation targeted picketing, outlawed protests near public buildings, made it illegal to distribute literature, and even outlawed political organizing among groups deemed subversive.

14. Len Holt, *The Summer That Didn't End* (New York: Morrow, 1965), 107. Some movement veterans referred to the Freedom Schools as "The Temples of Questions."

15. Sitton, "3 in Rights Drive Reported Missing."

16. John Herbers, "Civil Rights Drive Alters Mississippi," *New York Times*, August 20, 1964.

17. "The Limpid Shambles of Violence," *Life*, July 3, 1964, 32–37.

18. "Terrible Silence of the Decent," *Life*, July 10, 1964, 4.

19. "In a Mississippi Grave, the Three Missing Men," *Life*, August 14, 1964, 36.

20. Lawrence Davies, "California Democrats Join Drive to Unseat Mississippi Delegates," *New York Times*, June 28, 1964.

21. Claude Sitton, "Democrats Face Mississippi Split," *New York Times*, July 20, 1964; "Mississippi Freedom Party Bids for Democratic Convention Role," *New York Times*, July 21, 1964.

22. John Herbers, "Dr. King Starts Mississippi Tour," *New York Times*, July 22, 1964; "Dr. King Speaks to Negro Group at Philadelphia, Miss., Rally," *New York Times*, July 25, 1964.

23. "1952 Ruling Is Key in Delegate Fight," *New York Times*, July 27, 1964.

24. E. W. Kenworthy, "Mississippi Factions Clash Before Panel," *New York Times*, August 23, 1964.

25. Nan Robertson, "Mississippian Relates Struggle of Negro in Voter Registration," *New York Times*, August 24, 1964.

26. E. W. Kenworthy, "Mississippi Seats Taken by Negroes," *New York Times*, August 26, 1964; Jack Gould, "TV: A Bizarre Spectacular from Atlantic City," *New York Times*, August 27, 1964; "Johnson Criticized by Freedom Party," *New York Times*, August 30, 1964.

27. Both articles from *Time* were collected from the periodical's online archive.

28. The "Freedom Primer" is accessible on the Mississippi Department of Archives and History's website.

29. From the Mississippi Department of Archives and History online archive.

30. "The Senate Races," *Time*, October 16, 1964.

31. "Freedom Democrats Renew Mississippi Ballot Appeal," *New York Times*, October 30, 1964; "Mississippi Seizes 5 in a 'Freedom Vote,'" *New York Times*, October 31, 1964; "Negroes Holding a Mock Election in Mississippi," *New York Times*, November 1, 1964.

32. Peter Kihss, "21 Lawyers Begin Mississippi Drive," *New York Times*, January 1965. Kihss reported, "Twenty-one lawyers pledged here yesterday to go to Mississippi starting this week to take depositions in efforts to oust Mississippi's five present members from the United States House of Representatives."

33. John D. Morris, "Mississippi Seats Under Challenge," *New York Times*, December 6, 1964.

34. Joseph A. Loftus, "5 Mississippians Seated by House," *New York Times*, January 5, 1965.

35. There is a compelling photograph of Mississippi state patrolman Huey Krohn tearing an American flag out of the hands of five-year-old Anthony Quin accompanying Paul L. Montgomery's June 19 *New York Times* article, "103 More Pickets Held in Jail." The white police officer is lifting the black youth off the ground as he attempts to take the flag. Quin was jailed after being "disarmed."

36. "Selma: Beatings Start the Killing Season," *Life*, March 19, 1965, 30–37.

EPILOGUE: KEEPING THE FAITH

1. Office of the White House Press Secretary, *White House Press Release* (July 27, 2006).

2. Lawrence Guyot, interview by the author, September 2011.

3. David Dennis, "Mississippi—A Pregnant State in Need of an Abortion," memo from the field secretary, [November 1963], SNCC papers, reel 66.

4. "Black Elected Officials Increased Six-Fold Since 1970: Study," *Jet*, April 15, 2002.

5. US Bureau of the Census, *2005 Census of Population and Housing*.

6. http://www.mississippi.gov/ms_sub_sub_template.jsp?Category_ID=9.

7. CNN article posted online at http://www.cnn.com/2008/POLITICS/03/11/miss.primary/index.html.

BIBLIOGRAPHY

ARCHIVES AND LIBRARIES

Manuscripts and Archives Department at Yale University Library, New Haven, CT.
Mississippi Department of Archives and History, Jackson.
National Archives at the Museum of National History, Washington, DC.
Rare Book, Manuscript, and Special Collections Library at Duke University, Durham, NC.
Southern Historical Collection, Manuscripts Department, University of North Carolina at Chapel Hill.
Special Collections Southern Media Archive in the J. D. Williams Library at the University of Mississippi, Oxford.
Strozier Library, Florida State University, Tallahassee.
Yale University Divinity Library, New Haven, CT.

INTERVIEWS AND MEMOIRS

Andrews, Richard. Interview by the author. Durham, NC, August 2006.
Basler, Frank. Interview by the author. New York City, August 2006.
Carter, Hodding, III. Interview by the author. Durham, NC, August 2006.
Guyot, Lawrence. Interview by the author. Washington, DC, September 2011.
King, Edwin. Interview by the author. Jackson, MS, October 2005.
King, Edwin. "Mississippi Freedom Vote—Fall of 1963." Unpublished memoir.
McLaurin, Charles. Interview by the author. Indianola, MS, January 2005.
Payne, Bruce. Interview by the author. New York City, August 2006.
Payne, Bruce. "Non-Violence and the Politics of Change." Unpublished memoir.
Van Wagenen, Richard. "Mississippi Talk." Manuscripts and Archives, Yale University Library, Jodi Wilgore Collection.
Vaughn, Jim. "Reflections Resulting from Participation in Freedom Vote Campaign." Unpublished memoir.

BOOKS AND JOURNAL ARTICLES

Anatol, Karl W., and John R. Bittner. "Kennedy on King: The Rhetoric of Control." *Today's Speech* 16 (1968): 31–34.

Armada, Bernhard J. "'An Important Piece of American History': Memory, *Malcolm X*, and African American Collective Identity." *Review of Education/Pedagogy/Cultural Studies* 18 (1996): 421–431.

Asen, Robert. "A Discourse Theory of Citizenship." *Quarterly Journal of Speech* 90 (2004): 189–211.

Barry, Ann Marie S. *Visual Intelligence: Perception, Image, and Manipulation in Visual Communication.* Albany: State University of New York Press, 1997.

Bass, S. Jonathan. *Blessed Are the Peace Makers: Martin Luther King Jr., Eight White Religious Leaders, and the "Letter from Birmingham Jail."* Baton Rouge: Louisiana State University Press, 2001.

Benson, Thomas. "Rhetoric and Autobiography: The Case of Malcolm X." *Quarterly Journal of Speech* 60 (1974): 1–13.

Berry, Edward I. "Doing Time: King's 'Letter from Birmingham Jail.'" *Rhetoric & Public Affairs* 8 (2005): 109–131.

Birdsell, David S., and Leo Groarke. "Toward a Theory of Visual Argument." In *Visual Rhetoric in a Digital World*, edited by Carolyn Handa, 309–320. Boston: Bedford, 2004.

Blair, J. Anthony. "The Rhetoric of Visual Arguments." In *Defining Visual Rhetorics*, edited by Charles A. Hill and Marguerite Helmers, 41–62. Mahwah, NJ: Lawrence Erlbaum, 2004.

Branch, Taylor. *At Canaan's Edge: America in the King Years 1965–1968.* New York: Touchstone, 2007.

———. *Parting the Waters: America in the King Years 1954–1963.* New York: Touchstone, 1988.

———. *Pillar of Fire: America in the King Years 1963–1965.* New York: Touchstone, 1998.

Branham, Robert J. "'I Was Gone on Debating': Malcolm X's Prison Debates and Public Confrontations." *Argumentation and Advocacy* 31 (1995): 117–137.

Brinson, Susan. "The Myth of White Superiority in *Mississippi Burning*." *Southern Communication Journal* 63 (1998): 211–221.

Broadhurst, Allan. "Audience Adaptation: The Determining Factor." *Today's Speech* 11 (1963): 11–13.

Brooks, Meagan Parker, and Davis W. Houck. *The Speeches of Fannie Lou Hamer: To Tell It Like It Is.* Jackson: University Press of Mississippi, 2010.

Bryant, Donald. "Rhetoric: Its Functions and Its Scope." *Quarterly Journal of Speech* 39 (1953): 401–424.

Burner, Eric. *And Gently He Shall Lead Them: Robert Parris Moses and Civil Rights in Mississippi.* New York: New York University Press, 1994.

Campbell, Karlyn Kohrs. "Agency: Promiscuous and Protean." *Communication and Critical/Cultural Studies* 2 (2005): 1–19.

Carson, Clayborne. *In Struggle: SNCC and the Black Awakening of the 1960s.* Cambridge, MA: Harvard University Press, 1981.

Carson, Clayborne, David G. Garrow, Gerald Gill, Vincent Harding, and Darlene Clark Hine, gen. eds. *The Eyes on the Prize Civil Rights Reader.* New York: Penguin, 1991.

Chafe, William H. *Never Stop Running: Allard Lowenstein and the Struggle to Save American Liberalism.* New York: Basic Books, 1993.

Chappell, David L. *A Stone of Hope: Prophetic Religion and the Death of Jim Crow.* Chapel Hill: University of North Carolina Press, 2004.

Charland, Maurice. "Constitutive Rhetoric: The Case of the *Peuple Quebecois*." *Quarterly Journal of Speech* 73 (1987): 133–150.

Condit, Celeste M. "Democracy and Civil Rights: The Universalizing Influence of Public Argumentation." *Communication Monographs* 54 (1987): 1–18.

Condit, Celeste M., and John L. Lucaites. "Malcolm X and the Limits of the Rhetoric of Revolutionary Dissent." *Journal of Black Studies* 23 (1993): 291–313.

Cronon, E. David. *Black Moses: The Story of Marcus Garvey and the United Negro Improvement Association.* Madison: University of Wisconsin Press, 1965.

Cummings, Richard. *The Pied Piper: Allard K. Lowenstein and the Liberal Dream.* New York: Grove Press, 1985.

C. W. H. III. "Federal Legislation to Safeguard Voting Rights: The Civil Rights Act of 1960." *Virginia Law Review* 46 (1960): 958–959.

Delicath, John W., and Kevin Michael DeLuca. "Image Events, the Public Sphere, and Argumentative Practice: The Case of Radical Environmental Groups." *Argumentation* 17 (2003): 315–333.

DeLuca, Kevin Michael. *Image Politics: The New Rhetoric of Environmental Activism.* New York: Guilford, 1999.

DeLuca, Kevin Michael, and Jennifer Peebles. "From Public Sphere to Public Screen: Democracy, Activism, and the 'Violence' of Seattle." *Critical Studies in Media Communication* 19 (2002): 125–151.

DeLuca, Kevin Michael, Sean Lawson, and Ye Sun. "Occupy Wall Street on the Public Screens of Social Media: The Many Framings of the Birth of a Protest Movement." *Communication, Culture & Critique* 5 (2012): 483–509.

Dittmer, John. *Local People: The Struggle for Civil Rights in Mississippi.* Urbana: University of Illinois Press, 1994.

Doyle, William. *An American Insurrection: James Oxford and the Battle of Oxford, Mississippi, 1962.* New York: Anchor, 2001.

Durrheim, Kevin. "Denying Racism: Discursive Strategies Used by the South African Media." *Critical Arts* 19 (2005): 167–186.

Eagles, Charles. "Toward New Histories of the Civil Rights Era." *Journal of Southern History* 66 (2000): 815–848.

Edwards, Janis, and Carol Winkler. "Representative Form and the Visual Ideograph: The Iwo Jima Image in Editorial Cartoons." *Quarterly Journal of Speech* 83 (1997): 289–310.

Finnegan, Cara A. "Doing Rhetorical History of the Visual: The Photograph and the Archive." In *Defining Visual Rhetorics*, edited by Charles A. Hill and Marguerite Helmers, 195–214. Mahwah, NJ: Lawrence Erlbaum, 2004.

Flores, Lisa, Dreama Moon, and Thomas Nakayama. "Dynamic Rhetorics of Race: California's Racial Privacy Initiative and the Shifting Grounds of Racial Politics." *Communication and Critical/Cultural Studies* 3 (2006): 181–201.

Forman, James. *The Making of Black Revolutionaries: A Personal Account.* New York: Macmillan, 1972.

Franklin, John H., and Alfred A. Moss Jr. *From Slavery to Freedom: A History of African Americans.* 8th ed. New York: McGraw-Hill, 2000.

Gallagher, Victoria. "Black Power in Berkeley: Postmodern Constructions in the Rhetoric of Stokely Carmichael." *Quarterly Journal of Speech* 87 (2001): 144–158.

Gallagher, Victoria, and Kenneth S. Zagacki. "Visibility and Rhetoric: Epiphanies and Transformations in the *Life* Photographs of the Selma Marches of 1965." *Rhetoric Society Quarterly* 37 (2007): 113–135.

———. "Visibility and Rhetoric: The Power of Visual Images in Norman Rockwell's Depictions of Civil Rights." *Quarterly Journal of Speech* 91 (2005): 175–200.

Garrow, David. *Bearing the Cross: Martin Luther King, Jr., and the Southern Christian Leadership Conference*. New York: Vintage, 1988.

Genovese, Eugene D. "Martin Luther King, Jr.: Theology, Politics, Scholarship." *Reviews in American History* 23 (1995): 1–12.

Giltin, Todd. *The World Is Watching: Mass Media in the Making and Unmaking of the New Left*. Berkeley: University of California Press, 1980.

Goldzwig, Steven R. "Multiculturalism, Rhetoric and the Twenty-First Century." *Southern Communication Journal* 63 (1998): 273–291.

Griffin, Leland M. "The Rhetoric of Historical Movements." In *Readings in Rhetorical Criticism*, edited by Carl R. Burgchardt, 184–188. State College, PA: Strata Publishing, 1995.

Haley, Alex, and Malcolm X. *The Autobiography of Malcolm X*. New York: Ballantine Publishing Group, 1964.

Hall, Stuart. "Introduction." In *Representation: Cultural Representations and Signifying Practices*, edited by Stuart Hall, 1–12. Thousand Oaks, CA: Open University, 1997.

Hanson, Joyce Ann. *Mary McLeod Bethune and Black Women's Political Activism*. Columbia: University of Missouri Press, 2003.

Hariman, Robert, and John Louis Lucaites. *No Caption Needed: Iconic Photographs, Public Culture, and Liberal Democracy*. Chicago: University of Chicago Press, 2007.

Harlan, Louis R. *Booker T. Washington: The Making of a Black Political Leader, 1856–1901*. New York: Oxford University Press, 1972.

———. *Booker T. Washington: The Wizard of Tuskegee, 1901–1915*. New York: Oxford University Press, 1983.

Harold, Christine, and Kevin Michael DeLuca. "Behold the Corpse: Violent Images and the Case of Emmett Till." *Rhetoric & Public Affairs* 8 (2005): 263–286.

Hendrickson, Paul. *Sons of Mississippi*. New York: Alfred A. Knopf, 2003.

Henry, Aaron, and Constance Curry. *The Fire Ever Burning*. Jackson: University Press of Mississippi, 2000.

Holt, Len. *The Summer That Didn't End*. New York: William Morrow, 1965.

Houck, Davis W. "'By Any Means Necessary': Re-Reading Malcolm X's Mecca Conversion." *Communication Studies* 44 (1993): 285–298.

Houck, Davis W., and David E. Dixon, eds. *Rhetoric, Religion, and the Civil Rights Movement: 1954–1965*. Waco, TX: Baylor University Press, 2006.

———, eds. *Women and the Civil Rights Movement, 1954–1965*. Jackson: University Press of Mississippi, 2011.

Houck, Davis W., and Matthew A. Grindy. *Emmett Till and the Mississippi Press*. Jackson: University Press of Mississippi, 2010.

Huie, William Bradford. *Three Lives for Mississippi*. New York: WCC Books, 1965.

Illo, John. "The Rhetoric of Malcolm X." In *Classical Rhetoric for the Modern Student*, edited by Edward P. J. Corbett, 565–578. New York: Oxford University Press, 1971.

Jack, Jordynn, and Lucy Massagee. "Ladies and Lynching: Southern Women, Civil Rights, and the Rhetoric of Interracial Cooperation." *Rhetoric & Public Affairs* 14 (2011): 493–510.
Jefferson, Pat. "'Stokely's Cool': Style." *Today's Speech* 16 (1968): 19–24.
Jensen, Richard J., and John C. Hammerback. "'Your Tools Are Really the People': The Rhetoric of Robert Parris Moses." *Communications Monographs* 65 (1998): 126–140.
Johnson, Davi. "Martin Luther King Jr.'s 1963 Birmingham Campaign as Image Event." *Rhetoric & Public Affairs* 10 (2007): 1–26.
Johnson, Patrick E. "Performing Blackness Down Under: The Café of the Gate of Salvation." *Text and Performance Quarterly* 22 (2002): 99–120.
Journal of the Proceedings of the Constitutional Convention of the State of Mississippi. Jackson, MS: E. L. Martin, printer to the Convention, 1890.
Katagiri, Yasuhiro. *The Mississippi State Sovereignty Commission: Civil Rights and States' Rights*. Jackson: University Press of Mississippi, 2001.
Kauffman, Charles. "Names and Weapons." *Communication Monographs* 56 (1989): 271–285.
Keith, Jeanette. *Rich Man's War, Poor Man's Fight: Race, Class, and Power in the Rural South during the First World War*. Chapel Hill: University of North Carolina Press, 2004.
Kenney, Keith. "Building Visual Communication Theory by Borrowing from Rhetoric." In *Visual Rhetoric in a Digital World*, edited by Carolyn Handa, 321–343. Boston: Bedford, 2004.
Lawson, William H., and Jennifer Proffitt. "Standing as Empowering and Limiting: A Rhetorical Analysis of *Office of Communication of the United Church of Christ v. Federal Communications Commission (1966)*." *Communication Law Review* 9 (2009): 36–47.
Lawson, William H., and Scott A. Smith. "Defeat in Decision, Victory in Action: A Critical Legal Rhetoric Reading of *U.S. v. Patridge et al.* (1963)." *Communication Law Review* 12 (2012): 11–28.
Leeman, Richard W. *African-American Orators: A Bio-Critical Sourcebook*. Westport, CT: Greenwood Press, 1996.
Leff, Michael, and Fred Kauffles, eds. *Texts in Context*. Davis, CA: Hermagoras, 1989.
Lewis, David L. *W. E. B. Du Bois: Biography of a Race, 1868–1919*. New York: Henry Holt, 1993.
———. *W. E. B. Du Bois: The Fight for Equality and the American Century, 1919–1963*. New York: Henry Holt, 2000.
Lewis, Earl M. "The Negro Voter in Mississippi." *Journal of Negro Education* 26 (1957): 329–350.
Lipari, Lisbeth. "'Fearful of the Written Word': White Fear, Black Writing, and Lorraine Hansberry's *A Raisin in the Sun* Screenplay." *Quarterly Journal of Speech* 90 (2004): 81–102.
Luker, Ralph. "Quoting, Merging, and Sampling the Dream: Martin Luther King and Vernon Johns." *Southern Cultures* 9 (2003): 28–48.
Mabry, William A. "Disfranchisement of the Negro in Mississippi." *Journal of Southern History* 4 (1938): 318–333.
Makay, John J. "The Rhetoric of George C. Wallace and the 1964 Civil Rights Law." *Today's Speech* 18 (1970): 26–33.
Manis, Andrew M. *A Fire You Can't Put Out: The Civil Rights Life of Birmingham's Reverend Fred Shuttlesworth*. Tuscaloosa: University of Alabama Press, 1999.
Marsh, Charles. *God's Long Summer: Stories of Faith and Civil Rights*. Princeton, NJ: Princeton University Press, 1997.
Marshall, James. *Student Activism and Civil Rights in Mississippi: Protest Politics and the Struggle for Racial Justice, 1960–1965*. Baton Rouge: Louisiana State University Press, 2013.

Martin, Tony. *Race First: The Ideological and Organizational Struggles of Marcus Garvey and the Universal Negro Improvement Association.* Dover, MA: Majority Press, 1976.

Mayer, Michael S. "With Much Deliberation and Some Speed: Eisenhower and the *Brown* Decision." *Journal of Southern History* 52 (1986): 43–76.

McClymer, John F. *Mississippi Freedom Summer.* Belmont, CA: Wadsworth/Thomson, 2004.

McGee, Brian R. "Speaking about the Other: W. E. B. Du Bois Responds to the Klan." *Southern Communication Journal* 63 (1998): 208–219.

McGee, Michael. "The 'Ideograph': A Link Between Rhetoric and Ideology." *Quarterly Journal of Speech* 66 (1980): 1–16.

McKay, Robert B. "Racial Discrimination in the Electoral Process." *Annals of the American Academy of Political and Social Science* 407 (1973): 102–118.

McMillen, Neil R. "Black Enfranchisement in Mississippi: Federal Enforcement and Black Protest in the 1960s." *Journal of Southern History* 43 (1977): 351–372.

———. *The Citizens' Council: Organized Resistance to the Second Reconstruction, 1954–64.* Urbana: University of Illinois Press, 1971.

Medhurst, Martin J. "The Contemporary Study of Public Address: Renewal, Recovery, and Reconfiguration." *Rhetoric and Public Affairs* 4 (2001): 495–511.

———. "Public Address and Significant Scholarship: Four Challenges to the Rhetorical Renaissance." In *Texts in Context*, edited by Michael Leff and Fred Kauffeld, 29–42. Davis, CA: Hermagoras, 1989.

Medhurst, Martin J., and Michael DeSousa. "Political Cartoons as Rhetorical Form: A Taxonomy of Graphic Discourse." *Communication Monographs* 48 (1981): 197–236.

Moody, Anne. *Coming of Age in Mississippi.* New York: Laurel, 1968.

Murphree, Vanessa D. "The Selling of Civil Rights: The Communication Section of the Student Nonviolent Coordinating Committee." *Journalism History* 29 (2003): 21–31.

Murphy, John M. "Domesticating Dissent: The Kennedys and the Freedom Rides." *Communication Monographs* 59 (1992): 61–78.

Newman, Mark. *Divine Agitators: The Delta Ministry and Civil Rights in Mississippi.* Athens: University of Georgia Press, 2004.

O'Brien, M. J. *We Shall Not Be Moved: The Jackson Woolworth's Sit-In and the Movement It Inspired.* Jackson: University Press of Mississippi, 2013.

O'Rourke, Sean Patrick. "Circulation and Noncirculation of Photographic Texts in the Civil Rights Movement: A Case Study of the Rhetoric of Control." *Rhetoric & Public Affairs* 15 (2012): 685–694.

Parker, Frank R. *Black Votes Count: Political Empowerment in Mississippi after 1965.* Chapel Hill: University of North Carolina Press, 1990.

Pauley, Garth E. "John Lewis's 'Serious Revolution': Rhetoric, Resistance, and Revision at the March on Washington." *Quarterly Journal of Speech* 84 (1998): 320–341.

———. *LBJ's American Promise: The 1965 Voting Rights Address.* College Station: Texas A&M University Press, 2007.

———. "Presidential Rhetoric and Interest Group Politics: Lyndon B. Johnson and the Civil Rights Act of 1964." *Southern Communication Journal* 64 (1998): 1–19.

Payne, Charles. *I've Got the Light of Freedom.* Berkeley: University of California Press, 1995.

Pittman, Coretta. "Black Women Writers and the Trouble with Ethos: Harriet Jacobs, Billie Holiday, and Sister Souljah." *Rhetoric Society Quarterly* 37 (2007): 43–70.
Raboteau, Albert J. *A Fire in the Bones: Reflections on African-American Religious History.* Boston: Beacon, 1995.
Rachal, John. "'The Long, Hot Summer': The Mississippi Response to Freedom Summer, 1964." *Journal of Negro History* 34 (1992): 315–339.
Raiford, Leigh. "'Come Let Us Build a New World Together': SNCC and Photography of the Civil Rights Movement." *American Quarterly* (2007): 1129–1157.
Raines, Howell, ed. *My Soul Is Rested: Movement Days in the Deep South Remembered.* New York: G. P. Putnam's Sons, 1977.
Roberts, Gene, and Hank Klibanoff. *The Race Beat: The Press, the Civil Rights Struggle, and the Awakening of a Nation.* New York: Knopf, 2006.
Ross, Susan Dente. "'Their Rising Voices': A Study of Civil Rights, Social Movements, and Advertising in the New York Times." *Journalism and Mass Communication Quarterly* 75 (1998): 518–534.
Rosteck, Thomas. "Form and Cultural Context in Rhetorical Criticism: Re-Reading Wrage." *Quarterly Journal of Speech* 84 (1998): 471–490.
Rothschild, Mary Aickin. "The Volunteers and the Freedom School: Education for Social Change in Mississippi." *History of Education Quarterly* (1982): 401–420.
Santoro, Wayne. "The Civil Rights Movement and the Right to Vote: Black Protest, Segregationist Violence and the Audience." *Social Forces* 86 (2008): 1391–1414.
Schechter, Patricia A. *Ida B. Wells-Barnett & American Reform, 1880–1930.* Chapel Hill: University of North Carolina Press, 2001.
Schiappa, Edward. *Defining Reality: Definitions and the Politics of Meaning.* Carbondale: Southern Illinois University Press, 2003.
Scott, Paul D., David R. Goldfield, Sally G. McMillen, and Elizabeth Hayes Turner, eds. *Major Problems in the History of the American South.* 2nd ed. New York: Houghton Mifflin, 1999.
Sellers, Cleveland, and Robert Terrell. *River of No Return: Autobiography of a Black Militant and the Life and Death of SNCC.* New York: Morrow, 1973.
Sheckels, Theodore. "The Rhetoric of Thabo Mbeki on HIV/AIDS: Strategic Scapegoating?" *Howard Journal of Communication* 15 (2004): 69–82.
Simons, Herbert. "Patterns of Persuasion in the Civil Rights Struggle." *Today's Speech* 15 (1967): 25–27.
Sinsheimer, Joseph A. "The Freedom Vote of 1963: New Strategies of Racial Protest in Mississippi." *Journal of Southern History* 55 (1989): 217–244.
Smith, Arthur L. "Socio-Historical Perspectives of Black Oratory." *Quarterly Journal of Speech* 56 (1970): 264–269.
Sojourner, Sue. *Thunder of Freedom: Black Leadership and the Transformation of 1960s Mississippi.* Frankfort: University Press of Kentucky, 2013.
Stewart, Charles J. "The Evolution of a Revolution: Stokely Carmichael and the Rhetoric of Black Power." *Quarterly Journal of Speech* 83 (1997): 429–446.
———. "A Functional Approach to the Rhetoric of Social Movements." In *Readings on the Rhetoric of Social Protest*, 2nd ed., edited by Charles E. Morris III and Stephen H. Browne: 152–160. State College, PA: Strata, 2006.

Thompson, Julius E. *The Black Press in Mississippi, 1865–1985*. Gainesville: University Press of Florida, 1993.
Thurber, John H., and John L. Petelle. "The Negro Pulpit and Civil Rights." *Central States Speech Journal* (1968): 273–278.
Till-Mobley, Mamie, and Christopher Benson. *Death of Innocence: The Story of the Hate Crime That Changed America*. New York: Random House, 2003.
Tuchman, Gaye. *Making News: A Study in the Construction of Reality*. New York: Free Press, 1978.
Tyson, Timothy B. "Martin Luther King and the Southern Dream of Freedom." *Southern Cultures* 11 (2005): 96–107.
Vail, Mark. "The 'Integrative' Rhetoric of Martin Luther King Jr.'s 'I Have a Dream' Speech." *Rhetoric & Public Affairs* 9 (2006): 51–78.
Viorst, Milton. *Fire in the Streets: America in the 1960s*. New York: Simon & Schuster, 1980.
"Voting Rights Act of 1965." *Duke Law Journal* 1966 (Spring 1966).
Walter, Mildred P. *Mississippi Challenge*. New York: Bradbury Press, 1992.
Watson, Bruce. *Freedom Summer: The Savage Season of 1964 That Made Mississippi Burn and Made America a Democracy*. New York: Penguin, 2010.
Watts, Eric K. "Cultivating a Black Public Voice: W. E. B. Du Bois and the 'Criteria of Negro Art.'" *Rhetoric & Public Affairs* 4 (2001): 181–202.
Whitfield, Stephen J. *A Death in the Delta*. Baltimore: Johns Hopkins University Press, 1988.
Wilson, Kirt H. "The Racial Politics of Imitation in the Nineteenth Century." *Quarterly Journal of Speech* 89 (2003): 89–108.
Winquist, Thomas R. "Civil Rights: Legislation: The Civil Rights Act of 1957." *Michigan Law Review* 56 (1958): 619–630.
Zarefsky, David. "Civil Rights and Civil Conflict: Presidential Communication in Crisis." *Central States Speech Journal* 34 (1983): 59–66.
———. "Four Senses of Rhetorical History." In *Doing Rhetorical History*, edited by Kathleen J. Turner, 19–32 Tuscaloosa: University of Alabama Press, 1998.
Zinn, Howard. *SNCC: The New Abolitionists*. Boston: Beacon Press, 1965.

NEWSPAPERS AND MAGAZINES

Apple, R. W. "2 of Missing Men Feared for Lives." *New York Times*, June 25, 1964.
Baker, Robert E. "Miss. Negroes Plan 'Private' Election." *Washington Post*, October 27, 1963.
Chicago Daily Defender. "Bi-Racial Pair to Seek Top Miss. Office." October 16, 1963.
Chicago Daily Defender. "No Hopes of Victory for Negro in Mississippi Governor's Race." November 4, 1963.
Chicago Daily Defender. "Yale Students Aid Negro in Governor Race." October 21, 1963.
Clarion-Ledger. "Aaron Henry Being Run for Governor by NAACP." October 13, 1963.
Clarksdale Press Register. "Negro Says He's Running for Mississippi Governor." October 15, 1963.
Davies, Lawrence. "California Democrats Join Drive to Unseat Mississippi Delegates." *New York Times*, June 28, 1964.

Delta Democrat-Times. "Aaron Henry May Run for Governor." October 13, 1963.
Delta Democrat-Times. "Henry Announces for Governor." October 15, 1963.
Delta Democrat-Times. "Henry to Speak Here." October 14, 1963.
Dugger, Ronnie. "Negro Candidate's Aides Jailed." *Washington Post*, November 1, 1963.
Enterprise Journal. "Police Hold 14 Negro Leaflet Distributors." October 23, 1963.
Gould, Jack. "Johnson Criticized by Freedom Party." *New York Times*, August 30, 1964.
———. "TV: A Bizarre Spectacular from Atlantic City." *New York Times*, August 27, 1964.
Halberstam, David. "Tallahatchie County Acquits a Peckerwood." *The Reporter*, April 19, 1956.
Herbers, John. "Civil Rights Drive Alters Mississippi." *New York Times*, August, 20, 1964.
———. "Dr. King Speaks to Negro Group at Philadelphia, Miss., Rally." *New York Times*, July 25, 1964.
———. "Dr. King Starts Mississippi Tour." *New York Times*, July 22, 1964.
———. "50 Yale Men Aid Mississippi Negro." *New York Times*, October 30, 1963.
———. "Norman Thomas Mocks Mississippi." *New York Times*, November 1, 1963.
Herron, Jeannine. "Underground Election." *Nation*, December 7, 1963.
Huie, William Bradford. "The Shocking Story of Approved Killing in Mississippi." *Look*, January 24, 1956.
———. "What's Happened to the Emmett Till Killers." *Look*, January 22, 1957.
Jackson Advocate. "Aaron Henry Is Running for Governor." October 19, 1963.
Jet. "Black Elected Officials Increased Six-Fold since 1970: Study." April 15, 2002.
Kenworthy, E. W. "Mississippi Factions Clash Before Panel." *New York Times*, August 23, 1964.
———. "Mississippi Seats Taken by Negroes." *New York Times*, August 26, 1964.
Kihss, Peter. "21 Lawyers Begin Mississippi Drive." *New York Times*, January [day], 1965.
Life. "In a Mississippi Grave, the Three Missing Men." August 14, 1964.
Life. "The Limpid Shambles of Violence." July 3, 1964.
Life. "Selma: Beatings Start the Killing Season." March 19, 1965.
Life. "Terrible Silence of the Decent." July 10, 1964.
Loftus, Joseph A. "5 Mississippians Seated by House." *New York Times*, January 5, 1965.
Meridian Star. "Negro Is Candidate but Doesn't Expect to Get Many Votes." October 15, 1963.
Mississippi Free Press. "Convention to Set Off Mighty Freedom Vote." October 5, 1963.
Mississippi Free Press. "Negroes to File Freedom Votes." August 24, 1963.
Mississippi Free Press. "733 Vote for Freedom." August 10, 1963.
Mississippi Free Press. "'We Shall VOTE FOR FREEDOM.'" October 12, 1963.
Mississippi Free Press. "200,000 Negroes to Vote." September 21, 1963.
M. L. "The Mississippi Freedom Vote." *The New South* ([City], [State abbrev.]), December 1963.
Montgomery, Paul L. "103 More Pickets Held in Jail." *New York Times*, June 19, 1965.
Morris, John D. "Mississippi Seats Under Challenge." *New York Times*, December 6, 1964.
New York Times. "Freedom Democrats Renew Mississippi Ballot Appeal." October 30, 1964.
New York Times. "Mississippi Seizes 5 in a 'Freedom Vote.'" October 31, 1964.
New York Times. "Mississippi Tense Over Voter Drive." June 21, 1964.
New York Times. "Negroes Holding a Mock Election in Mississippi." November 1, 1964.
New York Times. "1952 Ruling Is Key in Delegate Fight." July 27, 1964.

New York Times. "Write-In Drive Started." October 15, 1963.

Presbyterian Life. "Four Yale University Divinity School Students Describe . . . a Week in Mississippi." December 15, 1963.

Robertson, Nan. "Mississippian Relates Struggle of Negro in Voter Registration." *New York Times,* August 24, 1964.

Sitton, Claude. "Democrats Face Mississippi Split." *New York Times,* July 20, 1964.

———. "400 Sailors Hunt 3 in Mississippi." *New York Times,* July 1, 1964.

———. "Mississippi Drags River in Search for Rights Aides." *New York Times,* June 28, 1964.

———. "Mississippi Freedom Party Bids for Democratic Convention Role." *New York Times,* July 21, 1964.

———. "Mississippi Is Gripped by Fear of Violence in Civil Rights Drive." *New York Times,* May 30, 1964.

———. "Tip Leads to Auto." *New York Times,* June 24, 1964.

———. "3 in Rights Drive Reported Missing." *New York Times,* June 23, 1964.

Southern Patriot. "A New Politics in Mississippi." November 1963.

Student Voice 4. "Henry-King Ticket Tops Mock Election." November 11, 1963.

Time. "The Senate Races." October 16, 1964.

INDEX

Allen, Lewis, murder of, 154–55
Arendt, Hannah, 94

Baker, Ella Jo, 25, 99; speech at Hattiesburg Freedom Day, 150–52
Baker, Robert E., 80–81
Barnes, James F., 18
Barnett, Ross, 104, 110
Basler, Frank, 72
Beittel, Daniel, 39
Bethune, Mary McLeod, 16
Bilbo, Theodore, 17–18
Blair, J. Anthony, 84, 94
Bloch, Marc, 4, 11
Blackwell, Fred, 30; sit-in photography, 34–39
Block, Samuel, 54, 73, 117, 123; and Freedom Singers, 131–32
Bosanquet, Nicolas, 99, 101, 103, 115
Bowman, Joan, internal report by, 74–75
Brady, Thomas, "Black Monday" address, 20
Branch, Taylor, 5, 175n5
Branton, Wiley, 26
Brooke, Edward, 13
Brown v. Board of Education, 16, 19–21, 60, 122
Bruce, Blanche, 13
Buchanan, William, 18
Bush, George W., 171

Carson, Clayborne, 4
Carter, Hodding, Jr., 61
Chaffee, Lois, 35
Chaney, James, 6, 157–58; media coverage, 161
Chappell, David, 98, 102, 145
Civil Rights Act of 1957, 23
Civil Rights Act of 1960, 25
Civil War Amendments, 13
Cobb, Charlie, 155
Coffin, William Sloane, 69

Committee on Elective Franchise, Apportionment, and Elections, 15
Congress of Racial Equality, 25, 54, 72, 131, 171
Council of Federated Organizations, 49, 149, 155; internal memo, 51–52; news release, 50
Courts, Gus, 22–23
Cox, William Harold, 25, 44

Davis, Jefferson, 13
Dee, Henry, body of, 161
De La Beckwith, Byron, 44, 124
Delicath, John W., 9–10, 96
DeLuca, Kevin, 9–10, 31–32, 55, 83, 96, 109, 120–21, 174
Dennis, Dave, 6, 54, 102, 116, 132, 155; aftermath of Freedom Vote, 171–72; letter to campaign policy committee, 71–72; speech at Freedom Vote rally, 110–11
Diggs, Charles, 21
Dittmer, John, 5, 20, 24, 39, 40, 148, 155, 167, 172; MFDP at Atlantic City, 159–60
Donaldson, Ivanhoe, speech in Greenwood, 125–26
Du Bois, W. E. B., 16
Duckworth, Roman, 54
Dugger, Ronnie, 101
Dylan, Bob, 109

Eastland, James O., 20, 25, 44, 142
Ellender, Allen, 18
Else, John, 144
Erskine, Doris, 116
Evers, Medgar, 29, 60, 102, 124, 136, 139; murder of, 40

Finnegan, Cara A., 89
Forman, James, 26, 132, 143, 182n10; speech at Greenwood, 118–25, 182n14
Freedom Days, 6, 148, 154

Freedom Rides, 25
Freedom Summer, 4, 155, 158; media coverage of, 160–65

Gallagher, Victoria, 33–34, 90
Garvey, Marcus, 16
Gitlin, Todd, 57–58
Goff, Fred, 116
Goodman, Andrew, 6, 157–58; media coverage, 161
Gore, Bob, 132
Gramsci, Antonio, 58
Green, George, 99, 116, 123, 124, 134, 140
Greene, Percy, 60, 64–65
Griffin, Leland, 8
Guyot, Lawrence, 148–49, 152, 171

H., C. W., III, 14, 23
Hall, Stuart, 56, 58
Hamer, Fannie Lou, 102, 124, 148–49, 150, 164, 167; legislation named after, 171; speech at Democratic National Convention, 159–60
Hampton, Henry, *Eyes on the Prize*, 164
Hariman, Robert, 83–84, 93, 95, 96, 159
Harold, Christine, 32, 120–21
Harris, Wiley P., 15
Henry, Aaron, 4, 53, 61–62, 66, 102, 172; campaign poster, 85–86; Freedom Vote of 1964, 166; speech at Freedom Vote rally, 111–15; speech at Hattiesburg, 148–49; speech at victory rally, 134–40
Herbers, John, 100, 161–63
Herron, Jeanine, 143
Hewitt, Theodus, 116
Higgins, Dorothy, 116
Honeysucker, Robert, 115
Houck, Davis, 98, 177n14, 179n13
Howard, T. R. M., 21

image events, 7, 31–32, 55, 68, 96

Jackson, Mississippi: Freedom Vote rally, 100–115; sit-in, 30, 34
Janson, Donald, 161
Jenkins, Tim, 64
Johnson, Davi, 9, 31
Johnson, Lyndon B., nationally televised address, 168

Johnson, Paul B., 76, 139–40, 161
Jones, Matt, 102; ballad for Medgar Evers, 109
Jordan, Andrew L., 54
Jordan, Reverend Cleveland, speech at Greenwood, 117–18, 122

Kauffman, Charles, 57
Kennedy, John F., 6, 112; nationally televised address, 40, 137
King, Coretta Scott, 171
King, Martin Luther, Jr., 24, 30, 31, 112, 137, 150, 173; March on Washington, 41; in Selma, 167
King, Reverend Edwin (Ed), 4, 53, 62, 68, 80, 95, 100, 102, 172; campaign poster, 85–88; speech at Freedom Vote rally, 105–9; speech at victory rally, 137–39
Klibanoff, Hank, 59–60
Klotz, Kenneth, 101, 144; letter to senator, 79–80

Lee, Herbert, 54, 154
Lee, Reverend George, 21, 33
Leff, Michael, 7–8
Lewis, Earl, 18
Lewis, John, 116, 132, 143, 149; speech at March on Washington, 41–42
Lewis, Pearlena, 34
Lowenstein, Allard, 29, 41, 64, 69, 134, 140; issuing of statement to federal authorities, 77–78; speech at Stanford University, 42–47; speech at Freedom Vote rally, 102–5
Lowry, Robert, 14
Lucaites, John L., 83–84, 93, 95, 96, 159
Lynch, James D., 60
Lynch, John R., 13

Mason, Henry, 59
McAdam, Doug, 4
McGee, Michael C., 84
McKay, Robert B., 14
McMillen, Neil, 14, 18–21, 24, 26
Medhurst, Martin, 60–61
Meredith, James, 26, 33
Middlebrook, Jonathan, personal letter, 78–79

Mississippi Freedom Democratic Party (MFDP), 5, 98, 134, 138, 142, 147; challenge at the Democratic National Convention, 159–60, 164; establishing of, 155–56
Mississippi Freedom Vote of 1963, 4–7, 49, 126, 129, 147; campaign flyers and posters, 83–97; composite poster, 89–91; "Freedom Candidates" poster, 85; literary citations of, 175n5; media coverage, 55, 61, 65, 75, 140; press release, 77; recruitment letters, 69–70; telegram to president, 81–82; "Stop Police Brutality" poster, 93–94; victory rally, 129; "Victory Rally" poster, 130; "What Does the Future Hold for the Farm Worker?" poster, 92–93
Mississippi Freedom Vote of 1964, 165–67
Mississippi Free Press, 67–69, 140–41
Mississippi state constitution, 14
Moncrief Collection, photos, 127
Moody, Ann, 34–38
Moore, Charles E., 161
Moses, Robert (Bob), 3, 24–25, 33, 41, 62, 68, 100, 116, 132, 143, 148, 153, 175n1; letter to Lowenstein, 69; speech at victory rally, 133–34
Myrdal, Gunnar, 60

National Association for the Advancement of Colored People, 16, 54, 131
Nielson, Vigo, 72–73
Norman, Memphis, 29–30; beating of, 35
Norris, Mildred W., 153

Obama, Barack, 173
Office of Communications for the United Church of Christ v. Federal Communications Commission, 52
Oliver, Benny, 30, 35
O'Neil, John, 61–62
O'Rourke, Sean Patrick, 36–37

Parker, Frank, 5
Parker, Mac, 54, 124, 178n3
Parks, Rosa, 171
Pauley, Garth, 168
Payne, Bruce, 69, 97–100, 115, 116, 143, 158
Payne, Charles, 5

Peacock, Willie, 73, 123; and Freedom Singers, 131
Peeples, Jennifer, 9, 31–32, 55
Plessy v. Ferguson, 16, 19
Ponder, Annell, 54, 149
Price, Cecil, 163

Rainey, Lawrence, 163
Raymond, George, 6, 116, 140
Regan, Cordell, and Freedom Singers, 131
Revels, Hiram, 13
Roberts, Gene, 59–60
Robertson, Nan, 164
Rockwell, Norman, 31
Roosevelt, Franklin Delano, Four Freedoms speech, 88, 97
Rustin, Bayard, 25

Salter, John, 34–39, 87
Santoro, Wayne, 37, 169
Schiappa, Edward, 57
Schwerner, Michael, 6, 156–58; media coverage, 161
Shaw, Willie, 116
Sinsheimer, Joseph, 175n5
Sitton, Claude, 161–63
Smith, Lamar, 21–22, 54
Smith v. Allwright, 17
Soltman, Nelson A., 75, 80
Southern Christian Leadership Council, 24, 54, 131, 149
South Pacific, 114
Sovereignty Commission, 21
State Sovereignty Commission, 21, 71
Stembridge, Jane, 116, 139
Stewart, Charles, 8
Stone, John M., 14
Student Nonviolent Coordinating Committee, 25, 33, 54, 72, 119, 131, 143, 148
Sugarman, Tracey, 4

Thomas, Norman, 100–101, 116
Thompson, Julius E., 59
Thurmond, Lenora, 116, 140
Till, Emmett, 22, 32, 60, 118, 120, 173; literary resources covering, 177n13
Toler, Ken, 39
Trumpauer, Joan, 34, 38

Tuchman, Gaye, 56–58
Turnbow, Hartman, 44
Tyler, Harold, Jr., 24

Van Wagenen, Richard, 69, 145
Vardaman, James K., 17
Vaughn, Jim, 49, 72, 144–45
Voter Education Project, 25–26
Voting Rights Act of 1965, 168–69

Walter, Mildred, 5
Washington, Booker T., 16
Watkins, Hollis, 132
Watson, Bruce, 4
Wells, Ida B., 16
White, Donald, 76, 80
White, William Wilson, 24
White Citizens' Council, 19–21, 22, 71, 124
Williams, Walter, 36

Yale Daily News, 180n25
Yale volunteers, 144–45; arrival, 72; personal letters, 78–80

Zagacki, Kenneth S., 33–34, 90
Zarefsky, David, 8, 32
Zinn, Howard, 149, 152–53

www.ingramcontent.com/pod-product-compliance
Lightning Source LLC
Chambersburg PA
CBHW030624230426
43661CB00053B/2126